The Plans that Failed

Studies in German History

Published in Association with the German Historical Institute, Washington, DC

General Editors:

Harmut Berghoff, Director of the German Historical Institute, Washington DC

Uwe Spiekermann, Deputy Director of the German Historical Institute, Washington DC

The Plans that Failed

An Economic History of the GDR

André Steiner

Translated from the German
by
Ewald Osers

berghahn
NEW YORK · OXFORD
www.berghahnbooks.com

Published in 2010 by

Berghahn Books

www.berghahnbooks.com

© English language translation Ewald Osers 2010, 2013
First paperback edition published in 2013

This book was originally published as *Von Plan zu Plan.*
Eine Wirtschaftsgeschichte der DDR, by André Steiner
© 2004 Deutsche Verlags-Anstalt, a division of Verlagsgruppe
Random House GmbH, München, Germany.

Library of Congress Cataloging-in-Publication Data

Steiner, André.
  [Von Plan zu Plan. English]
  The plans that failed : an economic history of the GDR / by André Steiner ;
translated from the German by Ewald Osers. -- 1st ed.
      p. cm. -- (Studies in German history ; v. 13)
  Includes bibliographical references and index.
  ISBN 978-1-84545-748-8 (hardback) — ISBN 978-1-78238-314-7 (paperback)
  1. Germany (East)--Economic conditions. 2. Germany (East)--Economic
  policy. 3. Central planning--Germany (East) I. Title.
  HC290.78.S74315 2010
  338.943'1009045--dc22

                                                                2010018531

British Library Cataloguing in Publication Data

A catalogue record for this book is available
from the British Library

Printed on acid-free paper.

ISBN 978-1-78238-314-7 paperback

Contents

List of Tables

Introduction

When Walter Ulbricht at the beginning of the fifties went into raptures on the radio, asserting: 'When I walk through the streets and see something new and beautiful, I point out proudly: this was done by my friend, my friend the plan', he may really have believed his own rhetoric.[1] Today the planned economy is thoroughly discredited, not least also by the history of the German Democratic Republic, the GDR. Nevertheless, it cannnot be simply inferred from the end result that the planned economy was at fault. We should ask why things happened the way they happened and, above all, what alternatives were available and why they were not chosen. In this book it is argued that the economic results of the GDR were in fact due chiefly to its economic system. There is no doubt that its poor starting conditions, the reparations to be paid to the Soviet Union, and the 'economic warfare' of the West played their part in the consolidation phase of the GDR's economy. These factors, however, were not decisive in the growing backwardness of the GDR compared to the Federal Republic. The crucial negative element was the planned-economy system.

The planned economy was part of a social system in which politics claimed to be able to shape and determine all parts of the system. It was ruled by the SED, the Socialist Unity Party of Germany, a party entirely in the Communist tradition, that had at its disposal far-reaching powers of decision in all social spheres. It justified its claim to leadership by arguing that the Party alone – based on the Marxist–Leninist ideology, declared to be a science – possessed the knowledge necessary for determining society's future development in advance. In accordance with Marxist theory the economy was to be so reshaped as to eliminate all the negative aspects of the capitalist economy.

For that reason the private ownership of the means of production was to be abolished and, on this basis, the economy was to be steered *in advance*, i.e., according to a plan and centrally. Thus – as Ulbricht put it at the Second SED Party Congress in September 1947 – the economy would be 'controlled in a way that would create the possibility of ruling out the danger of crises'. Planning, Ulbricht continued, would 'also create the prerequisites for preventing future crises. Labour will be freed from the fear of unemployment.'[2] In this vision, therefore, full employment and freedom from crises was to be guaranteed and the opportunity created for satisfying human needs. It was from the fulfilment of these claims for a planned economy that the SED also derived the legitimacy of its rule; the attempt to create a more humane system justified the state's intervention in economic life. The differentiation between politics and economy was largely discarded: economic rationality was subordinated to political considerations.

The GDR's 'new' society was deliberately conceived as a countermodel to the liberal and market-regulated system. The motivation for this was not only the socialist utopia, but also, and very largely, historical experience of the economic disorder of the period between the wars, especially the Great Depression at the beginning of the thirties and its political and social consequences. The Soviet system seemed to be an alternative; the more so as, simultaneously, it had achieved impressive growth rates with Stalin's industrialisation policy and had eliminated unemployment. In the perception of the Communists its overwhelming share in the smashing of the Third Reich was further proof of the efficiency of the Soviet economy. This fascination with a planned economy, found after the war not only in the East of Germany, was moreover due to the fact that advocates did not know, or did not wish to know, how many human lives and other sacrifices the Soviet Union's catch-up industrialisation had cost. The establishment of this social model in one part of Germany was a result of postwar international developments, of the Cold War waged by East and West and of the resultant partition of Germany. It was intended to safeguard for the principal protagonists – the German Communists – the political power they had seized in the wake of the Soviet occupation. That was largely why they leaned on the model of the Soviet Union, the leaders of which, however, either held back or promoted this process according to their political intentions with regard to Germany as a whole at any given time.

Nevertheless, the SED, in shaping its policy, also had to make allowances for the surrounding political and economic framework. As a result of the division of Germany and of its own claim that, in the east of Germany, it was developing an alternative to the market-governed economic system in the West, the Federal Republic became the referential society for the GDR. Comparison with the West was, for economic policy decisions, at times explicitly, but always implicitly, an important, indeed often the most important, parameter. At the same time the SED leadership had to remember the cohesion of the Eastern Bloc; after all, this was a main pillar of the GDR's existence – as much in political and military as in economic and ideological respects. Otto Reinhold, one of the master-minds of the later SED, expressed this idea with remarkable clarity in the GDR's final crisis in the summer and autumn of 1989: 'Without socialism in the GDR there will not be two German states in the long run.'[3] Since the SED leaders, in the interest of retaining their own power, were only able to divert slightly from the ideas of their Moscow patrons, their freedom of action in shaping their own system was limited. The Soviet planning system always remained the background against which they might reflect about changes in their own economic system. These basic conditions – the economic challenge from the West and the limited system variability because of its Bloc membership – were in latent opposition to one another. This might be described as a conflict between the safeguarding of the party's power and the achievement of economic efficiency, without which power could not be ultimately retained – after all, this system was not legitimated in a number of ways. As with other dictatorships, and more crucially than in liberal societies, there was a need in the GDR for minimum levels of consumption to be maintained in order to ensure the loyalty of the mass of the population and hence the stability of the system. Power alone, however, did not ensure economic efficiency.

In view of this situation and its ideological premises the Party found itself confronted with numerous dilemmas in its economic policy. In order to determine the optimal road of development in advance, decisions had to be made as to how much of the economic yield was to be assigned to consumption and how much to investments. Because of the continuous comparison with the Federal Republic a reduction of consumption was not possible in the GDR to the same extent as in other East European countries. Yet arguably, greater investments were necessary for the sake of future growth and subsequently increased consumption. The apportioning of yield between consumption and investment remained a political decision caught between short-term and long-term interests – a decision for which there were no objective criteria and in which, for the most part, the long-term safeguarding of power was favoured, and hence greater investments. In making such decisions, the SED leaders were guided by the dogma that the production of the means of production must always grow more rapidly than that of the means of consumption. This was based on an absolutist reading of Marxist theories of reproduction and guided by the Soviet experience of industrialisation. This idea not only encouraged a neglect of the consumer goods industry, which militated against a rise in the standard of living, but also increasingly proved an obstacle to structural change and hence to future growth.

The basic idea of the planning system was the coordination and control of the entire national economy, down to its sectors, i.e., all the way down to individual factories. This required institutions that differed from those in free market economies. In the GDR these new institutions – with slight exceptions at certain times – were organised strictly hierarchically. The institutional system consisted of two main pillars – the state's economic bureaucracy on the one side and the SED Party apparatus on the other. The responsibilities of both were overlapping and sometimes they were working against one another. However, both pillars were personally interwoven at the top. In the state's economic bureaucracy an outstanding part was played by the State Planning Commission (SPK). It had to work out the plans and be responsible for them, it had to establish the interdependencies of the various controlled economic fields and in so doing reject the interests of individual partial spheres that might run counter to the macroeconomic – but often politically determined – priorities. The immediate operational control of the economy was usually taken over by Ministries responsible for certain sectors or branches. The Association of People-Owned Enterprises (VVB) and the combines formed an intermediate level, which organised the individual firms of a sector or branch. Disregarding the purely formal approval of the plans by the People's Chamber, the final decision on all essential issues by the state was up to the Council of Ministers and its Presidium, to which the central authorities were subordinated and which represented the government. The most important members of the Presidium of the Council of Ministers were, at the same time, members of the top bodies of the SED.

In the SED, decision making on all fundamental economic questions was in the hands of the Politbüro or the Secretariat of the Central Committee (ZK). Key positions there were held by the Chief of the Party – i.e., Walter Ulbricht and, after 1971, Erich Honecker – as well as by the members of the Secretariat or the Politbüro responsible for the economy, who were also in charge of the work of the economic policy departments of the Party Central Committee. Similar economic policy departments also existed at the level of the regions and districts in the SED apparatus. Finally, the SED could exert its influence on the economy through the Party organisations active in all enterprises and their Secretaries. A crucial aspect of the relationship between the economic bureaucracy and the Party apparatus, however, was that decisions of the Party leadership had to be adopted by the state's authorities. The State Planning Commission was not to take any fundamental decisions: it had to submit them to the SED Politbüro and the Council of Ministers. As a result, economic rationality was subordinated, also institutionally, to political intentions and their justification. Moreover, the Party had the final say in filling the relevant leading positions not only in its own, but also in the state apparatus (Nomenklaturprinzip). In this way the SED apparatus became a corrective for any emerging economic problems as well as the final authority for deciding differences of opinion within the economic bureaucracy.

However, although the political leadership had the final say, the specialised authorities of the economic bureaucracy were often able to determine in advance its decisions by their submissions and studies.

The most important instrument of economic control was the annual plan, even though medium-term plans gained in importance in time. The main significance belonged to the production plan, followed by the investment plan with its significance for structural development. All these plans arose in a highly centralised bureaucratic process, in which the subordinate hierarchy levels were involved. Their assistance was necessary as the central authorities could not be aware of all capacities, resources or production functions. The process moreover provided an opportunity for creating an awareness of ownership among enterprises and their employees by providing them with a formal chance of participating in the decisions. On this basis it was hoped that they would identify with the plans and implement them eagerly. In actual fact, their participation was rather limited. Fundamentally all essential questions were decided centrally: establishment or closure of enterprises, their production profile and its changes, the distribution of production factors, the apportioning between consumption and investments, technological innovations to be introduced, imports and exports, issues of prices and finance.

Participation of the subordinate levels was possible only within the boundaries of the centrally set targets and their fulfilment. Within this tight framework the enterprises were allowed to draw on the profit they had made for bonuses and investments or else to receive funds from the state budget. Thus they had, at least formally, an incentive to fulfil the plan. If only for that reason the enterprises and their managers were anxious to be given the lowest possible plan targets and the largest possible resources. In order to fulfil present and future tasks more easily, existing capacities and stocks were often hidden and labour, equipment and material hoarded. This tendency towards 'soft' plans, immanent in the system, was further favoured by an asymmetrical distribution of information. The higher authorities were never fully informed of the situation and the available resources of the subordinate levels. From a financial point of view the striving for as many resources as possible was no problem for the 'people-owned' enterprises, since these, even if they produced negative results, were topped up by the state. If only to secure full employment and thereby to prove the superiority of its own system over the Western economy, the state found itself obliged to cover the financial needs of the enterprises and not to let any of them go bankrupt. This is also known as 'soft budget constraint'.

Thus the planned-economy system roughly sketched out here had two fundamental problems from the start: the information problem and the incentive problem. To take information first: in market economies, prices result from the ratio of supply and demand at a given time; price development is an indispensable source of information by which companies are guided in making their own decisions. The GDR's planning system, where the economic process was to be shaped deliberately and in advance, meant prices – unlike in a market economy – were no longer to be a source of uncertainty. This meant at the same time that prices as an independent information source generated from the economic process itself should be dispensed with. They continued to be maintained as largely rigid units of account for value that were contradictory to the dynamics of the economic process. The information required for economic decisions could be gained by the central authority only from the planning process, and these were falsified in this highly bureaucratic and hierarchical process by the diverse interests of superior and subordinate levels – as already shown in connection with the 'soft' plans. On this basis the central authority was not in a position to take economically optimal decisions. It therefore, in line with its leadership claims, oriented itself mainly by political priorities.

Secondly, with regard to incentive: the given system structure concealed an incentive problem. It was difficult to motivate enterprises and employees to the highest levels of efficiency. The initial ideal of a 'new man' under socialism soon revealed itself to be a fiction: formal ownership of machines and factories was no guarantee of higher work motivation. The conflict between economically necessary pressure to perform and the basic legitimation of the system, for example through commitment to full employment, gave rise to an incentive problem. Even though the SED leadership justified its rule as a state of 'workers and peasants', it had to confront the workforce as a kind of 'overall entrepreneur' who demanded ever higher performance. Each additional pressure to perform was therefore apt to endanger the legitimacy of the SED's power: yet dispensing with it could, of course, lead to the same result because of the loss of economic efficiency.

Throughout most of the GDR's history the planning mechanism was moreover so shaped that the enterprises were rewarded chiefly for quantitatively fulfilling their production targets. Qualitative considerations usually played a secondary role. From that point of view any innovation in the products or in the manufacturing process was seen as a disturbance. For their part, the enterprises – with some exceptions – were hardly interested in innovations; this was no problem for them since with the general shortage of goods they could (nearly) always sell their products. The state's foreign trade monopoly, intended to protect the domestic economy against 'disturbances' from outside by shuttering off the enterprises against competition from foreign companies, likewise played a part. The result was a system-immanent innovation weakness.

In case of shortages of raw materials or other supplies the enterprises' own stocks allowed them to help themselves independently and outside of the plans. Spontaneously and free from central administrative control, the enterprises exchanged their hoarded products amongst each other. This may have required high costs, but the benefit usually achieved by it was considerable and ensured plan fulfilment – the decisive criterion for which those responsible for the enterprises were rewarded or penalised. In the economy as a whole this 'grey market' contributed not inconsiderably to the functioning of the system. The fact that, in order to function, the system's own formal rules had to be bent was a symptom of its inefficiency. The resources of the national economy were thus not only not optimally distributed, but they were also insufficiently used. Permanent shortages and seemingly perpetual abundance were, as the stocks hoarded in the enterprises showed, typical of the GDR economy.

The manifold functional weaknesses of the economic system were known to those responsible. They were, however, regarded as 'teething troubles', as initial problems that would be solved. In the West, on the other hand, their fundamental nature was stressed from the beginning. How was it possible then that the system survived for more than forty years in spite of its being inefficient? There are several answers to this question. First, even the planned economy, despite all its system-immanent defects, had adjustment elasticities at its disposal, such as the 'grey market'. These resulted mainly from the imperfections and the gaps in planning: even in the GDR's greatly centralised system it was not possible to set up a 'total' plan. Second, the GDR – in spite of grave shortages of raw materials and in some other areas – had at its disposal a highly developed economic potential that was only gradually eroded by its inefficiencies. The control mechanism of the planned economy was in a relatively favourable position for opening up the extensive growth sources that were lying fallow after the war. Only when these were exhausted towards the end of the fifties did the limitations of the system become increasingly obvious. Even the GDR profited indirectly from the worldwide boom of the fifties and sixties, though not nearly to the same extent as the market-oriented economies. Third, considerable funds were flowing into it, directly and indirectly, from the Soviet Union, beginning at the end of the fifties, if not earlier, until at least the start of the eighties. From the seventies onwards there were also politically motivated inputs from the Federal Republic; these helped the GDR to cope with some economic problems. Only when the Soviet Union was no longer willing or able to support the GDR, could the deficits no longer to be offset even by transfers from the West. The livelihood-threatening economic weakness of the system became more or less obvious and the economic decline of the GDR was accelerated.

The account that follows concentrates on three crucial areas: first, we describe the origin and institutional development of the planned economy as an 'alternative' to the Western system. Secondly, the fundamental economic decisions of the SED leadership will be examined. And thirdly, we shall demonstrate the consequences of the specific shape of the planned economy and of the SED's economic policy. In this context, growth and productivity, as well as consumption and the living standards of the population, will be shown as indicators of the economic performance.[4] Essentially, this study focuses on investigating the macroeconomic level and, in doing so, chiefly discusses developments in industry and agriculture. The enterprise level plays its part mainly in connection with the incentive problem, but remains otherwise disregarded.

The division into periods follows political caesuras, preceded as they always were by economic crises. These crises were predominantly of political origin. What all of them had in common was the fact that the SED leadership tried to speed up growth. This placed a huge strain on the economy, magnified the imbalances in the economic process and exacerbated the shortages anyway caused by the system, which inevitably led to political unrest, and indeed in 1953 there was an uprising. The Party leadership reacted variously to these crises. In most cases the growth targets were lowered and the means earmarked for consumption increased. Alternatively reforms were initiated to make the system more efficient. As, however, these efforts failed for system-immanent reasons, the SED leadership, if only because of the competition with the West, soon found itself compelled to initiate the next mobilisation offensive. In this sense we can speak of a politically induced cycle of crises, taken into account by the division into periods.

The state of research into the various periods and problems of the GDR's economic history varies a great deal. The present study is not so much intended to fill in existing gaps as to sum up what exists, without, however, claiming completeness. It has been possible to go back to the many-sided results of the work of others, as well as to supplement these by my own research. In order to keep the notes brief, they refer as a rule only to quotations and figures. I have, in the interest of making the book more readable, dispensed with too much presentation of old and more recent research controversies.

It should also be pointed out that conversations and discussions with many colleagues and friends, too numerous to mention individually, have contributed to this study. Particular thanks, however, are due to Burghard Ciesla, Matthias Judt, Jennifer Schevardo, and Dietrich Staritz, who have not only read the manuscript as a whole or in parts, but also enriched it with criticism and suggestions. In the provision of the literature and data retrieval I was supported by Sven Schultze, who is likewise thanked here. I am, moreover, grateful to the staff of the Federal Archives in Berlin-Lichterfelde and the Foundation Archive of Parties and Mass Organisations in the GDR in the Federal Archive for their patience and helpfulness. Last but not least I would like to thank the German Historical Institute in Washington D.C. under the direction of Hartmut Berghoff and Berghahn Books under the direction of Marion Berghahn for making possible this English edition of my book.

Notes

1. Walter Ulbricht on the GDR radio, February 1953, quoted from *17. Juni 1953, Chronik des Volksaufstandes in the DDR*. CD-ROM, Bundeszentrale für politische Bildung/Deutschlandradio/Zentrum für Zeithistorische Forschung, Potsdam 2003.
2. *Protokoll der Verhandlungen des 2. Parteitages der SED. 20. bis 24. September 1947*, Berlin 1947, p. 320 f., 324.
3. Cf. Reinhold's contribution to the discussion at the Central Committee meeting in November 1989 and the bibliographical references therein listed: Hans-Hermann Hertle and Gerd Rüdiger Stephan (eds), *Das Ende der SED. Die letzten Tage des Zentralkomitees*, Berlin 1997, p. 334.
4. Unless Western studies are explicitly mentioned in the text, all numerical data are based on GDR statistics. As a rule it was possible to check these against internal records. These data should also be referred to in our historical account because they were essential decision parameters for the planners. Nevertheless they revealed fundamental inadequacies. Thus the production index figures were partly unrealistic since many products were unsaleable. Moreover, the enterprises had an interest in 'correcting' their reports to the statistical authority in one direction or another, according to the report index figure. Although these data are consistent within themselves and are suitable for intertemporal and structural comparison, they are not suitable for comparison with data from other statistical collection systems, especially Western ones. The economic totals and the data for the separate economic branches have been calculated on the basis of a uniform data base (Einheitliche Datenbasis) – as referred to in the notes – derived from the internal data of the GDR Statistical Authority for the total time span from 1949 to 1989. (Cf. *Statistisches Jahrbuch des gesellschaftlichen Gesamtproduktes und des Nationaleinkommens 1989*, BA Berlin DE2/23081/922135; *Ergänzungsband zum Statistischen Jahrbuch des gesellschaftlichen Gesamtproduktes und des Nationaleinkommens 1987*, BA Berlin DE2/30075/11546 (hereinafter: *Einheitliche Datenbasis*). Published in part in Oskar Schwarzer, *Sozialistische Zentralplanwirtschaft in der SBZ/DDR. Ergebnisse eines ordnungspolitischen Experiments (1945–1989)*, Stuttgart 1999.) Value added offered here as an indicator for economic performance is likewise based on this foundation and is therefore not free from the fundamental shortcomings of GDR statistics. Finally it should be pointed out that all data on the state budg-

et have been tidied up by specific aspects of the GDR state budget calculation. In order to ensure a rough comparability they now only contain expenditures financed from dues, taxes and credits. See André Steiner in collaboration with Matthias Judt and Thomas Reichel, *Statistische Übersichten zur Sozialpolitik in Deutschland seit 1945. Band SBZ/DDR (Bundesministerium für Arbeit und Soziales, Forschungsbericht 352)*, Bonn 2006.

Chapter 1

A Difficult Start? Initial Conditions in the Soviet Occupation Zone

Before the end of the Second World War, the Allies had already decided to jointly administer Germany – with its eastern territories severed – and to divide it into occupation zones. The area of the Soviet Occupation Zone (SBZ) included the Länder Mecklenburg–Vorpommern, Thuringia and Saxony, as well as the former Prussian provinces of Brandenburg and Saxony (later Saxony–Anhalt), which – following the dissolution of Prussia – were constituted as Länder in 1947. The Soviet Occupation Zone (excluding Berlin) took up 23 per cent of the area of the German Reich in its 1937 frontiers; in it lived 22 per cent of the population in 1939.[1]

Economic Potential and its Structure at the End of the War

What became the Soviet Occupation Zone was highly industrialised even before the war. Its degree of industrialisation in 1936, with 546 Reichsmark (RM) of net production per inhabitant, was somewhat above the average of 535 RM for Germany within the boundaries laid down at Potsdam.[2] Within the Soviet Occupation Zone the industrial density showed a marked south–north divide: industry was strongly developed in the south, especially in Saxony but also in Thuringia and Saxony–Anhalt, as well as in the Berlin metropolitan area. The province of Brandenburg, parts of Saxony–Anhalt and, above all, Mecklenburg, on the other hand, were characterised by agriculture. With reference to conditions in 1936 the Soviet Occupation Zone was thus an agricultural surplus area and more than able to feed itself. The traffic system before the war was roughly at the Reich average in extent and quality.

Within the framework of the Third Reich's rearmament and war economy Central Germany's industrial region – later part of the Soviet Occupation Zone – had, for strategic reasons, been considerably enlarged since 1936. By 1944 net industrial production in the future Soviet

Occupation Zone rose by 45 per cent, using adjusted prices.[3] Particularly fast-growing branches were mechanical engineering and vehicle manufacturing, precision mechanics and optics, electrical engineering, the iron and steel industries, as well as the chemical and fuel industries. The industrial structure changed accordingly, the share of the capital goods industry rising from 50 to 74 per cent of overall production.[4]

For important raw materials and other supplies the area of the Soviet Occupation Zone had been almost totally dependent on deliveries from other parts of Germany and on imports. In 1943 less than 2 per cent of hard coal and pig iron were produced there, as well as less than 8 per cent of the crude steel produced in the Reich in its 1937 frontiers. Only brown coal and potash were available in quantities exceeding demand. Even though 66 per cent of German copper ore was mined, the deposits were too small to meet demand. By way of contrast, some branches of the metal-working industry were relatively strongly developed, but this was heavily dependent on iron and steel, items which were scarcely produced in the Soviet Occupation Zone. This chiefly affected the manufacture of machine tools, textile machinery, office machines and vehicles of every kind, and in fact also electrical engineering and the precision mechanics and optical industry. In the chemical industry the production of basic products predominated, but their further processing was largely lacking. Thus, while 60 per cent of German synthetic rubber was produced in the Soviet Occupation Zone, there was no manufacture of vehicle tyres. Alongside the paper industry, the foodstuffs and textiles industries were strongly represented.[5]

The economic structure of the future Soviet Occupation Zone made trade with the other parts of Germany and foreign trade absolutely indispensable.

Table 1.1: Economic interweaving of the future Soviet Occupation Zone in 1936[6]

	Deliveries		Purchases	
	to other German territories	for abroad (export)	from other German territories	from abroad (import)
	as proportion of net production in per cent		as proportion of consumption in per cent	
Berlin	9.3	.	7.6	.
Western Germany (including the Saar)	27.8	.	29.3	.
Eastern territories	6.2	.	7.6	.
Total	43.3	11.3	44.5	7.6

The future West German zones before the war received a mere 18 per cent of their consumption from other German territories; in turn they supplied 18 per cent of their production to them. As Table 1.1 shows, even before the war the future Soviet Occupation Zone was far more dependent on intra-German regional trade than Western Germany. The future Soviet-occupied part depended mainly on hard coal supplies. In 1937 it received 4 million tons from Western Germany and 9 million tons from Silesia. Its mechanical engineering was similarly largely dependent on iron and steel supplies, especially from the Ruhr. Non-deliveries of even seemingly small supplies could paralyse entire production lines. Lack of hard coal, iron and steel was the crucial weakness in the structure of the economy of the Soviet Occupation Zone.[7] There is, of course, nothing unusual in the fact that geographic, local, economic and political factors lead over time to industries which are unevenly distributed across regions. So long as inter-relations over the whole economic area can be ensured, this might even result in higher productivity and enhanced welfare. However, as relations between the former allies deteriorated after the war, and the Western zones and the Soviet Occupation Zone separated themselves off during the Cold War, the consequences of these disproportions in the economic structure became increasingly negative for the East.

In 1947 the US and British zones first amalgamated as the Bizone and then, in 1948, with the French zone as the Trizone. This included a territory that was greater, economically more homogeneous, less dependent from the outset on intra-German trade and better able than the Soviet Occupation Zone to offset the deficits resulting from partition. An additional difficulty was the fact that an economic system was established in the East that – as will be shown – by its nature tended to obstruct foreign trade.

A further factor affecting the starting position was wartime destruction, estimated for the Soviet Occupation Zone as at most 15 per cent of the industrial capacities existing in 1944. This means that it was less than in the Western zones. In certain branches, however, such as vehicle manufacturing, electrical engineering, manufacture of printing machinery and machine tools, as well as the timber industry, destruction was higher. In agriculture the material war damage was estimated at about 2 per cent. Considerably higher, however, were the losses of livestock. In transport, war damage may have exceeded 10 per cent as this sector was a priority target of the Allies. In residential building the losses in the West were also higher than in the Soviet Occupation Zone: this can be explained by the fact that the Allied air war started about a year earlier in the West. Even so, some 14 per cent of homes on average were destroyed in the Soviet Occupation Zone, especially in the big towns, a circumstance which proved a long-term mortgage for the state.[8]

Numbers and structure of the population changed lastingly as a result of the heavy war losses and, above all, through the influx of refugees and expellees. The balance sheet records millions of dead, hundreds of thousands of war invalids and millions of men in captivity. Between 1939 and 1946 the old-established population in the Soviet Occupation Zone declined by nearly three million.[9] In the final phase of the war and in the immediate post-war period, however, more than 5 million refugees and expellees entered the Soviet Occupation Zone;[10] of these about 4.2 million were still settled there in 1950. Disproportionately many of them of working age moved on into the West. Bruno Gleitze, then President of the Central Statistical Office of the Soviet Occupation Zone, later said that 'the Soviet Occupation Zone acted like a sieve, holding back the aged, sick and single'.[11] Relative to the total population the Soviet Occupation Zone accommodated by far the greatest part of the displaced. This more than compensated for the war losses, so that by 1946 its population was considerably more numerous than before the war.

Table 1.2: Population in the GDR territory including East Berlin in 1939, and from 1946 to 1950, in millions[12]

1939	1946	1947	1948	1949	1950
16.7	17.8	18.9	19.1	18.9	18.4

At the same time, the percentage of the population that was fit for work declined from 67 to 60 per cent between 1939 and 1946. In consequence, in the postwar period, the same number of persons fit for work had to feed more children and elderly people. Whereas the number of persons capable of work remained more or less steady in absolute terms, wartime destruction and the start of Soviet dismantling meant that fewer workplaces were available. This explains the mass unemployment in the immediate postwar period. Despite a population exodus to the West, the number of persons capable of work rose between 1946 and 1950 thanks to the return of former prisoners of war. Among those capable of work, however, there was a lack above all of younger men, many of whom had lost their lives in the war or were still in captivity. As a result, compared to the pre-war situation, the share of women in the working population increased, as did the average age of those employable. These demographic strains, however, were mostly short-term. In the medium and long term expellees and returning prisoners of war offset the losses of those capable of work.[13]

All in all, the Soviet Occupation Zone at the end of the war had a considerable industrial potential at its disposal. Wartime destruction was limited and was generally less than in the Western zones. The workforce potential declined in the short term, but was offset again in the medium term. Moreover, the Soviet Occupation Zone was potentially an agricultural surplus area. Immediately after the end of the war the major starting handicap of the Soviet Occupation Zone, compared to the Western zones, was merely the imbalance in its economic structure: the lack of raw materials, of a metallurgical basis and of the second processing phase of the chemical industry. All of which, being the result of the rupture of a historically-grown economic area, could have been compensated for by foreign trade.

Plant Dismantling and Reparations

The war of annihilation waged against the Soviet Union by Germany led to an enormous loss of life and destruction. For that reason the Moscow Ministry of Foreign Affairs considered, even before the end of the war, what scale of reparation should be demanded from Germany. The essential elements of Soviet reparations policy were drafted in 1942/43 by the economist Eugen Varga: on the one hand they wanted to confine themselves to deliveries immediately after the end of the war and for the next few years. On the other hand, reparations were to be made 'not in money, but a) as non-recurrent withdrawals from the national wealth, b) as withdrawals from ongoing production and c) as labour performances'.[14] In the later adjustment process with the Western Allies the argument of restitution (*Wiedergutmachung*) was increasingly eclipsed by the intention of weakening Germany's war potential and achieving the greatest possible security for Germany's neighbours. Moreover, it was considered in Moscow that German reparations would serve not only Soviet reconstruction but also further industrialisation. Eventually, in Yalta, the Soviet Union demanded that Germany make total reparations of twenty billion dollars, of which it demanded one-half for itself. Here, however, the Soviets met with resistance from the Americans and British, whose reparation plans were based on different aims and principles: the US was interested in a multilateral global economic system and therefore 'altogether opposed to reparations and the British tended to incline towards the American view'.[15] The Western Allies were here drawing on the lessons of the difficulties caused by reparations after the First World War. The Soviet Union, with its planned economy, on the other hand, had no need to reflect that reparations as unpaid deliveries were, as a matter of principle, incompatible with free-enterprise tradeoffs. It gave pride of place to its security considerations and to the aspect of *Wiedergutmachung*.

The only contradiction in its concept was the fact that dismantling must inevitably impede deliveries from ongoing production.

These fundamental differences of opinion prevented inter-Allied agreement on the reparations issue. At the Potsdam Conference in July and August 1945 it was therefore decided that the occupation powers should each satisfy their reparation demands in their own zones. Moreover, the Soviet Union was awarded a certain share of the industrial plant to be dismantled in the Western zones. This meant that Germany was divided as to reparations policy, which provided the foundation stone for its political division. The originally planned joint procedure – Germany to be treated as an economic entity – became more and more illusory in view of the divergent interests and aims of the Allies. Moreover, extensive industrial dismantling in the Soviet-occupied areas and prematurely demanded deliveries out of ongoing production – details of which the Soviets prevented the other occupying powers from seeing – had, by 1947, progressively withdrawn the ground from a common occupation policy.

While still occupying East German regions (above all Upper Silesia and East Prussia) that were eventually placed under Polish administration, the Soviets, under their 'Trophies Action', dismantled industrial plant on a large scale. This continued on the territory of their subsequent Occupation Zone. Soviet dismantling activities reached an initial peak in June 1945, i.e., before the Potsdam Conference. In West Berlin, prior to the Western Allies' moving in, 605 objects were dismantled in that month alone.[16] In the final weeks of the war and immediately afterwards Soviet troops and special commandos hurriedly confiscated not only industrial plant and raw materials but also art objects and cultural assets. Moreover, tens of thousands of pigs, beef, cattle and horses were shipped to the Soviet Union, and about 10 per cent of the total household goods of 1945 were privately pillaged by soldiers and officers. The American and British troops likewise removed valuable raw materials, machinery, railway engines and rolling stock, as well as scientific documents from the part of the Soviet Occupation Zone that, up to June 1945, had been occupied by them. This affected, among others, the Zeiss works in Jena, and the IG Farben plants. Although no records were ever made of Anglo–American booty-taking on the territory of the Soviet Occupation Zone, its extent undoubtedly remained below that of the Soviets. Values lost through looting and irregular requisitions in the Soviet Occupation Zone are estimated at 1 billion RM (price basis 1944).[17] Although 'trophy actions' were to come to a stop with the creation of the Soviet Military Administration in Germany (SMAD) in June 1945, this was by no means the end of dismantling. But this was now credited to the reparations account.

After the Potsdam Conference a second wave of dismantling began which reached its peak in April 1946 and predominantly concerned Saxony. Dismantling of industrial plant here focused on large-scale enterprises. Dismantling teams, including the staff of Soviet industrial ministries and research institutions, swarmed about the Soviet Occupation Zone, chasing up dismantlable goods and eventually registering over six thousand objects suitable for dismantling.[18] These dismantlers, directly subordinate as they were to Moscow, worked according to the slogan 'Load up the lot!' (*Alles auf die Räder*).[19] This precipitate and often chaotic dismantling scarcely produced the hoped-for benefit: in the late summer of 1945 trains with dismantled equipment formed a line of over 100 km at the Soviet frontier station of Brest. Much of the equipment came to the Soviet Union unlabelled, parts and equipment from different plants got mixed up; others rotted away. Such a rapid reduction of industrial capacities would only have made sense if the Soviet leadership expected only a brief hold on power in its zone. Some of the Soviet leaders indeed pursued a strategy of getting as much out of Germany as possible and as fast as possible. Other representatives of the Moscow leadership however wanted to utilise the economic resources of the Soviet Occupation Zone in situ, mainly in the form of deliveries from ongoing production. The Soviet Military Administration representatives, more than anyone else, were familiar with the situation in the Soviet Occupation Zone. Their main task was to safeguard reparation deliveries, supplies for the their own occupation troops and supplies for the German population at least on a minimum level. Fearing an 'economic vacuum' in the event of further uncontrolled dismantling, they were interested in keeping a basic industrial core within in the Soviet Occupation Zone.[20]

The divergent interests in Moscow partly explain the inconsistent actions of the Soviets. When representatives of the Communist Party of Germany, the Social Democratic Party of Germany and later the Socialist Unity Party repeatedly begged the head of the Soviet Military Administration to reduce dismantling, he repeatedly announced (in May 1946, January 1947, and July 1947) that he would terminate dismantling. Such termination would also make sense as a reaction to the end of dismantling in the West in May 1946 and to the creation of the Bizone at the beginning of 1947. However, he did not succeed in actually enforcing an end to the dismantling work. As the Communist Party of Germany and the Socialist Unity Party of Germany only criticised the Soviet measures in private, while publicly going along with them, they found themselves discredited as the 'Russian Party'. While passive resistance to the rigorous dismantling policy, such as the destruction of dismantled items or the concealment of vital machine parts, was widespread, open protest remained the exception. After all, obstruction of dismantling work attracted draconic punishment. A very few workforces succeeded, by petitions to the head of the Soviet Military Administration, in preventing the threatened dismantling of their plant. In other enterprises, on which the future of entire regions depended, the Social Democratic Party and Communist Party leaderships, as well as representatives of German central administrations, sometimes achieved the same result. Such partial successes, however, were possible only because, beginning with the spring of 1946, the pragmatic concept of utilising East German resources in situ was gaining further ground in Moscow. A signal of that rethinking was the Soviet Military Administration Order No. 167 of 5 June 1946, according to which over two hundred large-scale industrial enterprises originally earmarked for dismantling were now to remain in Germany while being converted into Soviet property in the form of Soviet joint-stock companies (SAG). Even so a third wave of plant dismantling, now better organised, swept over the Soviet Occupation Zone from spring to autumn of 1946. Dismantling of plants was now more or less prepared with the help of German technicians. In many places dismantling and reconstruction took place in parallel, or rebuilt enterprises were dismantled for a second, and in a few cases a third, time. A fourth and fifth wave of dismantling work engulfed the Soviet Occupation Zone's economy between the autumn of 1946 and the spring of 1947, and again in the autumn of 1947. The final dismantling began in the spring of 1948.

All in all some 3,400 plants were dismantled in the Soviet Occupation Zone.[21] Admittedly this figure reveals little about the economic consequences. Relevant estimates may supply only rough data, but they convey an idea of the orders of magnitude.

Table 1.3: Development of gross invested capital in the Soviet Occupation Zone from 1936 to 1948 (1936=100)[22]

Gross invested capital 1936		100.0
+ Gross investments 1936–45	+ 75.3	
– Depreciation 1936–45	– 37.2	
– Wartime destruction	– 15.0	
Gross invested capital 1945		123.1
+ Gross investments 1946–48	+ 8.7	
– Depreciation 1946–48	– 11.5	
– Dismantling 1945–48	– 46.0	
Gross invested capital 1948		74.3

Although the gross invested capital in 1948 amounted to 74 per cent of the 1936 level, capacities only reached 70 per cent because the lack of even low-value parts resulted in the stoppage of entire plants and hence led to greater losses of capacity.[23] In the Bizone, on the other hand, the gross investment capital was 111 per cent, with greater war damage more than compensated by less dismantling, and was therefore already above the pre-war level.[24]

In some branches the cuts in capacity were especially serious – above all in the most modern and best equipped production places, such as aircraft construction, aluminium production, metallurgy, mineral oil extraction, machine tool manufacture and precision mechanics and optics, where there had been total dismantling of individual plants in order to destroy Germany's armament potential. Yet the majority of the dismantled plants were neither direct nor indirect armaments enterprises. In the very beginning the Soviets were anxious to dismantle equipment that was needed for the reconstruction of their own industry. The following table indicates, at a rough estimate, what proportions of capacities were lost through dismantling by different branches of industry in relation to capacities still available at the end of the war.

Table 1.4: Losses of capacity by dismantling in relation to the capacities still available at the end of the war in different branches of industry (in per cent)[25]

Motor vehicle industry	80
Iron production	75
Machine tool manufacture	75
Office machines	75
Railway engines	75
Electrical engineering	66
Optical industry	66
Textile machinery	66
Chemical industry (basic substances)	50
Precision mechanics	50
Artificial fibres	50
Brown coal mining and briquetting	33
Footwear	33
Pharmaceuticals	33
Textiles	20
Foodstuffs	20

The transport system was also greatly affected. By March 1947 railtrack of a total length of 11,800 km had been removed and the network nearly halved compared with 1938. By 1950 about one-quarter of the main lines and even more of the secondary lines had been removed. The most serious consequence, however, was the almost total dismantling of the second track on main lines; this engraved itself on the minds of the East

German population as *the* symbol of dismantling. The Reichsbahn, more-over, comparing its stock from 1936 to 1947/48, lost more than 60 per cent of its goods trucks and more than 40 per cent of its locomotives through war and dismantling.[26]

The creation of the Soviet joint-stock companies heralded a turn in Soviet reparation policy. The Soviets had indeed for some time been util-ising Soviet Occupation Zone potentials in situ, in particular the research and development capacities in the construction and engineering bureaux under their management and relevant to armaments. In October 1946 they eventually, in a cloak-and-dagger operation, moved the overwhelm-ing portion of 'specialists' employed there to the Soviet Union. Some 2,500 to 3,000 German specialists got into the Soviet Union in this way between 1945 and 1947. There they worked predominantly on armaments projects, returning to Germany between 1949 and 1958. The value of these 'intellectual' reparations – which were also a reaction to the American Operation 'Paperclip' that brought German researchers into the US – can-not be accurately determined. Yet compared to the Western zones, where 'the bringing along of know-how and the withdrawal of German scien-tists and technicians had contributed to Western Germany's integration into the Western hemisphere, the compulsory dispatch from the Soviet Occupation Zone into the USSR … had a negative medium and long-term effect' on the Soviet Occupation Zone and the GDR.[27]

The Soviet joint-stock companies were created by the Soviets so that they would keep their economic influence in the Soviet Occupation Zone in all circumstances. The future directors of these enterprises were sworn in in Moscow before their departure: 'Figuratively speaking you are Soviet colonists. If it were to happen that our government decides to withdraw our troops from Germany, you alone will remain there and wage a tough struggle with capitalist competitors.'[28] Seen from this angle, the creation of the joint-stock companies does not constitute evidence that the Soviet Union was already preparing for a separation of its zone. Generally, however, the Soviets were able in this way to control and influ-ence important spheres of the Soviet Occupation Zone's economy. After all, the share of the joint-stock companies in the industrial production of the Soviet Occupation Zone amounted to over 30 per cent at the end of the forties, with particular prominence in the chemical industry, brown coal mining and the energy industry, metallurgy and electrical engineer-ing. They played a decisive role in guaranteeing the reparation deliveries, of which they provided a little less than one-half at the end of the forties and as much as three-quarters in 1951/52. Because of the progressive handing-back of the enterprises their share declined in the following years.

If only because of this key function they were favoured in every way in the economy of the Soviet Occupation Zone: they received higher quotas of materials and electricity, they were allowed to pay higher wages in order to attract qualified workers who were in short supply and they were subsidised from Land budgets and from the Zone budget. The supplies provided by the enterprises for their employees were also better. All this ultimately explains their higher production growth. While they were able to assert themselves 'better and more ruthlessly' – the words of the Saxony–Anhalt economic ministry – when it came to fighting for resources in short supply, they soon developed into an obstacle to the attempt to steer the economy on the Land or Zone scale. In these companies, planning often played no greater part for the Soviet directors than it did for capitalist large-scale entrepreneurs. Although they displayed a greater degree of bureaucratisation, they could hardly be described as model examples of the planned economy, as advertised in the GDR.

A total of seventy-four mostly unprofitable Soviet joint-stock companies were handed back in February 1947 and transferred into Land ownership; in the spring of 1950 a further twenty-three were shed by the Soviets and a further sixty-six enterprises on 1 April 1952. Whereas in the case of the first returns in 1947 only the 'increase in value' had to be compensated for by the Soviet Union, the remaining joint-stock companies had to be bought back by the GDR: between 1947 and 1953 altogether 1,725 million DM (East) became payable at current prices. As part of the stabilisation efforts after the 17 June 1953 uprising in the GDR, all but one of the remaining thirty-three joint-stock companies were handed back at no charge at the beginning of 1954. The exception was the SAG Wismut, which was engaged in uranium mining and would cost the GDR dear at a later date. Thanks to the joint-stock companies, industrial centres and workplaces were preserved in the Soviet Occupation Zone on a major scale.

Reparation deliveries from ongoing production were supplied not only by the Soviet joint-stock companies, but also by state-owned enterprises and, to a lesser extent, by privately-owned enterprises. During the first few years in particular, the demands of the occupying power were often uncoordinated and indeed chaotic. This made it difficult for the German authorities to plan and manage them. Ultimately this procedure delayed the boosting of the economy generally. What most impeded the implementation of the reparation demands were shortages of materials, difficulties in interzonal trade and planning mistakes. The Soviets insisted on punctual delivery of reparations; otherwise they imposed draconian penalties on the enterprise managers concerned. On the other hand, the compulsion behind the reparation demands had a positive effect on reconstruction and growth by rapidly mobilising available resources.

Until 1948 all branches of the economy, including agriculture, had to make deliveries to the occupying power. After that date building of heavy machinery, ships and track vehicles moved more and more to the fore. The reparations accordingly also influenced the economic structure of the Soviet Occupation Zone and the future GDR. Direct deliveries from ongoing production from the Soviet Occupation Zone and East Berlin between 1945 and 1953 are estimated today at about 11.5 billion RM/DM-Ost at current prices. Added to these were indirect reparation deliveries – profits and leases of the Soviet joint-stock companies, as well as purchases of Soviet trading companies – so that the total came to roughly 15 billion RM/DM-Ost at current prices.[29]

However, this total does not include the contribution of the SAG Wismut. In the interests of its own nuclear bomb programme the Soviet Union had developed uranium mining in a few areas of Saxony and Thuringia from 1946 and extended this rapidly until 1951. The real costs of uranium mining for East Germany from 1946 to 1953 amounted to at least 7.3 billion RM/DM-Ost at current prices, though the Soviets recognised no more than one-half of that as reparations.[30] In the period from 1945 to 1953 the Soviet Occupation Zone/GDR moreover had to cope with occupation costs amounting to 16.8 billion RM/DM-Ost at current prices. Added to this were losses from the issue of occupation money of about 5 billion RM, as well as foreign trade losses due to price discrimination in import and export; these were also the responsibility of the occupying power.

Reparation contributions altogether, at current prices, amounted to about 12.1 billion RM of non-recurrent withdrawals within the framework of the trophies action and dismantling, as well as 41.8 billion RM/DM-Ost of ongoing deliveries between 1945 and 1953. This corresponded to a minimum amount of 14 billion dollars at 1938 prices, to which about 1 to 2 billion RM must be added for 'intellectual' reparations.[31] These data, based as they are on internal records, are clearly below most earlier estimates. Even so the reparations to the Soviet Union represented a considerable burden for the economy of the Soviet Occupation Zone/GDR, especially during the first postwar years, a burden that diminished only gradually (Table 1.5).

Table 1.5: Reparation yields as a proportion of the gross domestic product of the Soviet Occupation Zone/GDR from 1946 to 1953 (in per cent)[32]

1946	1947	1948	1949	1950	1951	1952	1953
48.8	38.4	31.1	19.9	18.4	16.4	14.6	12.9

Comparison with the Western zones, or the Federal Republic, has shown that while war destruction was somewhat greater there, the East was more seriously affected by booty-taking and dismantling. The loss of substance, assessed at 1944 prices, amounted to 16 per cent of the national wealth in the Western zones and to 18.5 per cent in the Soviet Occupation Zone. Yet this conveys an incomplete picture as capacity losses due to dismantling considerably surpassed the loss of value, as explained above. Capacity losses were in effect ten times higher in the East of Germany than in the West. Added to this was the fact that this reduced capital equipment was only inadequately evened out in the years that followed because the ongoing reparation deliveries to the Soviet Union were systematically depriving the Soviet Occupation Zone/GDR of the means for reconstruction. The sum-total of ongoing deliveries in the years up to 1953, assessed at 1944 prices, amounted to 34.4 billion RM for the Western zones/the Federal Republic and to 31.7 billion RM for the Soviet Occupation Zone/GDR. In view of the disparate size of the territories concerned and their economic potential, these absolute data should, for the purpose of comparison, be recalculated as per-head figures (Table 1.6).[33]

Table 1.6: Loss of capital assets and ongoing reparation of the Western zones/the Federal Republic and the Soviet Occupation Zone/GDR until 1953 per inhabitant in RM (at 1944 prices)

	Western zones / Federal Republic	Soviet Occupation Zone / GDR
Loss of capital assets	899	1,027
Ongoing reparations total	713	1,997
Ongoing reparations without occupation costs	23	1,349

Losses of capital assets were therefore a little greater in the East than in the West, with the greater dismantling losses having a greater effect because, due to the reparation deliveries, they could not be offset very quickly. Above all, the Soviet Occupation Zone had to make nearly three times the ongoing reparations of the Western zones. If the occupation costs, which were an almost equal burden per head in both parts of the country, are excluded, the imbalance of burdens between West and East in the immediate postwar period is seen to its full extent.[34] These are often confronted with the extensive payments of the Federal Republic after 1953 for liquidation of debts payments and restitution to the victims of the Nazi regime. They cannot, however, be compared to the burdens in the Soviet Occupation Zone in the period up to 1953, if only because, for one thing, they stretched over a very long span of time and, for another, were made by a then prospering economy. Moreover, the Soviet Occupation Zone/GDR in the postwar period received only insignificant support from outside, whereas the Western zones, and later the Federal Republic, were receiving extensive foreign help. Although there, too, the balance of burdens and donations was negative, the imports rendered possible by dollar help first safeguarded the nutrition of the population, later the importation of the required industrial raw materials and, not least, the success of the economic and currency reform of 1948. Rightly, therefore, the 'enormous importance of foreign aid for Western Germany' has been emphasised time and again, while its burdens were described as rather secondary.[35] All in all, of all the loser states of the Second World War, Eastern Germany supplied the most restitution. However, the markedly higher reparation burdens of the Soviet Occupation Zone/GDR, which greatly impeded its start, cannot by themselves explain the subsequently observed growth arrears compared to the Federal Republic. They are above all a consequence of the economic system.

Political Forces in the Soviet Occupation Zone and their Ideas on Economic Policy

The decisive political factor in the Soviet Occupation Zone was initially the Soviet Union. What concept it had for the development of its occupation zone is a controversial question among historians to this day. Some believe they can observe an intention to Sovietise it from the start, while others see a hesitant world power that was being urged by the German Communists to install a Soviet-type system in the East of Germany. In point of fact there are many indications that, at the end of the war, the Soviet Union had no clear concept of its policy towards Germany. The Soviet leaders' ideas on their treatment of Germany developed from the practice of occupation and from their cooperation with the Western Allies. The Soviet Union intended to use the part of Germany occupied by it as a bargaining counter in the struggle for the reshaping of the world order after the Second World War. For a long time a Sovietised part-Germany was not at the forefront of their intentions. A neutral Germany, entire within the frontiers of Yalta and Potsdam, disarmed and denazified, with a political order modelled on the Weimar Republic but with Prussian *Junkers* and big capital stripped of their power, initially seemed sufficient to the Soviets and gradually even advantageous. This goal was also in line with the common Allied positions at the Moscow conference of foreign ministers in October 1943, where agreement had been reached on a common policy towards Germany on the basis of denazification, democratisation, economic unity and reparations. However, there seem to have also been alternative approaches in Moscow, and various measures in the Soviet Occupation Zone were already tending towards Sovietisation. This was critically noted by the Western Allies and influenced their own policy but also confirmed the German Communists in their expectation that Stalin would continue along that road.[36]

In view of the Soviet occupation, the leadership of the Communist Party of Germany (KPD) was playing a major political part. In an appeal by the Central Committee of the Communist Party, dated 11 June 1945, ideas on the reshaping of the economy were – for tactical reasons – rather limited: the appeal was aimed at gaining the broad approval of all strata of society and at a close alliance of all political parties. It demanded a land reform, the protection of the working people against arbitrary actions by employers and unacceptable exploitation. At the same time the appeal supported private initiative by entrepreneurs and private property. Nazi bigwigs and war criminals, on the other hand, were to be expropriated. In line with Soviet ideas the German Communists had to accept that under a joint occupation and administration of Germany there would be democratisation, but not a planned economy on the Soviet model. This was also the attitude of the appeal, which kept to ideas of a social economy. It was only the foundation document of the SED, the Socialist Unity Party of Germany, in April 1946, that explicitly envisaged a future socialism and hence, indirectly, a planned economy. Nevertheless the KPD appeal of 1945 already revealed the essential goals to be pursued in future by the KPD and later the SED leaders through a planned economy, goals that moulded this economy well into the eighties. What mattered above all was the 'struggle against hunger, unemployment and homelessness',[37] that derived from experiences of the Great Depression at the beginning of the thirties and decisively influenced the thinking and actions of the Party leaders right to the end. These arguments were being seriously put forward by those responsible as reasons for the introduction and maintenance of a planned economy; and as its legitimation.

The Communists were not the only ones to call for state intervention and planned-economy instruments, immediately after the war. The Social Democratic Party of Germany, in its foundation appeal of June 1945, already demanded socialism in the economy and society, though with different forms of property continuing to exist side-by-side in a mixed economy. Their cooperation was to be ensured by united and comprehensive planning. Initially the Liberal Democratic Party only reluctantly agreed with these ideas. While it accepted them for a period of most urgent need, for the future it proposed a reform on market-economy lines, oriented along the ideas of early Liberalism. Like the CDU, the Christian Democratic Union, it rejected economic domination by private cartels and concerns, demanding a free-market economy based on small and medium enterprises. The Eastern CDU, on the other hand, tended more towards supporting a planned economy. It based its philosophy on 'Christian socialism' and on 'socialism through Christian responsibility' and aimed at economic planning, public ownership of key enterprises and co-determination of employees in the running of enterprises. Planning, however, was only to mark out the framework, while private initiative would manage economic activity. With the exception of 'Nazi and war criminals' it rejected expropriation without compensation, but supported the nationalisation of certain sectors. It was therefore not only the Communists, but also other political groups that, immediately after the war, were in favour of controlling intervention by the state, all the way to using planning instruments in the economy. This consensus – which lasted only until 1948 – was based first on memories of the Great Depression and its social and political consequences: at the time that crisis was seen as the failure of the capitalist system. Secondly, there was the example of the Soviet Union, where impressive growth rates had been achieved in the thirties. Finally it was believed that the economic plight of the immediate postwar years could only be tackled by an overarching control of the economy.

Land Reform and Nationalisation of Industry

Land reform was one of the first measures by which the Soviets and the German Communists intervened in East German ownership relations. Especially in the areas east of the river Elbe, land ownership had until then been very uneven. The break-up of the large estates was seen as an element of Germany's denazification and democratisation. Because individual ownership would give rise to more production incentives and because the new peasants were to be given a subsistence basis with the expropriated land, it was believed that this would result in better food supplies. Moreover, refugees and expellees could thus be integrated into the postwar society. At the beginning of September 1945 the provincial administration of Saxony issued a land reform decree that was subsequently followed also by the other Länder. This decree was evidently based on a draft prepared in the Soviet Foreign Ministry. It provided for the expropriation, without compensation, of the land of leading Nazis and representatives of the Third Reich, as well as of all landowners with more than one hundred hectares. Large farms and lands owned by the Churches were not affected. The confiscated land, along with its livestock and equipment, was assigned chiefly to agricultural labourers, landless peasants and expelled persons. Machines were to be concentrated with committees for mutual farm help. The land assigned to the new peasants was to comprise five to eight hectares, or ten hectares at the most, and was not to be subdivided, sold, leased, or pawned, but was required to be worked individually.

By October 1947 some 32 per cent of the Soviet Occupation Zone's farmland had been expropriated and by 1950 some 66 per cent of the expropriated land had been handed over to individual recipients. In 1950, some 210,276 new peasants owned an average of 8.1 hectares each. Peasants who had previously had too little land were additionally given 3.3 hectares on average; small leaseholders, part-time farmers and 'old-established peasants' (persons who had been in agriculture even before the land reform) were also given some additional land. A little over one-fifth of the expropriated land – chiefly seed-cultivating and stockbreeding estates as well as schools – were transferred into Land or 'people's' ownership. The proportion of enterprises with more than one hundred hectares had been reduced by the land reform from 28 per cent to just under 4 per cent of the farmland. Farms between 5 and 10 hectares, which until then had accounted for over 11 per cent of the agriculturally useful acreage, now accounted for 32 per cent. In consequence the agrarian structure had undergone a fundamental change.[38] In labour-intensive stockfarming, small farms actually perform best. Against this, however, was the inadequate endowment of new small farms: at the end of 1946 only one-quarter of these enterprises had pigs and only one-third had cows. The shortage of draught animals – three-quarters of the new peasants were working without horses – greatly impaired the facilities of these farms. Only one in four farmers owned a plough, only one in five owned a harrow. Only one in seven new-peasant farms had their own residential or working premises. Sometimes the new peasants had received nothing but the bare land.[39] Thus the structural problem of small and very small peasants suffering from poverty and insufficient resources was exacerbated – a problem not existing on the territory of the Soviet Occupation Zone on the same scale as in Western Germany until then. The new peasants had to be economically stabilised and integrated into rural society.

Given the unsatisfactory results of the reform for many of these new peasants, KPD and SED leaders' hopes of winning their loyalty by means of the land reform were only partially fulfilled. At the same time the overall expropriation without compensation, the harsh treatment of the former estate owners and the rapid uncompromising enforcement of the land reform weakened the 'anti-fascist' consensus and the cooperation of the main political parties. The Christian Democratic Party, in particular, opposed expropriation without compensation. At the peak of the conflict the Soviet Military Administration compelled the two CDU chairmen,

Andreas Hermes and Walther Schreiber, to resign their posts. The membership of the two workers' parties, the SPD and the KPD, tended to favour a nationalisation of the big estates and the creation of cooperatives, though this was not the official position of these parties. Such intentions, however, were rejected by the KPD leadership with reference to Soviet directives. The Soviet Union still seemed reluctant to rule out a consensus with the Western Allies. It regarded the land reform primarily as a measure for stripping militarism and Nazism of power. This was initially also the intention of the Western Allies. However, the manner of the Soviet procedure did not bode well for the future. It promoted dissent among the Allies and compromised the land reform in the West.

Intervention in ownership structure was not, however, confined to agriculture. At the Potsdam Conference the Allies had agreed that German concerns and banks should be decentralised and decartellised and that active Nazis were to be removed from responsible posts in important private enterprises.[40] The Allied Control Council confiscated the property of IG Farben and issued several legal norms for the 'punishment of … industrialists … who had promoted and supported the National Socialist regime'[41] and whose property was now to be confiscated.

In the East, in many places, workers and employees took over their enterprises as soon as the Red Army moved in. Several Länder issued decrees in the summer or early autumn of 1945 concerning the confiscation and expropriation of Nazi property. But it was only the Soviet Military Administration's Order No.124 of 30 October 1945 that made such confiscations binding: under it the property of the German state, of leading members of the Nazi Party, as well as of persons named by the Soviet military command, and all unclaimed property was to be placed under sequestration, i.e., to be confiscated. The following day, Order No. 126 confiscated the assets of the Nazi Party and other Nazi organisations. Apart from the punitive aspect, the Soviet Military Administration was also anxious to put an end to uncoordinated and uncontrollable dismantling – though this hope was not fulfilled. In addition, the entrepreneurial control over their business was to be curtailed in order to safeguard reparations from Eastern Germany.

Sequestration commissions made up of representatives of all political parties, organisations and administrations were to examine each case individually before deciding which enterprise or what owner was to be regarded as a Nazi activist or war profiteer and therefore to be expropriated. Whereas the commission members of the SED and of the Free German Trade Union Association applied their incriminating criteria rather generously, the Christian Democratic and Liberal Party members wanted to keep the number of those affected as small as possible. The Christian Democratic Party chairman, Jakob Kaiser, pointed out that 'such far-reaching decisions

... could genuinely jeopardise the universally desired restitution of the unity of the Reich'.[42] In practice enterprises were regarded as 'deserving of expropriation' if they had a certain economic size, regardless of whether their proprietor or owner was in fact politically incriminated. In consequence virtually all large-scale industrial enterprises were included, as well as large numbers of medium-sized businesses. Such a general transformation of the socioeconomic structure was entirely in line with the Party leaders' intentions, as Fritz Selbmann, Vice President of the Saxony Administration for Economy and Labour, emphasised at a closed meeting of functionaries: it did not matter whether someone was 'incriminated or not; it is a question of class'.[43]

At the beginning of February 1946 Stalin had agreed to the suggestion of Walter Ulbricht, the 'strong man' of the Soviet Occupation Zone and deputy chairman of the SED, that in highly industrialised Saxony the expropriation of confiscated enterprises should be legitimated by a referendum. In consequence this measure would not be seen as an act of Soviet policy, but as the will of the new anti-fascist Germany. There is no doubt that the success of the referendum was also a result of a massive propaganda by the SED. However, an even greater part may have been played by the widespread view that the Nazi dictatorship had very largely been a consequence of capitalism. Even so, all strata of the population were disquieted: workers feared to lose their jobs, peasants thought that 'every farm would become a [Soviet-type] Kolkhoz', tradesmen and the middle classes were expecting further expropriations. Last but not least there were rumours, launched by the Soviets that punitive measures would be taken against the population if the referendum failed.[44] On 30 June 1946 – with a participation of 94 per cent – 78 per cent of all those entitled to vote voted in favour of the law on the expropriation of 'war and Nazi criminals'.[45]

According to the law, the expropriated enterprises became 'people's property'; in economic terms, however, they were state property, as the state – initially in the form of Länder and communes, and later in the shape of the Republic and its central institutions – functioned as the owner of the legal title. The other Länder followed Saxony's lead, without, however, seeking legitimation through a referendum. But conflicts about the expropriations continued. As adjudications were needed for the decisions of the commissions, for hearing appeals and complaints, these dragged on until the summer of 1948. In April 1948 the Soviet Military Administration issued Order No. 64, 'in response to a German request', formally concluding the expropriations.

At the end of 1948 the state sector, together with the Soviet joint-stock companies, accounted for more than three-fifths of industrial gross production. The rest was supplied by private enterprises and, to a small degree, by firms administered by trustees. Over the years that followed the state sector was further enlarged by being assigned more material and, above all, more investments. Simultaneously the private enterprises were further disadvantaged and the full harshness of economic law and tax legislation was applied against them. Already in 1948/49 more and more private entrepreneurs went bankrupt; others just gave up and quite a number fled to the West. In 1950, eventually, three-quarters of gross industrial production came from the state sector (including the Soviet joint-stock companies); by 1955 it was more than four-fifths.[46]

This change in the ownership structure also produced a change in the elite in the enterprises, a change that had begun at the end of the war when Nazi-incriminated managers had fled before the Red Army or had been deposed by the workers. In the course of denazification, management personnel were dismissed or moved into lower posts – which again induced further persons to flee to the West. Soviet commanders, on the other hand, often proceeded more pragmatically in matters of denazification. Whenever it seemed necessary in the interest of production, incriminated specialists were recalled to the enterprises. In many cases, however, the posts were filled by workers or through sideways appointment; these persons often had political qualifications rather than knowledge of the job. To the SED leaders this process was largely a power issue. In Saxony in mid-1948 more than half of all managers of state enterprises were former workers; 80 per cent of them had only elementary school education. For this reason the Party offered special economic classes at its district and regional schools, as well as in specialised economic colleges. The low level of qualifications of managers in the economy, however, persisted well into the fifties and was often used as an argument for the strong centralisation of the control of the economy. Nevertheless a considerable number of leading posts in industry continued to be held by representatives of the 'old' economic elite; with the development of the planned economy and the growing complexity of demands they were increasingly needed again. Towards the end of the fifties the new – GDR-socialised – intelligentsia moved up into leading positions.[47] This succession of elites, moreover, consolidated the new ownership patterns: the new opportunities of promotion should not be underrated for the socially and politically binding power they represented: this would determine the identification with the new order for a long time.

Admittedly, the authority of the management in the enterprises still had to be upheld vis-à-vis the works councils. In August 1946 Selbmann observed in this connection that 'we don't want an enterprise parliament, where the works council has to be consulted about every screw that has to be obtained, but … a tight leadership aware of its responsibility upwards and downwards'.[48] The works councils, moreover, orientated themselves by the interests of their enterprises and their workforce rather than by the requirements of the economy as a whole. This was one of the reasons why they were abolished in 1948. The Free German Trade Union Association (FDGB) increasingly acted as the representative of the new state 'overall entrepreneur' and largely ceased to represent the interests of the employees. Thus there was no institution that would have enabled the workers to share in decision making and that would therefore have been an incentive to higher performance.

Restarting Production

The economic situation after the war was marked for the bulk of the population by shortages. Many, especially refugees and expellees, lacked adequate living space and food. In addition to wartime destruction, uncoordinated dismantling and arbitrary confiscation by the Soviet occupying power paralysed entire sectors; important enterprises, now Soviet joint-stock companies, were only partially available, with their products, to the economy of the Soviet Occupation Zone. As the separate Länder and then the Western zones and the Soviet Occupation Zone increasingly cut themselves off from each other, many enterprises lost their traditional suppliers. Because of the difficulties of obtaining the usual raw materials and because of the lack of machines, many products only had a limited practical value. Moreover, there was a considerable surplus of money in circulation with the result that its function as a universal means of exchange was also limited. Together with the disrupted interconnections, the result was that enterprises exchanged their products for foodstuffs for their employees and for raw materials in order to maintain their production. Enterprises were thus able to pay part of their staff's wages in kind. Under these conditions the black or the grey market was indispensable not only for the survival of individual, but also for the maintenance of production. According to various estimates one-quarter of the national income or of industrial durables was still, in 1948, turned over by the black market or by compensation deals.[49]

Against this background the two crucial economic tasks of the immediate postwar period were paying reparations to the Soviet Union and promoting reconstruction in order to eliminate the worst hardships. As the Soviets were interested in reparations out of ongoing production, they had a direct interest in economic recovery. Expropriations and the first steps towards a command economy and a planned economy were considered by them necessary in order to safeguard reparations. This approach also accorded with the ambitions of the Communist and Socialist Unity Parties to reshape society along Communist ideas, even though they initially pursued a tactical concept with regard to Soviet policies which did not seek socialism as the immediate task. Moreover, many people regarded state control of the economy as indispensable because of the shortages. Finally, the growing number of state-owned enterprises demanded the same thing.

Local commanders of the Soviet army had ordered a resumption of production immediately after the arrival of the troops. On 21 July 1945 the chief of the Soviet Military Administration issued Order No. 9, which specified the industrial branches to be prioritised. It demanded a 'project plan' for the production in the final quarter of 1945 and a listing of available stocks. Furthermore the prices were frozen. Under Soviet Military Administration Order No. 17 of 27 July 1945 eleven central administrations were to be created in the Soviet Occupation Zone, the economically most important being those for fuel, industry, agriculture, trade and food supplies, transport, communications, finance, as well as labour and social welfare. Their rights and competences, however, remained unregulated. In addition, economic authorities were set up in the Länder and provinces. Thus the outlines of a controlled economy with price controls and rationing of goods appeared at a very early stage without, however, linking up with the Nazi wartime economy directly. The Third Reich's controlling institutions, such as the Wirtschaftsgruppen, tried, as a federation of commercial enterprises, to assert some planning demands, but these ambitions were soon quashed. There were, however, continuities especially in personnel: the central administrations depended on experts from the Third Reich's private economy and administration who were open-minded to planning and bureaucratic procedures. There were scarcely any other qualified persons for such tasks.

Until 1948 planning was done for the manageable period of one quarter. The difficulty of any planning was to register what was available and to secure the conditions for orderly production. Uncoordinated dismantling and increasing reparation seizures were undermining the basis of planning, even though this was to guarantee the restitution deliveries. Moreover, enterprises concealed their capacities, their raw material and other material reserves from the planning authorities because in an uncertain situation they wanted to hold on to their reserves and because they feared confiscations. For this reason the Soviet Military Administration introduced rationing of raw materials – a bureaucratic and inflexible system that soon proved to be an obstacle to production. Besides, production, demand and distribution were not attuned to each other in the plans. In any case, the coordination of economic activities for the Zone as a whole was exceedingly limited. The central administrations had few rights and the Länder, anxious to serve their own interests, resisted their instructions, mostly successfully, and separated themselves off against one another. Thus the planning efforts often worked against each other and many regarded them as purely playing with figures by the occupying power – the more so as the continuing dismantling operated against the implementation of the reparation demands. Selbmann, the Saxon Minister for the Economy, spoke of a 'chaotic situation', in which, 'because of the totally confused measures of the Soviet Military Administration', there was no such thing as economic planning.[50] In this sense the economy of the Soviet Occupation Zone was, until 1947/48, steered operationally, and not very successfully, according to rough targets.

After the end of the war conditions for increasing production were initially favourable as there were sufficient unused capacities available and enterprises still had reserves of raw materials and other materials from wartime. Many destroyed capacities were put on stream again with only slight effort. This resulted in rapid and surprising successes until the end of 1946; after that, however, reserves were exhausted. Moreover, the development of production was decisively determined by available supplies of raw materials, fuel and power. Besides, compensation deals were playing a major part in the economic results of individual enterprises. Although the raw materials and semi-finished goods not available in the Soviet Occupation Zone could have been obtained mostly by interzonal trade, this was difficult from the start because of restrictive Allied regulations. It is thought that grey and black market deals across the zonal boundary initially amounted to a greater volume than interzonal trade. Not until 1946/47 did legal imports of iron, steel and engineering products from the Western zones increase. Vital deliveries of hard coal, however, very nearly stagnated and, compared to requirements and to the pre-war level, remained slight. In 1947 the Soviet Occupation Zone received less than one-third of the 1938 volume of hard coal, hard-coal coke and pig iron from the Ruhr.[51] Moreover, these deliveries were 'quite openly used to bring pressure to bear'. In line with their strategic intentions regarding Germany 'the Western powers were increasingly trying to impose an indirect embargo by limiting or delaying such deliveries'. In turn the Soviet authorities prevented some deliveries going to the West for fear of losing reparation assets. The Soviet Occupation Zone needed 13 to 14 million tonnes of hard coal: with a domestic production of 0.15 million tonnes it received 1.5 million tonnes from the Western zones and 0.43 million tonnes from Upper Silesia, which only covered 15 to 16 per cent of its requirements.[52]

In agriculture the yields per hectare in 1946 amounted to only 57 per cent of the 1936 figure for grain and to about 70 per cent for potatoes and sugar beet.[53] Farmland and means of production had been damaged by the war; in particular livestock had been greatly reduced through war, escape and confiscation. The number of horses in 1946 was 20 per cent below the 1935/38 level, that of cows was 30 per cent below, that of sheep 54 per cent and even that of pigs 66 per cent below.[54] As the number of livestock diminished, so did the amount of natural manure. Chemical fertiliser was also in short supply. The land reform, finally, prevented any rapid increase in agrarian production: the newly created enterprises were too small and inadequately provided with means of production; moreover, the new peasants lacked experience. In addition, the numbers and quality of the machines available at the Machine Lending Stations (MAS) were insufficient. Not until the fifties were the Machine Lending Stations able to improve their stock. As a result the new peasants had to borrow equipment and machines from the long-established 'old' peasants; this made them dependent on them and represented a financial burden. In order to improve the livestock numbers of the new peasants the Soviet Military Administration, in November 1945, ordered a livestock equalisation within the Soviet Occupation Zone in favour of Mecklenburg and Brandenburg. By August 1946 Saxony–Anhalt alone supplied 9,000 horses and 22,500 head of cattle. Such redistributions were repeated several times in the late forties. They weakened stock farming in the southern regions of the Soviet Occupation Zone and inflamed conflicts between old and new peasants. Even so, this was not enough to consolidate the position of the new peasants. Thousands of them gave up as early as 1946.[55]

Because of the low agricultural production the population – which had meanwhile grown – could not be sufficiently fed. Its nutrition was regulated by food rationing cards and was graduated according to the holder's occupation: the biggest rations went to workers in heavy and very heavy occupations. Next came other manual workers, then office workers and all the rest. This lowest category nevertheless included nearly one-half of the card holders in 1947/48.[56] The rations were sold at relatively low prices. Even so, the cost of living rose by 24 per cent, according to 'legal' prices only, from 1944 to October 1946.[57] Only very rarely did the population have enough money or objects of value to supplement their rations by purchases on the black market. According to an estimate at the time foodstuffs on the black market cost sixteen times as much and consumer goods ten times as much as in 1935.[58] Alongside the black market, two recollections have engraved themselves on the collective memory of the postwar period: 'hoarding trips' into the countryside and 'field stubbling', i.e., picking up the left-overs on harvested fields. The scale and food supply effect of these can no longer be established. But poverty was certainly widespread immediately after the war. Malnutrition, inadequate clothing, especially footwear, and a shortage of domestic fuel had a negative effect on the health and performance of the population. Deficiency diseases such as tuberculosis were spreading, demanding victims. For men the average mortality was about twice that of before the war and only normalised in 1950; for women it did so in 1948.[59]

During the first eighteen months after the end of the war production rose relatively fast, but in the exceptionally harsh winter of 1946/47 it collapsed. Foodstuffs and fuel became ever scarcer, and the poor food conditions seriously impaired the performance of the workers. After the harvest failure of the summer of 1947 the prospects for the coming winter were even grimmer. Industry had exhausted its wartime stocks of material, and the distribution system was unable to relieve the situation as, due to the transport crisis, its performance and productivity declined. To this crisis the East German Communists and the occupying power reacted by tightening their economic control, by offering more incentives to the workers and by more strongly supporting the new peasants.

Notes

1. Calculated from Länderrat des amerikanischen Besatzungsgebietes (ed.), *Statistisches Handbuch von Deutschland 1928–1944*, Munich 1949, p. 8.
2. Including the Saar territory calculated according to: *Wirtschaftsstatistik der deutschen Besatzungszonen 1945–1948 in Verbindung mit der deutschen Produktionsstatistik der Vorkriegszeit (Dokumente und Berichte des Europa-Archivs, Vol. 3)*, Oberursel 1948, p. 33; *Statistisches Handbuch 1928–1944*, p. 8.
3. Calculated according to: Bruno Gleitze, *Ostdeutsche Wirtschaft. Industrielle Standorte und volkswirtschaftliche Kapazitäten des ungeteilten Deutschlands*, Berlin (West) 1956, p. 173.
4. This admittedly refers to the gross value; see Rainer Karlsch, *Allein bezahlt? Die Reparationsleistungen der SBZ/DDR 1945–1953*, Berlin 1993, p. 36.
5. All numerical data refer to the area of the later Soviet Occupation Zone (excluding Berlin) as a share of production or sale in the German Reich in its 1937 frontiers; they are calculated according to Gleitze, *Ostdeutsche Wirtschaft*, pp. 191–208. Cf., with figures calculated differently, Werner Matschke, *Die industrielle Entwicklung in der Sowjetischen Besatzungszone Deutschlands (SBZ) von 1945 bis 1948*, Berlin (West) 1988, pp. 60 ff., 99–103.
6. Calculated according to Gleitze, *Ostdeutsche Wirtschaft*, pp. 167 f.
7. Lothar Baar, Rainer Karlsch and Werner Matschke, 'Kriegsschäden, Demontagen und Reparationen', in Deutscher Bundestag (ed.), *Materialien der Enquete-Kommission 'Aufarbeitung von Geschichte und Folgen der SED-Diktatur in Deutschland'*, Baden-Baden 1995, Vol II/2, pp. 868–988, here 894 f.
8. Karlsch, *Allein bezahlt?*, pp. 44 ff.; Matschke, *Industrielle Entwicklung*, p. 301; Jörg Roesler, Veronika Siedt and Michael Elle, *Wirtschaftswachstum in der Industrie der DDR 1945–1970*, Berlin (East) 1986, pp. 71, 77.
9. Unless otherwise stated the following data are based on Wolfgang Zank, *Wirtschaft und Arbeit in Ostdeutschland 1945–1949. Probleme des Wiederaufbaus in der Sowjetischen Besatzungszone Deutschlands*, Munich 1987, pp. 30–34.
10. This results from the total of registered resettlers in the Soviet Occupation Zone between 1946 and 1949 according to Marcel Boldorf, *Sozialfürsorge in der SBZ/DDR 1945–1953. Ursachen, Ausmaß und Bewältigung der Nachkriegsarmut*, Stuttgart 1998, p. 24, Table 2.

11. Bruno Gleitze, 'Die Forderungen der Sowjetzone aus der mitteldeutschen Fluchtbewegung', *Allgemeines Statistisches Archiv 1967*, p. 384, quoted from Zank, *Wirtschaft und Arbeit*, p. 38.
12. Zank, *Wirtschaft und Arbeit*, p. 31.
13. All data according to Zank, *Wirtschaft und Arbeit*, pp. 30 ff.
14. On this and also on the following: Jochen Laufer: 'Die Reparationsplanungen im sowjetischen Außenministerium während des Zweiten Weltkrieges' in: Christoph Buchheim (ed.): *Wirtschaftliche Folgelasten des Krieges in der SBZ/DDR*, Baden-Baden 1995, pp. 21–43, quotation p. 32.
15. On the following cf. also Christoph Buchheim, 'Kriegsschäden, Demontagen und Reparationen. Deutschland nach dem Zweiten Weltkrieg', in Deutscher Bundestag, *Materialien der Enquete-Kommission*, pp. 1030–69, quotation p. 1038.
16. Jochen Laufer, 'Von den Demontagen zur Währungsreform – Besatzungspolitik und Sowjetisierung Ostdeutschlands 1945–1948', in Michael Lemke (ed.), *Sowjetisierung und Eigenständigkeit in der SBZ/DDR (1945–1953)*, Cologne 1999, pp. 163–86, here 168 ff.
17. Karlsch, *Allein bezahlt?*, pp. 55–60; Baar et al., *Kriegsschäden*, pp. 900–3.
18. Laufer, 'Von den Demontagen zur Währungsreform', p. 170.
19. The following, unless stated otherwise, according to Karlsch, *Allein bezahlt?* pp. 60–84.
20. Jochen Laufer, 'Politik und Bilanz der sowjetischen Demontagen in der SBZ/DDR 1945–1950', in Rainer Karlsch and Jochen Laufer (eds), *Sowjetische Demontagen in Deutschland 1944–1949. Hintergründe, Ziele und Wirkungen*, Berlin 2002, pp. 31–77, here 52.
21. Rainer Karlsch, 'Die Reparationsleistungen der SBZ/DDR im Spiegel deutscher und russischer Quellen', in Karl Eckart and Jörg Roesler (eds), *Die Wirtschaft im geteilten und vereinten Deutschland*, Berlin 1999, pp. 9–30, here 11; Laufer, 'Von den Demontagen zur Währungsreform', p. 169.
22. Karlsch, 'Reparationsleistungen', p. 13.
23. Karlsch, *Allein bezahlt?* p. 88.
24. Werner Abelshauser, *Wirtschaftsgeschichte der Bundesrepublik Deutschland 1945–1980*, Frankfurt 1983, p. 20.
25. Matschke, *Industrielle Entwicklung*, p. 195.
26. Rüdiger Kühr, *Die Reparationspolitik der UdSSR und die Sowjetisierung des Verkehrswesens der SBZ. Eine Untersuchung der Entwicklung der Deutschen Reichsbahn 1945–1949*, Bochum 1996, quoted from Karlsch, Reparationsleistungen, p. 17.
27. On this complex cf. Burghard Ciesla, '"Intellektuelle Reparationen" der SBZ an die alliierten Siegermächte? Begriffsgeschichte, Diskussionsaspekte und ein Fallbeispiel – Die deutsche Flugzeugindustrie 1945–1946', in Buchheim, *Wirtschaftliche Folgelasten*, pp. 79–109, quotation p. 93.
28. These and the following data on the SAGs according to: Rainer Karlsch and Johannes Bähr, 'Die Sowjetischen Aktiengesellschaften (SAG) in der SBZ/DDR. Bildung, Struktur und Probleme ihrer inneren Entwicklung', in Karl Lauschke and Thomas Welskopp (eds), *Mikropolitik im Unternehmen.*

Arbeitsbeziehungen und Machtstrukturen in industriellen Großbetrieben des 20. Jahrhunderts, Essen 1994, pp. 214–55.

29. Karlsch, *Allein bezahlt?* pp. 194–96.
30. Heinz Köhler, *Economic Integration in the Soviet Bloc, with an East German Case Study*, New York 1965, p. 23. This estimate is also used by Rainer Kalsch for his calculations.
31. Kalsch, *Allein bezahlt?* pp. 200–5, 217–22, 230 f.
32. Kalsch, *Allein bezahlt?* p. 234.
33. All the above data, as well as the table and the following according to Karlsch, *Allein bezahlt?* pp. 232–36.
34. Jörg Fisch, *Reparationen nach dem Zweiten Weltkrieg*, Munich 1992, p. 225; Buchheim, 'Kriegsschäden', p. 1066.
35. Christoph Buchheim, *Die Wiedereingliederung Westdeutschlands in die Weltwirtschaft 1945–1958*, Munich 1990, pp. 98 f.; Fisch, *Reparationen*, pp. 226, 307.
36. Cf., inter alia: Jan Foitzik, *Sowjetische Militäradministration in Deutschland (SMAD) 1945–1949. Struktur und Funktion*, Berlin 1999; Laufer, *Von den Demontagen zur Währungsreform*; Wilfried Loth, *Stalins ungeliebtes Kind. Warum Moskau die DDR nicht wollte*, Berlin 1994; Elke Scherstjanoi, 'Die deutschlandpolitischen Absichten der UdSSR 1948. Erkenntnisstand und forschungsleitende Problematisierungen', in Dierk Hoffmann and Hermann Wentker (eds), *Das letzte Jahr der SBZ. Politische Weichenstellungen und Kontinuitäten im Prozeß der Gründung der DDR*, Munich 2000, pp. 39–54.
37. 'Aufruf des ZK der KPD vom 11. Juni 1945', in Peter Erler, Horst Laude and Manfred Wilke (eds), *'Nach Hitler kommen wir'. Dokumente zur Programmatik der Moskauer KPD-Führung 1944–1945 für Nachkriegsdeutschland*, Berlin 1994, p. 395.
38. Figures according to 'Ergebnisse der Bodenreform', in Matthias Judt (ed.), *DDR-Geschichte in Dokumenten. Beschlüsse, Berichte, interne Materialien und Alltagszeugnisse*, Berlin 1997, pp. 103 f.; Arnd Bauerkämper, 'Problemdruck und Ressourcenverbrauch. Wirtschaftliche Auswirkungen der Bodenreform in der SBZ/DDR 1945–1952', in Buchheim, *Wirtschaftliche Folgelasten*, pp. 295–322, here 301 f.; Staatliche Zentralverwaltung für Statistik (ed.), *Statistisches Jahrbuch der DDR 1956*, Berlin (East) 1957 (hereinafter *Statistisches Jahrbuch*), pp. 348 f.
39. Zank, *Wirtschaft und Arbeit*, p. 154.
40. Alexander Fischer (ed.), *Teheran, Jalta, Potsdam. Die sowjetischen Protokolle von den Kriegskonferenzen der 'Großen Drei'*, Cologne 1985, pp. 394 ff.
41. Control Council Directive No. 38 of 12.10.1946, quoted according to Tilman Bezzenberger, 'Wie das Volkseigentum geschaffen wurde. Die Unternehmensenteignungen in der Sowjetischen Besatzungszone 1945–1948', *Zeitschrift für neuere Rechtsgeschichte* 19, 1997, pp. 210–48, here 218 f.
42. 'Protokoll der Sitzung des gemeinsamen Einheitsfront-Ausschusses am 16.5.46', in Siegfried Suckut, *Blockpolitik in der SBZ/DDR 1945–1949. Die Sitzungsprotokolle des Zentralen Einheitsfront-Ausschusses. Quellenedition*, Cologne 1986, p. 137.

43. Quoted according to Winfrid Halder, 'Prüfstein ... für die politische Lauterbarkeit der Führenden? Der Volksentscheid zur "Enteignung der Kriegs- und Naziverbrecher" in Sachsen im Juni 1946', *Geschichte und Gesellschaft* 25, 1999, pp. 589–612, here 610.

44. Halder, 'Prüfstein', pp. 600–6, quotations pp. 603, 606.

45. Werner Krause, *Die Entstehung des Volkseigentums in der Industrie der DDR*, Berlin (East) 1958, p. 75.

46. Calculated according to Krause, *Entstehung des Volkseigentums*, p. 108; *Statistisches Jahrbuch 1955*, p. 126.

47. Fritz Selbmann, *Demokratische Wirtschaft*, Dresden 1948, p. 66. Cf. Matschke, *Industrielle Entwicklung*, pp. 234 f.; Peter Hübner, 'Durch Planung zur Improvisation, Zur Geschichte des Leitungspersonals in der staatlichen Industrie der DDR', *Archiv für Sozialgeschichte* 39, 1999, pp. 197–233, here 212 f.; Armin Müller, *Institutionelle Brüche und personelle Brücken. Werkleiter in Volkseigenen Betrieben der DDR in der Ära Ulbricht*, Cologne 2006.

48. Referat Selbmann vor den Direktoren der Industrieverwaltungen, 5.8.1946, Sächsisches Hauptstaatsarchiv LRS MfW No. 2276, quoted according to Winfrid Halder, *'Modell für Deutschland'. Wirtschaftspolitik in Sachsen 1945–1948*, Paderborn 2001, p. 259.

49. Leuschner, 'Kritische Betrachtungen über die Wirtschaftsplanung in der sowjetischen Besatzungszone', 10.8.1946, SAPMO-BA NY4182/951; Horst Barthel, 'Die Einführung des doppelten Preissystems für Einzelhandelsverkaufspreise in der DDR durch die Schaffung der HO-Laden von 1948 bis 1950/51 als komplexe Maßnahme der Wirtschaftspolitik', in *Jahrbuch für Geschichte, Vol. 31*, Berlin (East) 1984, pp. 273–97, here 276; Dietrich Staritz, *Die Gründung der DDR. Von der sowjetischen Besatzungsherrschaft zum sozialistischen Staat*, Munich 1995, p. 135.

50. Selbmann to Leuschner, 16.8.1946, SAPMO-BA NY4113/16.

51. Matschke, *Industrielle Entwicklung*, p. 178.

52. Quotation and all details according to: Gunther Mai, *Der Alliierte Kontrollrat in Deutschland 1945–1948. Alliierte Einheit – deutsche Teilung?*, Munich 1995, p. 186.

53. Horst Barthel, *Die wirtschaftlichen Ausgangsbedingungen der DDR. Zur Wirtschaftsentwicklung auf dem Gebiet der DDR 1945–1949/50*, Berlin (East) 1979, pp. 45–50; Bauerkämper, 'Problemdruck und Ressourcenverbrauch', pp. 297, 302.

54. Matthias Kramer, *Die Landwirtschaft in der Sowjetischen Besatzungszone. Die Entwicklung in den Jahren 1945–1955. Textteil (Bonner Berichte aus Mittel- und Ostdeutschland)*, Bonn 1957, p. 102.

55. Zank, *Wirtschaft und Arbeit*, p. 156; Bauerkämper, 'Problemdruck und Ressourcenverbrauch', pp. 302 ff.

56. Boldorf, *Sozialfürsorge*, p. 63.

57. Vorläufige Untersuchung über die Entwicklung von Preisen und Löhnen seit 1944, 24.10.1946, SAPMO-BA DY30 IV 2/602/88.

58. Rainer Gries, *Die Rationen-Gesellschaft. Versorgungskampf und Vergleichsmentalität: Leipzig, München und Köln nach dem Kriege*, Münster 1991, p. 110.

59. See Zank, *Wirtschaft und Arbeit*, pp. 78 ff.

Chapter 2

The Establishment of the
Planned Economy 1948–1953

Whereas initially it was the poor economic situation that led to the development of a controlled economy, subsequently the establishment of the planned economy became increasingly an instrument of the Socialist Unity Party's power policy. The Soviet Union pursued an ambivalent course in this respect: on the one hand, driven by the constraints of the poor economy, it supported the transition to a planned economy. On the other, it was anxious, for security as well as political and economic reasons, to avoid an open confrontation with the Western Allies. For quite some time it had favoured a united neutral Germany. For this reason, the Soviets only yielded to the SED's urgings for further steps in socioeconomic transformation and the creation of state structures in the Soviet Occupation Zone to the extent that measures for state-building were similarly being taken in the Western zones. The simultaneous introduction of the Marshall Plan (in which the East European countries, under pressure from Stalin, were not permitted to participate); the establishment of the Ruhr Authority; the reform of the Bizone; and the abandonment of nationalisation in the British zone, appeared to the Soviets in 1947 like the installation of a 'Western Bloc'. An all-German solution seemed increasingly improbable. This lent additional impulses to the transformation process in the Soviet Occupation Zone. Soon the Socialist Unity Party's officials were no longer able or willing to rely on the fact that the Soviet Occupation Zone would receive the same volume of raw materials and commodities from the West as before the war. That was why they believed the deficits in the economic structure caused by the disruption of traditional economic ties had to be offset by the creation of their own capacities. This structural policy was complemented by imports of scarce raw materials from those Eastern and Southeastern European countries which had carried out their socioeconomic transformations on the Soviet model by the beginning of the fifties.

German Economic Commission and Currency Reform

In order to meet the 1947 crisis the Soviet Military Administration on 4 June 1947 issued Order No. 138 which approved an agreement among the economic central administrations: economic activities were to be better coordinated. For this purpose the German Economic Commission (DWK) was established. Until then the Soviet Union had avoided creating an all-embracing authority for its zone because it continued to prefer an all-German solution. But after the creation of the Economic Council of the Bizone it evidently no longer saw any reason for such constraint. Yet initially even the German Economic Commission was scarcely able, because of its limited powers, to assert itself vis-à-vis the Länder. The attitude of the Thurinigian Ministry of Economic Affairs was: 'of the decisions of the Berlin Economic Commission we will implement whatever we consider advisable and correct'.[1] In practice the separatism of the Länder and the centralising tendencies of the German Economic Commission continued to lead to conflicting rulings and decisions. Even though the occupying power had the final say, it was unable to enhance the efficiency of economic control.

Consequently, Party leaders urged Moscow to widen the powers of the German Economic Commission – a move that had already been under consideration there. After all, the weakness of economic control so far would have to be overcome and the dismal economic situation improved to ensure that reparation demands were fulfilled. But it was only when the Western Allies, after the failure of the London foreign ministers' conference at the end of 1947, extended the powers of the Frankfurt Economic Council, that the German Economic Commission was newly constituted in February 1948 by Soviet Military Administration Order No. 32. A little later it was given a general and mandatory authority vis-à-vis the administrative bodies and the population. The central administrations were integrated into the German Economic Commission. This now represented a uniform authority under the chairmanship of the former Minister of Economic Affairs of the Brandenburg Land, Heinrich Rau. By the summer of 1948 it had created the foundations of the new economic order: first, the hierarchy of economic direction was unified and centralised and the economic administrations of the Länder were subordinated to the directives of the German Economic Commission; this meant that their responsibilities for economic policy were in fact abolished. These powers were now held by the German Economic Commission and, for planning especially, by their Hauptverwaltung Wirtschaftsplanung (Main Administration for Economic Planning) under the direction of Bruno Leuschner. Secondly, the time span of the plans was extended. Following consultation with the Soviet Military Administration, a production plan for the second half of 1948 was issued in the spring of

1948, followed by the Two-Year Plan for 1949/50 'in the interest of recon-struction and the development of a peacetime economy'.[2] The Party leaders here quite openly demonstrated their prerogative: at the end of June 1948 they laid down the directives for the six-month plan and the Two-Year Plan, which were taken over by the German Economic Commission, who made them the basis of the plan. What to many seemed initially merely something necessary for rapid reconstruction, now assumed a political power dimen-sion which shook the consensus of the East German political parties. Ever since the autumn of 1947 the Socialist Unity Party had been aiming at a Soviet-type planned economy. The Liberal Democratic Party in particular opposed this development, but, together with the other East German par-ties, conformed to the political goals after massive pressure from the Soviets and from the Socialist Unity Party. Thirdly, the foundations had to be creat-ed for an orderly economic activity: the existing surplus of money had to be liquidated.

The 'noiseless' financing of the war by the Nazis had increased the amount of money from 1939 to the end of April 1945 sevenfold, which contrasted with the clearly declined real domestic product.[3] The thereby threatening inflation had been held back in the Third Reich by strict price regulation, and the Soviet occupying power now continued this with a price stop at the 1944 level. During the final days of the war the Soviet commander in Berlin gave orders to halt all bank transactions. Similar orders were issued elsewhere. Accounts were blocked and a payment prohibition was issued at the end of July 1945. With a few exceptions all banks in the Soviet Occupation Zone were closed; simultaneously, upon a Soviet Military Administration Order, a single Land or provincial bank was set up in every Land or Province. This was intended to avoid a run of depositors on remaining cash accounts, to freeze monetary means and to check inflation. There was an increased need for such measures because the Red Army, on entry, had confiscated all monies within reach and, according to its own requirements, brought them into circulation. The Allies, moreover, issued occupation money, the 'Military Mark' – in all about 6 billion RM, of which 5 billion RM went to the Soviet Union.[4] This influx further inflated the circulation of cash. In all four occupation zones it amounted in the summer of 1948, prior to the currency reforms, to about 65 billion RM. Added to this were large amounts of deposit money – the bank accounts due at any time. Cash and deposit money together represented a volume of money that probably amounted to between 170 and 190 billion RM in 1948.[5]

The disparity between the inflated volume of money and the goods available to the public stimulated the black and grey markets, where sig-nificantly higher prices were current than those officially controlled. Fewer and fewer commodities could be found at the controlled prices.

The Reichsmark was increasingly rejected as currency; secondary currencies came into existence, such as cigarettes, which better performed the function of money. In consequence of the shortage of goods the official price stop was not tenable – in defiance of it, wholesale prices, up to the currency reform in June 1948, rose by 22 per cent compared with 1944; investment goods rose by more (60 per cent) than consumer goods (27 per cent).[6] The surplus of money and the rejection of the Reichmark as currency eventually made a currency reform indispensable.

Generally speaking, it was assumed that the currency would have to be devalued 10:1. However, the divergent economic policies in the separate zones and the Cold War made it seem increasingly improbable that a unified currency policy could be maintained across Germany. In their negotiations both the Soviet Union and the Western Allies backed a double strategy, in which 'on the basis of one's own ideas the others' ability to compromise was to be sounded out'. Both sides wanted to be able, 'in the event of a failure of the four-power negotiations, to shift the blame for a final division of Germany due to separate currency reforms away from themselves'. Information about separate preparations on the other side reciprocally accelerated this process, the more so as the East–West conflict became generally exacerbated during those weeks and a quasi-state development was being promoted both in the Western zones and in the Soviet Occupation Zone. By their walk-out from the Control Council on 20 March 1948 the Soviets eventually anticipated the American withdrawal from the negotiations.[7]

In the same month the head of the Soviet Military Administration's financial administration reported to Moscow that preparations for a currency reform had been completed. For technical reasons, however, the new banknotes could not be printed in time. When, on 17 June 1948, the Western Allies announced the currency reform for the Western zones on 20 June, the Soviets prohibited the circulation of the new Western money in the Soviet Occupation Zone. Similar measures now had to be taken swiftly, because otherwise there was the danger that the Reichsmark, now worthless in the West, might flow into Eastern Germany. Because of the non-existence of new banknotes the devaluation in the East had to be done in two steps. First the old Reichsmark notes had special coupons stuck on. Because of their poor glue these coupons often came off the banknotes, which therefore earned themselves the name of 'wallpaper Marks'. Starting on 24 June, the inhabitants of the Soviet Occupation Zone and Berlin (including its Western sectors) each received 70 such coupon Marks at the rate of 1:1 against the old currency. Further cash was to be deposited in accounts and exchanged at a rate of 10:1, but not to become available until later. In the case of accounts exceeding 5,000 RM the owner had to prove the 'honest origin' of the money – a measure intended to hit mainly the black marketeers. Prices, wages, salaries, pensions, stipends and taxes were converted at 1:1. Between 25 and 28 July a second cash exchange took place, during which the coupon Mark was exchanged at 1:1 against the Deutsche Mark der Deutschen Notenbank. This – hereinafter simply called Mark – was now the exclusive legal currency in the Soviet Occupation Zone and the future GDR. After the reform, cash in circulation amounted to about 15 per cent of the surrendered old cash, which corresponds to a devaluation ratio of 6.8:1 only (as against the desired 10:1) (see Table 2.1).

Not only was the cash revaluation unsatisfactory, but so was the revaluation of deposits at credit institutions. If one includes the account blocking of 1945 and leaves the deposits of the credit institutions unconsidered, deposit money, at an estimate, was devalued only at a rate of 8:1. First of all special rules for state-owned enterprises and political parties, politically motivated, led to a considerable portion of accounts accumulated between 1945 and 1948 being almost totally converted. Ultimately the total amount of money per head of population was twice as great in the East as in the Western zones (Table 2.1).

Table 2.1: Results of the 1948 currency reform in the Soviet Occupation Zone compared to the Western zones: amounts of money in old and new currency, revaluation ratios and relation to population total[8]

	Old money		New money		Revaluation ratio
	Total million RM	per head RM	Total million DM	per head DM	
Soviet Occupation Zone					
Cash	27,940	1,471	4,112	216	6.8:1
Deposit money	51,823	2,728	6,508	343	8.0:1
Money in circulation	79,763	4,198	10,620	559	7.5:1
Western Zones					
Cash	.	.	6,850	143	.
Deposit money	.	.	6,400	133	.
Money in circulation	144,508	3,011	13,250	276	10.9:1

The currency reform in Western Germany was not only more thorough, but also had a totally different character, as it, as a matter of principle, abolished price regulation by the state as well as rationing, and instead reintroduced a market economy. By way of contrast, the East German currency reform with its massive favouring of state-owned enterprises further advanced the development of a planned economy. Accordingly, the banking and financial system was likewise reorganised following the currency reform. From July 1948 the Deutsche Notenbank functioned as 'the house bank of the state' and as a central bank. Its brief was 'actively to support economic planning with the instruments of monetary and credit policy'.[9]

About the same time, therefore, in 1948, the German Economic Commission was newly constituted, the controlling hierarchy centralised, preparations advanced for the Two-Year Plan, and the currency reformed. The coincidence of these political steps created the impression among contemporaries that Germany was already being increasingly divided into West and East, each with its separate currency reforms and its own money – the more so as the Soviets took the Western currency reform as an opportunity for blocking the Western sectors of Berlin. The separate solutions of the currency problem, following upon the separation of reparations policy, represented a further step towards the political division of Germany.

Problems of Economic Control

In order to deal with the economic crisis of 1947 the incentives of employed workers needed to be increased. In the immediate postwar period the workers had often used unclear managerial relations in the enterprises to enable them to reduce or abolish detested work norms or do away with piecework wages, discredited as a means of exploitation. In view of the crisis, the Soviet Military Administration in October 1947 issued Order No. 234 to the effect that in state-owned enterprises and Soviet joint-stock companies 'social improvements should be directly linked to the compliance of the given performance level, above all to performance increases'. Additional supplies thus granted via the enterprises, for instance of clothing, could be withdrawn if the plan was not fulfilled; in case of 'refusal to work', the food ration card was to be confiscated.

In addition, piecework wages were to be reintroduced. To forestall possible resistance a directive issued in the autumn of 1948 no longer provided for an upper limit to income increments in the event of targets being exceeded. Besides, the norms were only to be adjusted in consultation with the workforce, and only when technical conditions had changed – not as a result of higher performance by the workers. These innovations of the traditional piecework wage – now called incentive pay – produced disastrous economic consequences: the progressively growing wage increment for target overfulfilment produced higher wages for top workers and increased wage differentials, which further stimulated performance. For the workforce there was no longer the danger that permanently exceeded targets might be raised and in consequence the wages might be reduced.[10] But at the same time the ratio between growth of productivity and of wages was bound to become more unfavourable because the new rules laid down that the wages were rising faster as the work norms were overfulfilled. In any case, work norms were rarely checked and, if new norms were laid down, they were often 'soft' so as not to endanger enterprise consensus. With such internal enterprise arrangements, not too much was to be demanded from the workforce; in return the workers did not entirely refuse the demands of the leadership personnel.[11] The fact that the share of industrial workers working for incentive pay rose from one-third at the end of 1948 to just under two-thirds in 1951,[12] has probably less to do with the 'high-performance shift' organised on the Soviet model for the miner Adolf Hennecke, which was meant to promote the incentive pay. This event was subsequently stylised into the foundation myth of the activists' movement. Instead, the new rules on wage calculation and the slowly improving range of consumer goods on offer produced some effect; as a result, monetary wages again acquired more weight in relation to payment in kind. However, the compensation-in-kind component of income was not entirely lost even in the following decades: more and more especially big enterprises supplied their employees direct with foodstuffs, industrial goods and holiday opportunities. What had been an improvisation strategy in the years immediately after the war gradually became an integral element in the incentive structure.

Alongside the incentive problem the attempt to steer the economy centrally also ran into difficulty in 1948 with the Soviet authorities arbitrarily changing their targets or confiscating products and equipment. The 'prerequisites for the execution of regulated economic planning' had therefore to be urged upon the Soviets time and again.[13] In doing so those responsible often proceeded from perfectionist expectations. Selbmann formulated this as follows: 'A planned economy means that production is regulated by plans from top to bottom, from front to back, that every economic procedure, raw material acquisition, transportation, processing within the enterprise and marketing are laid down in advance by plans.'[14] Realisation of such 'total planning', however, was an illusion, if only because of the complexity of a national economy.

Equally utopian was the idea that prices could be altogether dispensed with in future and that planning would be possible merely on the basis of user value. This sprang from the Marxist idea that money, and hence prices, would no longer be needed as an exchange medium once work was immediately performed societally, which was the goal of the socialist utopia. Admittedly, where more producers were needed than in industry, and where material incentives were urgently needed, as for instance in agriculture with its multiplicity of peasants and their key function in the food supply, prices were used, alongside plans, as steering instruments. For their delivery quotas, demanded with the threat of sanctions, the peasants received only low prices; on the other hand they were free to sell their surplus as 'free peak produce' at rural markets or to the state purchasing centres at significantly higher prices. This was to offer an incentive to peasants to increase their production beyond their targets and gradually improve food supplies. Nor could prices be dispensed with in industry. Many aspects could only be expressed in terms of value, which is why a new price structure was to be established after the currency reform.

The prevailing prices consisted partly of the ceiling prices of 1944 – sometimes with surcharges – and partly of calculated prices from the subsequent years. In consequence, the prices of different goods were in an increasingly unrealistic relation to each other. For some products they were actually lower than the prices of their raw materials. Real costs had less and less to do with the prices laid down in the plans. It was almost impossible to discover whether an enterprise was working well or badly. In the event of losses the enterprises were subsidised. In the early fifties, Rau, now head of the State Planning Commission, summed the situation up as follows: 'So much stupidity in price policy probably exists only with us.' From those responsible he demanded the solution of these problems on a 'totally new basis'.[15] As a result, in February 1953 new 'Principles of Price Policy' were issued; these envisaged the formation of uniform fixed prices for every product in its different qualities. This step was logical in the context of the move towards a planned economy. Changes and imponderabilities were to be excluded and the price system was to be consistent within itself. Henceforth price formation was to be on the basis of the average cost of the industrial sector concerned, as envisaged in the plan. These cost prices, however, provided no information on supply and demand, which was also the reason why they offered no indication of where the resources should be directed in order to achieve the maximum utility. Prices lost their guiding function and it was necessary, in advance and according to a valuation of needs, to determine what the enterprises were to produce and in what quantity.

In the eyes of the Marxist-trained economic politicians, influenced additionally by Soviet experience, structural policy had to comply with macroeconomic interests of overriding importance; this should yield one of the significant advantages of the control of the economy as a whole. The question, however, was: who was to lay down the 'macroeconomic requirements' and thereby determine which sectors or enterprises were to be supported and which not. With prices frozen and an unreliable information flow from the enterprises, the central authorities had no economic criteria for making such macroeconomic decisions. As a result the economic aims could only be politically defined – which enabled the Socialist Unity Party to impose them on the economy. In order to enforce such a structural policy, the state enterprises had to hand over to the state at first almost the total of their profits and one-half of any writings-off; in the event of additional requirements they were to take up credits. Sectors and enterprises prioritised by the German Economic Commission were assigned additional funds by the state. This concentration of funds on a few industrial sectors deprived others of the means for the maintenance and renewal of their manufacturing facilities and led to asset erosion. At the same time, with such a redistribution, enterprises had scarcely any incentives left for increasing their profitability, their productivity or their production. Slight modifications of the regulations in subsequent years did not greatly change the situation.

In consequence, a typical feature of the planned economy began to appear as early as the end of the forties: the so-called 'soft' plans, which resulted in an increase of stocks of raw materials, other input requirements and unsellable products. At the beginning of the fifties these 'stock investments' were higher than fixed-asset investments. Their share of the use of the gross domestic product, up to 1953, amounted to 7 per cent to 9 per cent, which was much higher than the 1 per cent to 4 per cent customary in the Federal Republic at the time.[16] This was largely due to the constraint exerted on enterprises to show as large a gross output as possible. In the early fifties, admittedly, this had the advantage of stimulating the mobilisation of idle capacities and resources, because all costs and inputs went into the value on the basis of which enterprises were rewarded or penalised. But even then this plan indicator was a temptation to wastefulness.

Generally speaking, the plans of the forties were full of gaps, and practical planning lagged behind the expectations of the leaders. In spite of this, planning was extended in subsequent years from the initially focal production to other sectors and soon covered nearly all aspects of economic life. In addition, since the beginning of the fifties the foreign trade monopoly, a typical element of a planned economy, was imposed. Henceforth only the state was permitted to engage in foreign trade transactions, including foreign currency transactions: only the Ministry of Foreign Trade and state-owned foreign trade enterprises were responsible for exports and imports. Moreover, domestic prices were separated from prices in foreign markets and the domestic currency could no longer be exchanged for foreign currencies. Private payment traffic with other countries was monopolised by the state; commercial foreign currency transactions were totally centralised in order to create foreign currency reserves and the 'uniform foreign currency policy of the GDR'. Offences against these regulations were severely punished. As a result, the Ost-

Mark became a purely domestic currency. However, in the fifties it was not yet possible to enforce this state monopoly completely.[17]

The intention of the foreign trade and foreign currency monopoly was, first of all, to protect the domestic economy against incalculable and undesirable foreign influences. At the same time, however, the enterprises were no longer in international competition. Soon they no longer knew what demand existed in the world market for their products; nor did they have any incentive to find out and adapt their products accordingly. After all, their products were accepted anyway, and at the planned prices. This lessened the constraint to innovate and reduced international competitiveness in the medium term.

With the foundation of the GDR in 1949, the German Economic Commission formed the nucleus of the GDR government. From November 1950 the State Planning Commission enjoyed an outstanding position – long demanded by the Party leaders – compared to the other institutions concerned with the economy. Heavy industry, engineering, light industry, as well as agriculture and forestry were now administered by their own ministries and the large-scale enterprises were directly subordinated to the Main Administrations (Hauptverwaltung) of the ministries. Moreover, the Ministries of Finance, of Foreign Trade and Intra-German Trade, of Trade and Supplies, as well as for Labour concerned themselves with cross-sectional tasks in the economy. The 'Main Directorate for the Protection of the National Economy' (Hauptverwaltung zum Schutze der Volkswirtschaft), hitherto subordinated to the Minister of the Interior, was transformed in February 1950 into the Ministry for State Security (Ministerium für Staatssicherheit), which was to strengthen its grip on the economy in the future. The establishment of a Soviet-type planned economy was eventually completed in the GDR in 1949/50, simultaneously with most of the Eastern European 'people's democracies', by the preparation of a Five-Year Plan for 1951–1955.

Reorientation of Foreign Trade and Industrial Development

The regional structure of foreign trade also changed fundamentally in 1948. Although the first trade links with Eastern neighbours were established as early as 1945, this trade remained generally slight and was unable to make up for the loss of traditional suppliers. In 1947 the countries of East and South-East Europe had a share of only 9 per cent of the foreign trade turnover of the Soviet Occupation Zone; by 1948 it amounted to 45 per cent and by 1950 to 68 per cent. By then the Soviet

Occupation Zone / GDR was heavily dependent on raw material supplies from the Soviet Union and the Eastern Bloc countries. In 1949 some 59 per cent of coke imports, 70 per cent of rolled metal and all cotton imports came from that area.[18]

The fact that from 1948 onwards the Soviet Occupation Zone increasingly oriented its foreign trade towards the East and South-East European area was primarily due to political factors: the realignment in economic regulatory policy in Eastern Germany, the separate currency reforms in West and East in 1948, as well as the Soviet blockade of Berlin and the West's countermeasures. Moreover, the countries of Western and Northern Europe were less and less willing to import industrial products as they did not have the US dollars available with which they had to pay for the imports. Besides, a beginning was made in Western Europe in 1948 to liberalise trade relations – something that the Soviet Occupation Zone was unable to participate in because of its foreign trade regime. Within the framework of the Cold War the US further restricted Western trade with the East by means of its Coordinating Committee for East–West Trade Policy (COCOM) list – a list of high-technology items that must not be exported to the East. As a result, the trade of the Western zones with the Soviet Occupation Zone / GDR only amounted to a small part of their total trade, whereas the interzonal trade for East Germany amounted to one-third of its trade volume. It was easy to instrumentalise this imbalance politically, which is why the East wanted to reduce its dependence on the West. Therefore the relevant Central Administration regarded it in 1948 as a 'natural commandment' for the Soviet Occupation Zone to turn towards Eastern and South-Eastern Europe. Besides, in those countries the foreign trade was similarly monopolised by the state. Arrangements between two states seemed incomparably more reliable than arrangements with a multiplicity of individual enterprises in countries with a market economy.[19]

The increasing closing off of relations with the West induced the responsible persons in the Soviet Occupation Zone / GDR to look elsewhere to supplement the capacities that were lacking in the available manufacturing chains. Until 1948 – mainly because of the heavy reparations – it was not possible even to secure a replacement of the used-up capital assets; in other words, there were no net investments. But in the autumn of 1947 Ulbricht announced that mining and, more particularly, the modest metallurgical capacities in East Germany were to be speedily developed. The Two-Year Plan of 1949/50 provided not only for the reconstruction and full utilisation of the existing economic potential, but also for a transformation of the industrial structure. Priority was given to steel production, as well as to fuel and energy production and to certain sectors of engineering. Of the industrial investments of 1949 two-thirds went to metallurgy and engineering only.[20] The reparations prior to 1949 had already preshaped such a change in the industrial structure: initially it was supplies of foodstuffs and light industry products that predominated, but from 1947 onwards it was vehicles, general engineering and heavy engineering products. In 1949 three-quarters of all reparations came from these sectors. Some entire branches, such as deep-sea ship-building, had been created specially for reparations, while others were greatly expanded. Because manpower was concentrated in these branches, the reconstruction speed in others was slowed down. Moreover, the 'reparations industries' were as a rule material-intensive, which increased the deficits of iron, steel and energy and thereby increased the country's dependence on supplies of Soviet raw materials. The structural effect of reparations should not therefore be underrated.[21] By the beginning of the fifties primary and metal-processing industries already accounted for a higher proportion of industrial production than before the war; light industry, on the other hand, lost in importance.[22]

The Two-Year Plan 1949/50 marked the beginning of the structural transformations intended to reshape the Soviet Occupation Zone / GDR economy into a national economy of its own. The first Five-Year Plan, 1951 to 1955, envisaged deeper intervention in the economic structure: industrial production was to almost double compared to 1936. Metallurgy continued to stand at the centre. In addition, manufacturing capacities for heavy-machine building were to be newly established in order to meet the requirements of the Soviet Union and the other Eastern Bloc countries for industrialisation and rearmament. Such plants, however, were needed also by the domestic economy in order to open up raw material deposits and to develop the metallurgy and energy industries. The investment funds, slight as they were because of reparations, continued to be centralised in the hands of the state and were applied in concentrated form in priority sectors. For that the central authority took fifty-eight projects under its direct control. In particular, primary industry continued to benefit from this at the expense of the light and foodstuffs industries.[23]

Nevertheless, production recovered quickly enough, due chiefly to the reconstruction effect: existing gaps in capacity were often closed with modest means, achieving high growth effects. However, these opportunities were soon exhausted, with the result that growth rates declined. It is interesting, however, that industrial production in the Soviet Occupation Zone up to the currency reform developed more rapidly than in the Western zones (Table 2.2). This was probably due to the fact that the economic order in the East was more homogeneous in the immediate postwar period than in the West: rationing measures and price control were in line with the nationalised large-scale enterprises. By contrast, the control measures in the West did not correspond to the system of property ownership: entrepreneurial autonomy on the basis of private ownership of the means of production conflicted with the state's rationing measures. As the entrepreneurs were unable, in the prevailing conditions of the money and price system, to enforce their profit interests, they embarked on a 'production strike against which the state authorities could act to a limited degree only, because not they but the entrepreneurs were controlling the enterprises'.[24] It was only the currency and economic reform in the West that resolved this contradiction; industrial production there then developed more rapidly than in the Soviet Occupation Zone (Table 2.2).

Table 2.2: Development of industrial production in the German occupation zones 1946 to 1950 (1936 = 100)[25]

	American zone		British zone	French zone	Soviet zone
1946	41		34	36	42
1947		44		45	54
1948		63		58	60
1949		86		78	68
1950		.		.	75

The growth in the Soviet Occupation Zone was reflected also in the labour market. In 1947 employment in the East already exceeded the pre-war level. There were two reasons for this: first, a great many people found a livelihood in agriculture: by the end of 1946, 25 per cent more persons were gainfully employed in that sector than before the war. Second, enterprises had begun to hoard labour. The unemployment rate fell from over 9 per cent at the end of 1945 to slightly above 1 per cent by mid 1948. From the end of 1948 to the beginning of 1950, however, it rose again to 5 per cent – a short-term result of the Soviet blockade of Berlin, which resulted in the non-arrival of Western deliveries needed for production. In spite of the end of the blockade in May 1949 unemployment remained at this level because overstaffing in agriculture was diminishing. The improving food situation and the relatively low wages made work in agriculture less and less attractive. Moreover, the number of persons employed in domestic services declined considerably – by 1950 to one-half of 1939 levels – as the potential employers disappeared with socioeconomic changes. Closure of enterprises, due to the growing pressure on the private sector, further increased the number of unemployed. Moreover, the duty to work, already existing in fact, the statistical shift of welfare recipients towards the unemployed compelled to register, as well as the returning prisoners of war, all contributed to a rise in unemployment. However, from the spring of 1950 onwards it once again diminished.[26]

Agriculture and Supplies for the Population

In the agrarian sphere, the severe winter of 1946/47 and the subsequent drought in the summer of 1947 had so exacerbated the situation that, in September 1947, the Soviet Military Administration ordered an auxiliary programme for the new peasants, to deal with the shortage of buildings resulting from the land reform. The big estates, mainly in Mecklenburg and Brandenburg, had often been divided up into a hundred new peasant holdings, 'so that in practice entire new villages had to be planned and established'.[27] The German Economic Commission concentrated building materials and building workers on the new peasant projects. At the same time, estate buildings were torn down, both to gain building materials and also to remove the symbols of the aristocratical system. By 1953 it had proved possible to establish 94,668 residential buildings, 104,235 byres and 38,406 barns. This 'helped to consolidate the new peasant holdings … but clearly lagged behind requirements';[28] it also proved a heavy burden on the economy.

By 1949/50 just about one-third of the new peasants had stabilised themselves economically, but 30 per cent of all medium-sized and 'small peasants' – smallholders – were working at a loss.[29] Arable and stock farming remained below their potential capacities. That was the price that had to be paid for the land reform. Mostly because they were unable to meet their annually increasing delivery quotas, some 60,000 new peasants (or 29 per cent) had returned their land by 1952.[30] The further heavily indebted 20,000 peasants, for the most part new peasants, were offered a new chance in agriculture by the creation of Agricultural Production Cooperatives (LPG). In consequence new and less successful peasants were overrepresented among the members of the first Agricultural Production Cooperatives.[31]

In 1949 the old-established peasants continued to run the majority of agricultural units, of which they accounted for 71 per cent.[32] Right from the start, however, they received less manure and similar supplies, they had to pay higher taxes and meet a higher delivery quota. From 1948 onwards the Party's policy was increasingly directed against the 'big farmers' with more than twenty hectares. First, their delivery quotas were further raised and the traditional rural cooperatives under their influence were marginalised. As the higher delivery quotas were not supported by greater material help, quota shortfalls increased on many farms. By 1949, in addition to the roughly 4,000 'big farmers' expropriated by the land reform, a further 5,600 gave up their farms. As a result, the number of enterprises with a farmland of twenty to one hundred hectares declined by 18 per cent compared to 1939. It was not only the annually increasing delivery quotas that increased the pressure on the 'big farmers' over the next few years: in 1952/53 there were numerous additional expropriations, with the result that between 1950 and 1953 their number declined by just under 40 per cent.[33]

The return of new peasant enterprises and the flight of many 'big farmers' to the West were symptoms of the failure of the Party's agrarian policy. Besides, its aim of equalling the 'peacetime yields per hectare' by 1950 was nowhere near reached: only for grain crops were the yields, averaged over 1951 to 1955, at the pre-war level. For oleaginous crops, potatoes and sugar beet they were not surpassed until the second half of the sixties. In spite of the heavy losses of livestock during the war and immediately after it, the pig population in 1950 was again at the pre-war level. In the case of cows the pre-war level was not surpassed until 1952.[34] Admittedly though, owing to a shortage of fodder, the live weight of the animals remained low and their susceptibility to diseases high. In consequence, meat supplies were not significantly improved. Agricultural production generally in 1946 was about one-half of the 1936 level and in 1947, due to a failed harvest, it declined again. Not until the following years did it slowly recover and, according to Western estimates, reach 70 per cent of the 1936 level in 1950 and 91 per cent in 1952.[35]

This increase in production made it possible for the rations on food cards to be gradually increased. The nutritional standard – in calories – increased in the lowest card category for adults, relevant to the bulk of the (urban) population, from about 1,100 kcal in 1945, to just under 1,300 kcal in 1946, to slightly more than 1,500 kcal in 1947/48 and finally to just under 1,800 kcal by the end of 1949. If one goes by the contemporary data – which are far lower than our present-day data – of a working person's minimum requirements of 1,500 to 2,000 kcal, the calories available for town dwellers reached the subsistence level in the autumn of 1948 at the earliest. From May 1949 potatoes and from December 1950 bread and nutrients were no longer on rations. In 1949/50 the rations of meat, fat and sugar were further increased, but the bulk of the GDR's population probably remained undersupplied in calories until the early fifties.[36]

Other consumer goods were even more difficult to acquire in the post-war years: fuel and cleaning materials were strictly rationed; shoes and clothing (in simple style and in small quantities) as well as a few household goods were all that was offered at horrendous prices. Watches, cameras, radio receivers and bicycles were added later. Rising production made it possible in December 1948 to introduce a 'points card' for manufactured consumer goods. Only then did the bulk of the population get a chance to buy new textiles or footwear instead of having to patch and repair, as they had had to do till then.

In November 1948 the State Trade Organisation (HO) was set up: in its shops and restaurants foodstuffs and industrial goods were sold without ration cards, but at prices well above the ration prices and just under the black market prices. The intention was to 'absorb' surplus purchasing power, to increase tax revenue and to dry up the black market. However, what was offered by these HOs was beyond the reach of the bulk of the population; also, initially, it was not varied enough to change buyer's attitudes significantly. It only became attractive gradually as a result of massive price cuts (Table 2.3).

Table 2.3: HO prices for basic foodstuffs in Marks per kg, and monthly net wages of workers and employees, 1948 to 1958[37]

	Butter	Margarine	Meat (pork chop)	Sugar	Wheat flour	Milk	Monthly net wage
1948	130.00	110.00	82.50	33.00	20.00	–	ca. 175.00*
1949	100.00/ 60.00	70.00/ 36.00	67.50/ 40.00	24.00/ 12.00	20.00/ 6.00	–	.
1950	48.00/ 24.00	18.00/ 14.00	30.00/ 15.00	12.00	4.80/ 1.60	2.50	218.91
1951	24.00	14.00	15.00	7.60/ 7.40	1.32	2.00	238.63
1952	20.00	12.00	11.20	3.00/ 2.80	1.32	2.00	256.23
1955–58	20.00	4.00	11.20	3.00	1.32	1.12	308.12 (1955)

* merely workers

According to data of the German Institute for Economic Research (DIW) in West Berlin, the reduction of the HO prices chiefly benefited high-income households, whose living costs, as a result, declined by 10 per cent between 1950 and the end of 1952. For low-income households, on the other hand, costs rose by 19 per cent because, along with the price reductions, rationing came to an end for various commodities. These goods could now no longer be purchased at the low ration-card prices, but only in the HOs, whose prices amounted to between double and four times the former ration-card prices. To repeal these double price levels, the supply of goods would have had to be greatly improved. As it was, even the card rations were not always available. Consumers were therefore compelled 'to buy other goods whenever possible or else to satisfy their needs by expensive round-about routes. The real cost of living was therefore much higher than can be expressed in numbers.'[38]

According to Western estimates the price-adjusted private consumption per head of the GDR population in 1950 was a good third to one-half of the 1936 level. Much the same applied in relation to the levels in the Federal Republic. By 1952 the GDR reached only one-half to three-quarters of the consumption per head in the Federal Republic.[39] This lagging behind the living standard in the West was the result of the low gross domestic product per head, as well as of the still considerable quantities of products flowing to the Soviet Union as reparations: in 1952 these still amounted to about 15 per cent of the gross domestic product. Just when the reparation obligations were lowered at the beginning of the fifties, military expenses rose to such an extent that the economy experienced hardly any relief. In addition, the low standard of living was due to shortcomings that were immanent within the system. Hoarding of resources by enterprises tied down considerable means, which were then not available for consumption. Added to this was the fact that most investments went into heavy industry, so that other enterprises could not even ensure for themselves a replacement of written-off capital goods. This affected the production of consumer goods more than anything else: its capital stock declined over several years.

According to Western estimates the gross domestic product per head of the GDR population only amounted to 69 per cent of the pre-war figure in 1950, which was two-thirds of the level reached in Western Germany.[40] This was due to several factors: first, the losses of capacity due to wartime destruction and, to a greater extent, dismantling; this lowered productivity especially where it took place in bottleneck areas. Second, there were the reparations from ongoing production: while they stimulated growth in the short term, the investment goods contained in the reparations and the possible gains in productivity that resulted from these investment goods did not benefit the East German economy, and so had a negative effect in the medium and long term. Moreover, the orientation of the economy towards reparations resulted in a structural change in industry that was, in the long run, bound to lower efficiency. Its lasting effect was due mainly to the fact that the planned economy tended to shut itself off from the world market. In consequence it was not possible to compensate by way of foreign trade either this structural change or the gaps in economic structure caused by the division of Germany. Admittedly, given the postwar development with the strong presence and interests of the Soviet Union, there was hardly an alternative to a planned economy. Even so, a less centralised variant would have been imaginable. Finally, the costs of transformation to a planned economy were the third essential factor causing the lagging of productivity until 1950. As a result of the exchange of elites the Soviet Occupation Zone / GDR lost entrepreneurial potential and specialised competence. By 1953 more than 4,000 industrial firms, i.e., every seventh industrial enterprise in East Germany, were relocated to the West, along with their managing and specialised staff.[41] Added to this was the fact that planning endeavours were for a long time marked by unrealistic assumptions, boundless optimism, widespread incompetence and sometimes chaos – all of which was dismissed at the time as teething troubles. In principle the Party leaders were convinced that a Soviet-type planned economy would result in higher productivity than capitalism and that the GDR could eventually act like a magnet on the West. As we know today, this assumption of German Communist policy turned out to be illusionary.

The Resolution to 'Construction of Socialism'

In view of the GDR's backwardness compared to Western Germany, the Resolution of the Second Socialist Unity Party Conference in July 1952 to construct socialism in the GDR also aimed at overtaking the competitor. When the Western powers rejected the proposals of Stalin's Notes of the spring of 1952,[42] the SED leadership believed their road was now clear for pushing ahead with socioeconomic transformation. The possibility that the Soviet Union might, after all, come to an agreement with the Western powers on Germany's unity and neutrality seemed increasingly remote. Once Western integration of the Federal Republic could no longer be prevented, Stalin for his part endeavoured to develop his East German outpost. In a conversation with the SED Party leaders at the beginning of April 1952 he demanded a 'trained army' and the 'creation of production cooperatives (*Produktiv-Genossenschaften*) in the villages'. In this way the GDR was to be brought onto the 'way to socialism … without shouting'.[43] These 'suggestions' were taken up by the Party leaders, who now made internal preparations for a change of policy. At the beginning of July 1952 the East Berlin leadership sent a letter to Stalin, pointing out that a 'socialist planned economy' was established in the GDR, that 'socialist ownership' predominated in industry, and that the conditions existed in agriculture for the voluntary association of farm workers and 'working peasants' into production cooperatives. Thus the 'decisive prerequisites for the transition to the construction of socialism' had been created; the letter requested Stalin to permit the announcement of this goal.[44] The Soviets had no objections and Ulbricht made the new programme public at the Second Party Conference in July 1952. This policy followed the pattern that had already been established in the other Eastern Bloc countries since 1948.

Since the beginning of June 1952 early cooperative associations had been revived and indeed promoted on the initiative of the Party leaders; now, at the Second Party Conference, the leaders called on peasants and farm workers to unite in cooperatives voluntarily. However, this new degree of interventions in the agrarian economy should not be understood merely as an aspect of a deliberate Sovietisation. These were primarily attempts to consolidate agricultural production. By creating a large-scale agrarian structure through collectivisation, the Party leaders were hoping to increase agrarian production at a leap. This step was now to be enforced at high speed: even though the harvest had failed in 1952, the delivery quotas of the peasants were further raised for 1953, which overstrained their economic capabilities. Many peasants thereupon fled to the West. Any large or medium farmer who did not deliver his quota was suspected as a 'black marketeer', 'speculator' or 'saboteur'. From July 1952 to the end of January 1953 GDR courts sentenced just under 1,250 peasants to penalties or detention for non-fulfilment of mandatory deliveries or 'black slaughtering'. Quite a lot were expropriated and their farms handed over to Agricultural Production Cooperatives to be worked by them. At the beginning of 1953 the delivery quota was substantially increased even for 'very small farms'.[45] State authorities increasingly interfered with the management of the peasants. At the same time the peasants – sometimes compulsorily – were united in cooperatives. Their number eventually rose from 1,906 to 5,074 in the first five months of 1953.[46] The cooperatives were increasingly granted privileges: lower delivery quotas, tax reductions and cheap credits, as well as priority supplies of seedstock, manure, livestock and building materials. Whenever goods in short supply, such as margarine, jam or chocolate, reached the villages, the cooperative members were, in many places, allowed to shop first. In December 1952 Ulbricht confirmed this policy: 'First it's the turn of the production cooperative, then it's again the turn of the production cooperative, and only then is it the turn of the small and medium peasants.'[47] But the spring cultivation in 1953 revealed serious shortages, especially in the Agricultural Production Cooperatives: they had too few machines and too little manpower, and there was a lack of specialists. Supplies of basic foodstuffs were tight anyway and the situation in the countryside did not promise a good harvest. The Soviets therefore advised Ulbricht 'tactfully' to halt collectivisation for the moment. Until the completion of the harvest no new members were to be accepted into the Agricultural Production Cooperatives; the cooperatives were first to be consolidated. However, a directive along these lines proved just lip service.[48]

Similarly as in agriculture, action was also taken in 1952/53 against private manufacturing and service enterprises. Until then, policy towards the private sector had alternated between ideology and pragmatism. On the one hand it was to be pushed back, but on the other it accounted for about one-fifth of industrial production; it was therefore of considerable economic importance and was urgently needed for supplying industry and the population with inputs, consumer goods and services. Now rigorous judicial sanctions were imposed in the event of genuine or presumed offences against the state's steering measures. Dues, already raised in the spring of 1952, and outstanding taxes, were inexorably collected from the autumn onwards, credits were called in or refused altogether, and enterprises were confiscated. Many proprietors therefore fled to the West, and hence the supply of input requirements and consumer goods declined even further. Within a little less than six months the number of private enterprises and their production had shrunk by more than one-tenth.[49]

The build-up of the army also had its economic consequences. Because of the Korean War and a growing fear of wider war, rearmament was stepped up in both West and East. Earlier attempts by the Party leaders to rearm in secret kept such activities within limits. As a reaction to Stalin's above-mentioned 'suggestions' of April 1952, promoted by the Party, a gigantic rearmament programme was now to be put into effect at short notice, in parallel with the development of heavy industry, in spite of the fact that economic resources were already overstretched. The Soviets recommended that 1.5 billion Marks be set aside in the plan for the 'creation of national armed forces' and that economies be made instead in social insurance and welfare, that consumption by the population be reduced, and that property and income taxes be raised. Armament production demanded considerable funds, raw materials, manpower and building capacities. It soon turned out that the national economy was overstretched with these projects. In 1952 military expenditure almost doubled compared to the previous year; in 1953 it stayed at the same level. Between summer 1952 and summer 1953 the armaments programme devoured over 2 billion Marks.[50]

When the 'construction of socialism' was to be further speeded up after autumn 1952, the Party leaders found themselves compelled, at the beginning of 1953, to admit to the Soviet leadership that it was impossible simultaneously to achieve all their economic tasks – reparation deliveries, export obligations, rearmament, fast development of primary industry and heavy industry, improved supplies for the population, as well as a strengthening of the state's reserves. The overall plan was not in balance. The lagging production of raw materials and intermediate inputs resulted in delays in exports and investments, which in turn impaired production and resulted in new deficits. There was a shortage not only of money, but also of the necessary materials and goods. In consequence it was expected 'that the complications with supplying the population with foodstuffs and industrial products would become even greater than in 1952. Given the present economic situation of the GDR a simultaneous solution of the listed main tasks is impossible', the Party leaders summed up, requesting Moscow to review them.[51] The Soviet government thereupon, in April 1953, decided to remit part of the East German debts, to reduce its reparation demands and to deliver more coke, iron ore and grain to the GDR. In addition, military expenditure was to be cut down by one-third.[52] These measures, however, were not enough to relieve the situation fast enough. The situation of consumers in the spring of 1953 was dramatic: there was a shortage, above all, of butter, margarine, vegetables, meat and sugar. In addition there were frequent power cuts. Also woollen clothing, leather footwear and overcoats could only rarely be found.

Meanwhile items of clothing, which because of their quality and their prices had no market, were piling up in the trade and with producers. When rationing of textiles and footwear was discontinued in April 1953, the HO prices were lowered by 15 to 20 per cent, which nevertheless meant an increase of 50 per cent and more over the former ration-card prices. Of particular importance was the fact that even the ration-card prices for meat and meat products were raised by 10 to 15 per cent. Eggs, too, became more expensive. Prices for honey substitute and jam rose by 40 per cent. Moreover, the reductions for workers' travel tickets (up to 75 per cent) were cut. All these measures were intended to reduce private demand and subsidies and to relieve the state budget. As a consequence the cost of living of all income groups went up.[53]

As, however, the means for the additional tasks continued to be insufficient and as the workers, the 'ruling class', were not to be burdened, the Party tried to find new sources of money among the middle strata: in the spring of 1953 income and crafts taxes were raised, self-employed persons were excluded from general health and social insurance, so that they could only insure themselves at higher rates with a newly formed insurance, and the cheap 'extra ration' for the 'working intelligentsia' was stopped. GDR citizens working in West Berlin, self-employed and freelance workers, including their dependents (except for children under fifteen) – altogether about 2 million people – were deprived of their food rationing cards, so that they could satisfy their needs only in the free shops. At the same time butter, margarine, oil and sugar had completely disappeared from the HO stores and meat was very largely absent. This created a situation of hardship from which flight seemed the only way out. It was chiefly peasants, craftsmen and private entrepreneurs who emigrated to the West. During 1950 to 1952 some 15,000 persons escaped from the GDR on average on a monthly basis; in the first six months of 1953 the monthly average reached as high as 37,500. In the end 'the sums thus saved and additional state income … created "bad blood" without closing the financial gap'.[54] Nor was it possible in this way to increase the range of goods on offer.

Up to this point the workers had been relatively protected, although, like everyone, they had to contend with higher prices and the shortage of consumer goods. Given the economic situation, it became necessary for them to be called upon to make a greater contribution to the 'construction of socialism'. To this end, wage development was to be more closely adjusted to labour productivity – a problem causally related to the long-simmering problem of production norms. The norms were in fact too low and were being fulfilled by 175 to 200 per cent. At the same time basic wages were so low in relation to prices that a tolerable standard of living could only be achieved with the surcharges for overfulfilled norms, especially in the lower wage categories. For this reason alone the workers opposed higher norms.

To begin with, the Party leaders conducted a campaign for a voluntary raising of norms. When, in the face of the disastrous supply situation and rising prices, this did not succeed, the Party leaders on 14 May 1953 decided to persuade the Council of Ministers to raise 'the work norms crucial for production by an average of at least 10 per cent'.[55] Because of its dilemma of wishing to legitimate its rule as 'worker and peasant power', while at the same time confronting the workers as a kind of 'overall entrepreneur', the Party leaders had until then always acted cautiously on the question of norms. The new Resolution now discarded the hitherto observed principle of voluntariness and caution.

The Events of 17 June 1953

Moscow had, since the end of April 1953, become aware of the exacerbating crisis in the GDR and was now urging the Party to make a U-turn in its economic policy, following the Soviet model. Ever since Stalin's death in March, economic relief for the GDR had been considered. In a 'New Course' the consumer goods industry was now to be more vigorously developed. At the beginning of June the SED Party leaders were confronted in Moscow with a critical analysis that referred to the 'extremely unsatisfactory political and economic situation' in the GDR. The Soviet leaders recorded 'serious dissatisfaction ... among the broad masses of the population', the cause of which they saw in the Resolution, earlier approved by themselves, for the 'accelerated construction of socialism'. In economic policy they criticised the forced development of heavy industry, the increasing restrictions on private entrepreneurs, the precipitate creation of cooperatives, and the inadequate supplies for the population. Forcibly created nonviable Agricultural Production Cooperatives were to be dissolved. Private craftsmen, shopkeepers and peasants were, in the Soviet view, to revive the economy. Their tax burden was to be reduced. Finally, the development of heavy industry was to be stopped in favour of the consumer goods industry, so that food rationing cards could be abolished.[56]

These course corrections demanded by Moscow were not uncontroversial among the Party leaders. The redistribution of resources at the expense of primary and heavy industry was, in the opinion of several top officials, including Ulbricht, bound to disorganise the economy. The only way out they saw was a reduction of reparations or some Soviet aid for the GDR on the lines of the Marshall Plan in the West. At the same time a power struggle erupted among the East German leaders: the role of Ulbricht and his political style were criticised. On 11 June 1953 a statement was eventually arrived at and published, in which the Party leaders admitted 'mistakes'. The restrictive measures against individual peasants and the middle strata were to be corrected. Confiscated property was to be handed back to persons returning from the West or else compensation made to them. Price increases of sugar-containing goods and of workers' travel tickets were to be revoked. Generally the New Course was to improve the standard of living of the population. Although reports were available about the exceedingly tense atmosphere in the enterprises, raising norms continued to be ignored as a crisis element. In view of the poor supply situation and the price increases, the high incomes of Party and trade union officials were causing bitterness. In this situation the Politbüro paper acted as a detonator: all groups who had been disadvantaged until then had concessions made to them, except the industrial workers. Minor strikes had already occurred in the winter of 1952/53 and in May 1953. Even the demonstrations of thousands of workers in Plzen (Czechoslovakia) at the beginning of June, caused by similar economic problems, were not seen by the East German Party leaders as a warning signal. Although they saw themselves as the representatives of the (supposedly ruling) working class, they disadvantaged these very people compared to the other strata, which showed a lack of political tact.

The fact that the increase of the production norms was not revoked was the last straw. On 15 June for the first time the East Berlin construction workers in the Stalin-Allee were to down tools. When the trade union paper *Tribüne* argued again on 16 June that the norm increases were correct, even though the government abolished the increases the same day, the fury of the workers rose further. By the time the cancellation was publicised on 17 June, the individual strikes had turned into a movement. Along with the lowering of norms and prices, the workers' demands now also included free elections, the resignation of the government and 'butter instead of cannons'.[57] Only when the Soviet occupying power sent tanks into the streets were the demonstrations forcibly ended and the situation brought under control.

The strike movement did not remain confined to Berlin, but spread throughout the GDR. Most affected were the industrial regions of Magdeburg and Halle, where the protests continued well into July. Altogether there were strikes and demonstrations in over five hundred localities, including all the major cities. More than half a million people participated in the first wave of protest between 16 and 21 June. The rebellion was crushed by a massive presence of troops and tanks. The strike activists and 'provocateurs', altogether between five thousand and ten thousand people, were arrested; a great many persons were wounded. The number of dead cannot be reliably established; reports vary between fifty-one and over one hundred.[58]

The Party leaders initially reacted with confusion to the disturbances and only recovered their determination on 19 June. Ulbricht's overthrow in the internal power struggles was prevented with Soviet help: according to the Soviet governors in East Berlin he guaranteed better than anyone else the overcoming of the week-long 'serious panic' among the Party leaders and hence the stability of the GDR.[59] To this end the country had to be economically unburdened. In August 1953 the Soviet Union renounced the still outstanding reparation demands and returned the remaining thirty-three Soviet joint-stock companies to the GDR. East German debts were remitted. In addition, the Soviet Union granted a credit of 485 million roubles – partly in convertible foreign currency – and promised additional foodstuff supplies. The stationing costs of its troops were to be lowered and three-quarters of them to be borne by the Soviet Union itself.

With the New Course the envisaged growth rates of heavy industry were lowered and those of light industry increased. Imports of foodstuffs rose. Raw materials and investments were to be redistributed in favour of the food and light industries and at the expense of metallurgy, chemicals and engineering. Armament expenses were likewise put partly aside. Even so it did not prove possible in general to increase production of consumer goods. Although private enterprises were granted tax relief, their number continued to decline. Of the 5,074 Agricultural Production Cooperatives, 564 were dissolved by February 1954 and at least 33,000 members left them.[60] Concessions concerning delivery quotas were made to cooperatives and individual peasants. For a while it even seemed as if individual peasants were to be supported and the Agricultural Production Cooperatives made disposable. However, from the autumn of 1953 they were once more patronised. Anyway, most peasants, entrepreneurs, small traders and craftsmen did not believe that their situation would improve in the long run. In spite of the concessions granted and the growing profits or incomes there continued to be, as a situation report of the Soviet embassy stated, 'a negative attitude to the policy of the GDR government among the broad masses of this part of the population'.[61]

By using the production norms valid until the beginning of April again as a basis for wages, the fatal resolution on norms was to be undone. Even a cautious increase of norms was unthinkable in the near future. The 'norms issue' and the events of 17 June became the trauma of the Party leaders. This first mass protest in the Eastern Bloc determined the thinking of the rulers right to the end. As late as the spring of 1989 State Security Chief Erich Mielke asked nervously whether another 17 June was around the corner. In future, conflicts were to be kept below the threshold of such an uprising. In the interest of safeguarding the state's power the supply and private consumption of, at least, the workers must not be impaired too much. Similarly, no measures were permitted any longer that might have led to a lowering of wages. The principle of 'wage safety' developed, which of course reduced the possibilities of perform-ance-enhancing incentives. While, as a result, incomes began to rise too fast in relation to labour productivity – something that had happened repeatedly already – a tendency also arose towards surplus money in cir-culation as the developing purchasing power was not matched by enough produced goods. In order to pacify the workers, the rates, chiefly in the lower wage categories, were increased in the second half of 1953, cuts in wages and salaries annulled and income tax tariffs reduced. In consequence, the wages of workers in state industries in the first five months of 1954 were more than 12 per cent higher than in the same peri-od of the preceding year, whereas the labour productivity had only increased by just under 7 per cent. Altogether, according to a statement by the Party leaders to the Soviet leadership, the purchasing power of the population had grown by 21 per cent by 1954 since 1953, owing to wage increases and price cuts during the New Course. However, there was a significantly smaller increase in goods available in the retail trade in 1954, with the result that the excess of money in circulation among the popula-tion trebled by the end of 1954.[62]

The measures of the New Course eventually led to a deterioration of the state budget. Because of higher wages the enterprises were operating more unprofitably, their profit transfers declined and they even demand-ed further subsidies. In addition, rising costs caused foreign trade losses to increase, so that exports and subsequently imports were limited. Relatively small imports, which could only be raised slowly, in turn pre-vented surplus purchasing power being absorbed by imported consumer goods. Nor was it possible to cover steel requirements by imports from abroad. In the medium run, therefore, it was necessary to increase heavy industry production and thus to throttle back private consumption. In consequence, the New Course had to be abandoned again. In the 1956 plan, eventually, heavy industry was also formally assigned a higher rank.

Notes

1. DWK, Abteilung für Wirtschaftsfragen: Bericht über die Ergebnisse der bisherigen Arbeit des Abschnitts IV – Kontrolle vom 7.10.47, SAPMO-BA DY30 IV 2/602/33.
2. DWK: Beschluß S 41/48 of 12.5.48: Aufstellung eines Zwei-Jahresplanes für die Sowjetische Besatzungszone, SAPMO-BA DY30 IV 2/602/114.
3. Frank Zschaler, 'Die vergessene Währungsreform. Vorgeschichte, Durchführung und Ergebnisse der Geldumstellung in der SBZ 1948', *Vierteljahreshefte für Zeitgeschichte* 45, 1997, pp. 191–224, here 193 f.
4. This estimate lies clearly below contemporary data: Baar et al., 'Kriegsschäden', p. 943.
5. On cash circulation, see Zschaler, 'Die vergessene Währungsreform', p. 195; Karsten Broosch, *Die Währungsreform 1948 in der sowjetischen Besatzungszone Deutschlands. Eine Untersuchung zur Rolle des Geldes beim Übergang zur sozialistischen Planwirtschaft in der SBZ/DDR*, Herdecke 1998, pp. 48 f.; For the total money in circulation see Matthias Ermer, *Von der Reichsmark zur Deutschen Mark der Deutschen Notenbank. Zum Binnenwährungsumtausch in der Sowjetischen Besatzungszone Deutschlands (Juni/Juli 1948)*, Stuttgart 2000, p. 73. The upper limit is obtained from the results of the currency reform (excluding the deposits of the credit institutions).
6. Calculated according to Index der Großhandelspreise in der DDR, BA Berlin DE1/28332.
7. Christoph Buchheim, 'Die Errichtung der Bank deutscher Länder und die Währungsreform in Westdeutschland', in Deutsche Bundesbank (ed.), *Fünfzig Jahre Deutsche Mark. Notenbank und Währung in Deutschland seit 1948*, Munich 1998, pp. 91–138, quotations p. 127. On the following, see Jochen Laufer, 'Die UdSSR und die deutsche Währungsfrage 1944–1948', *Vierteljahreshefte für Zeitgeschichte* 46, 1998, pp. 455–85.
8. All previous data from Zschaler, 'Vergessene Währungsreform', pp. 207–19. The table is based, for the Soviet Occupation Zone, on Zschaler's primary data. The figures for deposit money had to be newly estimated as deposits with the credit institutions were not allowed for. For that purpose, for old money, the relation of deposits in banks to those in non-banks in the West, as well as Zschaler's estimate of blocked total deposits in 1945 were drawn upon. For new money the ratio of total deposits in the Soviet Occupation Zone to Greater Berlin had to be used for estimating the deposits at non-banks in Berlin. (Cf. ibid.) The data for the Western zones were corrected according to Deutsche Bundesbank (ed.), *Deutsches Geld- und Bankwesen in Zahlen 1876–1975*, Frankfurt 1976, pp. 24 f. against Zschaler. The same was

done about the population figure for the Soviet Occupation Zone in 1948 on the basis of *Statistisches Jahrbuch 1990*, p. 63.

9. BA Berlin DN1/835, quoted from Frank Zschaler, 'Von der Emissions- und Girobank zur Deutschen Notenbank. Zu den Umständen der Gründung einer Staatsbank für Ostdeutschland', *Bankhistorisches Archiv* 18, 1992, pp. 59–68, here 65.

10. Jörg Roesler, 'Vom Akkordlohn zum Leistungslohn', *Zeitschrift für Geschichtswissenschaft* 32, 1984, pp. 778–95, here 787; Peter Hübner, *Konsens, Konflikt und Kompromiß. Soziale Arbeiterinteressen und Sozialpolitik in der SBZ/DDR 1945–1970*, Berlin 1995, p. 33.

11. Hübner, *Konsens*, pp. 39 ff.

12. Hübner, *Konsens*, p. 41.

13. [Selbmann:] Voraussetzungen für die Durchführung einer geregelten Wirtschaftsplanung vom 5.1.1948, SAPMO-BA NY4113/5.

14. Fritz Selbmann, *Demokratische Wirtschaft*, Dresden 1948, pp. 93, 95 f.

15. Rau to Strassenberger, 7.9.1951, SAPMO-BA NY4090/333.

16. Cf. Wolfgang F. Stolper, *The Structure of the East German Economy*, Cambridge 1960, p. 437; Christoph Buchheim, 'Wirtschaftliche Hintergründe des Arbeiteraufstandes vom 17. Juni 1953 in der DDR', *Vierteljahreshefte für Zeitgeschichte* 38, 1990, pp. 415–33, here 426.

17. Tzschorn to Rumpf and Kuckhoff, 26.6.1952, SAPMO-BA NY4090/316. Cf. Christoph Buchheim, 'Wirtschaftliche Folgen der Integration der DDR in den RGW', in idem (ed.), *Wirtschaftliche Folgelasten*, pp. 341–61, here 314–45; Peter E. Fäßler, *Durch den 'Eisernen Vorhang'. Die deutsch-deutschen Wirtschaftsbeziehungen 1949–1969*, Cologne 2006, pp. 85 ff.

18. Ralf Ahrens, *Gegenseitige Wirtschaftshilfe? Die DDR im RGW–Strukturen und handelspolitische Strategien 1963–1976*, Cologne 2000, pp. 90 f.

19. Buchheim, 'Wirtschaftliche Folgen', pp. 348–52, quotation p. 349; Mai, *Kontrollrat*, p. 197; Ahrens, *Gegenseitige Wirtschaftshilfe?*, p. 91.

20. Rainer Karlsch, 'Die Auswirkungen der Reparationsentnahmen auf die Wettbewerbsfähigkeit der Wirtschaft in der SBZ/DDR', in Jürgen Schneider and Wolfgang Harbrecht (eds), *Wirtschaftsordnung und Wirtschaftspolitik in Deutschland (1933–1993)*, Stuttgart 1996, pp. 139–72, here 148 ff.; *Industriezweige in der DDR 1945 bis 1985* (*Jahrbuch für Wirtschaftsgeschichte*, Sonderband 1988), Berlin (East) 1989, pp. 10 f.

21. Karlsch, *Allein bezahlt?*, pp. 176, 182 ff.

22. André Steiner, 'Wirtschaftliche Lenkungsverfahren in der Industrie der DDR Mitte der fünfziger Jahre. Resultate und Alternativen', in Buchheim, *Wirtschaftliche Folgelasten*, pp. 271–93, here 283.

23. Jörg Roesler, *Die Herausbildung der sozialistischen Planwirtschaft in der DDR. Aufgaben, Methoden und Ergebnisse der Wirtschaftsplanung in der zentralgeleiteten volkseigenen Industrie während der Übergangsperiode vom Kapitalismus zum Sozialismus*, Berlin (East) 1978, p. 18.

24. Christoph Buchheim, 'Die Wirtschaftsordnung als Barriere des gesamtwirtschaftlichen Wachstums in der DDR', *Vierteljahrschrift für Sozial- und Wirtschaftsgeschichte* 82, 1995, pp. 194–210, here 200.

25. Abelhauser, *Wirtschaftsgeschichte der Bundesrepublik*, p. 34. For the Soviet Occupation Zone/GDR according to Zank, *Wirtschaft und Arbeit*, pp. 192 f.

26. Zank, *Wirtschaft und Arbeit*, pp. 170 ff.; Boldorf, *Sozialfürsorge*, p. 236; Dierk Hoffmann, *Aufbau und Krise der Planwirtschaft. Die Arbeitskräftelenkung in der SBZ/DDR 1945 bis 1963*, Munich 2002, pp. 108, 269 ff. Data on persons gainfully employed according to *Arbeitsmarktstatistiken 1946–1951*, BA Berlin DE1/28332; *Statistisches Handbuch 1928–1944*, p. 43. Unemployment figures according to Steiner, *Statistische Übersichten*, Table 3.2.2.

27. BA Berlin DK1/7375, quoted according to Arnd Bauerkämper, *Ländliche Gesellschaft in der kommunistischen Diktatur. Zwangsmodernisierung und Tradition in Brandenburg von 1945 bis zu den frühen sechziger Jahren*, Cologne 2002, p. 269.

28. Zank, *Wirtschaft und Arbeit*, pp. 156–59; Bauerkämper, 'Problemdruck und Ressourcenverbrauch', pp. 308–16, quotation p. 313.

29. Zank, *Wirtschaft und Arbeit*, p. 160; Bauerkämper, *Ländliche Gesellschaft*, p. 281.

30. Bauerkämper, *Ländliche Gesellschaft*, p. 165.

31. Bauerkämper, 'Problemdruck und Ressourcenverbrauch', pp. 321 f.; Dieter Schulz, 'Probleme der sozialen und politischen Entwicklung der Bauern und Landarbeiter in der DDR von 1949 bis 1955', Dissertation, Humboldt-Universität zu Berlin 1984, p. 53.

32. Schulz, 'Probleme', pp. 2 f.

33. Calculated according to: *Statistisches Jahrbuch 1956*, pp. 349 ff. See also Arnd Bauerkämper, 'Auf dem Wege zum "Sozialismus auf dem Lande". Die Politik der SED 1948/49 und die Reaktionen im dörflich-agrarischen Milieu', in Hoffmann and Wentker, *Das letzte Jahr der SBZ*, pp. 245–68, here 258.

34. *Statistisches Jahrbuch 1990*, pp. 38, 42.

35. Barthel, *Wirtschaftliche Ausgangsbedingungen*, p. 163; Stolper, *Structure*, p. 417.

36. Boldorf, *Sozialfürsorge*, pp. 73–77, 82; Hübner, *Konsens*, p. 146.

37. Prices according to Boldorf, *Sozialfürsorge*, p. 85, Table 16. Net wages 1948 estimated according to Ergebnisse der Lohnerhebungen in der Sowjetischen Besatzungszone 1947 und 1948, BA Berlin DE1/28327; Net wages 1950–55 according to *Statistisches Jahrbuch 1956*, p. 202.

38. 'Preise und Lebenshaltungskosten im sowjetischen Besatzungsgebiet', in *DIW-Wochenbericht* 20, 1953, pp. 25 ff.; 'Die Entwicklung der Lebenshaltungskosten im sowjetischen Besatzungsgebiet', in ibid., pp.107–9, quotation p. 109.

39. All data – some of them calculated – according to Stolper, *Structure*, pp. 434, 437, 440.

40. Stolper, *Structure*, pp. 436, 440.

41. Johannes Bähr, 'Die Firmenabwanderung aus der SBZ/DDR und aus Ost-Berlin (1945–1953)', in Wolfram Fischer, Uwe Müller and Frank Zschaler (eds), *Wirtschaft im Umbruch. Strukturveränderungen und Wirtschaftspolitik im 19. und 20. Jahrhundert*, St. Katharinen 1997, pp. 229–49.

42. Stalin offered the Western Allied Powers negotiations concerning Germany as a united state, a peace treaty and the permission to form national armed forces for its own defence. In reaction he demanded the withdrawal of all occupational forces from Germany and the neutrality of the united Germany.

Western powers perceived the proposals as a tactically motivated attempt to prevent the integration of the Federal Republic in the Western alliance. See: Gerhard Wettig, *Stalin and the Cold War in Europe. The Emergence and Development of East–West Conflict, 1939–1953*, Lanham 2008, pp. 212–21.

43. Besprechung am 1.4.1952 und Schlußbesprechung am 7.4.1952, in Rolf Badstübner and Wilfried Loth (eds), *Wilhelm Pieck – Aufzeichnungen zur Deutschlandpolitik 1945–1953*, Berlin 1994, pp. 395 ff.; Wladimir K. Wolkow, 'Die deutsche Frage aus Stalins Sicht (1947–1952)', *Zeitschrift für Geschichtswissenschaft* 48, 2000, pp. 20–49, here 45 f.

44. Brief der SED-Führung an Stalin, 2.7.52, in Staritz, *Gründung*, pp. 261–64. On the reply see Elke Scherstjanoi and Rolf Semmelmann, 'Die Gespräche Stalins mit der SED-Führung im Dezember 1948 und im April 1952 (Teil 2)', *Zeitschrift für Geschichtswissenschaft* 52, 2004, pp. 238–69, here 245 f.

45. Dietrich Staritz, *Geschichte der DDR* (new enlarged edition), Frankfurt 1996, p. 104; Falco Werkentin, *Politische Strafjustiz in der Ära Ulbricht*, Berlin 1995, p. 69; Dieter Schulz, 'Ruhe im Dorf? Die Agrarpolitik von 1952/53 und ihre Folgen', in Jochen Černý, (ed.), *Brüche, Krisen, Wendepunkte*, Leipzig 1990, pp. 103–110, here 106; Ulrich Kluge, 'Die verhinderte Rebellion. Bauern, Genossenschaften und SED im Umfeld der Juni-Krise 1953 in der DDR', in Wolther von Kieseritzky and Klaus-Peter Sick (eds), *Demokratie in Deutschland. Chancen und Gefährdungen im 19. und 20. Jahrhundert*, Munich 1999, pp. 317–35, here 323.

46. Schulz, *Ruhe im Dorf?*, pp. 107 f. Cf. Kluge, 'Verhinderte Rebellion', pp. 324 ff.

47. Quoted according to Schulz, *Ruhe im Dorf?*, p. 107. On the whole passage, Bauerkämper, *Ländliche Gesellschaft*, p. 169.

48. Christian Ostermann, *Uprising in East Germany 1953. The Cold War, the German Question and the First Major Upheaval behind the Iron Curtain*, Budapest 2001, p. 11; Jens Schöne, *Frühling auf dem Lande? Die Kollektivierung der DDR-Landwirtschaft*, Berlin 2005, pp. 136–39.

49. Monika Tatzkow, 'Privatindustrie ohne Perspektive. Der Versuch zur Liquidierung der mittleren privaten Warenproduzenten', in Jochen Černý (ed.), *Brüche, Krisen, Wendepunkte*, Leipzig 1990, pp. 97–103, here 100.

50. Torsten Diedrich, 'Aufrüstungsvorbereitung und -finanzierung in der SBZ/DDR in den Jahren 1948 bis 1953 und deren Rückwirkungen auf die Wirtschaft', in Bruno Thoß (ed.), *Volksarmee schaffen – ohne Geschrei*, Munich 1994, pp. 273–336; Torsten Diedrich and Rüdiger Wenzke, *Die getarnte Armee. Geschichte der Kasernierten Volkspolizei der DDR 1952–1956*, Berlin 2001, pp. 89 f., 268–74, 307–11.

51. Die Sicherung der Durchführung des Fünfjahrplanes und des Aufbaus der nationalen bewaffneten Streitkräfte in der DDR [February 1953], SAPMO-BA DY30/3697.

52. Chuykov to the SED Central Committee, 13.4.1953, SAPMO-BA DY30/3697; Ministry of Foreign Affairs to Grotewohl, 27.4.1953, ibid.; Diedrich, 'Aufrüstungsvorbereitung', p. 332.

53. Die Entwicklung der Lebenshaltungskosten im sowjetischen Besatzungsgebiet, in *DIW-Wochenbericht* 20, 1953, pp. 107 ff.

54. Staritz, *Geschichte der DDR*, pp. 101, 107; Buchheim, 'Wirtschaftliche Hintergründe', p. 418; Die Entwicklung der Lebenshaltungskosten im sowjetischen Besatzungsgebiet, in *DIW-Wochenbericht* 20, 1953, pp. 107 ff.

55. Staritz, *Geschichte der DDR*, p. 102; Buchheim, 'Wirtschaftliche Hintergründe', pp. 422, 428 f.

56. 'Über die Maßnahmen zur Gesundung der politischen Lage in der Deutschen Demokratischen Republik', in Dierk Hoffmann, Karl-Heinz Schmidt and Peter Skyba (eds), *Die DDR vor dem Mauerbau. Dokumente zur Geschichte des anderen deutschen Staates 1949–1961*, Munich 1993, pp. 152–58.

57. Cf. Ostermann, *Uprising*, p. 164.

58. *17. Juni 1953. Chronik* (CD-Rom 2003). See also in Ostermann, *Uprising*, the Soviet documents with figures especially pp. 283 f.

59. 'Report from Sokolovskij, Semyonov and Yudin', in Ostermann, *Uprising*, p. 275.

60. Schulz, *Ruhe im Dorf?*, p. 108.

61. 'Abteilung für politische Fragen der DDR bei der Botschaft der UdSSR in der DDR: Über die Lage der Privatunternehmer, Händler und Handwerker in der DDR in Verbindung mit dem Neuen Kurs', in Jan Foitzik, 'Berichte des Hohen Kommissars der UdSSR in Deutschland aus den Jahren 1953/54. Dokumente aus dem Archiv für Außenpolitik der Russischen Föderation', in Deutscher Bundestag (ed.), *Materialien der Enquete-Kommission, Aufarbeitung von Geschichte und Folgen der SED-Diktatur in Deutschland'*, Baden-Baden 1995, Vol. II/2, pp. 1474–83, here 1479 f.

62. 'Abteilung für ökonomische Fragen der Botschaft der UdSSR in der DDR und des Hohen Kommissars der UdSSR in Deutschland: Wirtschaftliche Lage der DDR [im ersten Halbjahr 1954]', in Foitzik, 'Berichte des Hohen Kommissars', pp. 1429–73; Grotewohl, Ulbricht to Khrushchev, 17.2.1955, SAPMO-BA DY30/3700; DNB, Kuckhoff to Grotewohl, 8.7.1954, SAPMO-BA NY4090/336. On the following see also Buchheim, 'Wirtschaftliche Hintergründe', p. 432.

Chapter 3

Between Shortages and Growth
1953–1961

After Stalin's death in 1953, the new Moscow leadership began to question not just the priorities in economic policy but also other concepts. Eventually at the Twentieth Congress of the Communist Party of the Soviet Union in February 1956 Stalin's ruling regime was also criticized. All this opened some room for discussion, and throughout the Eastern Bloc a 'thaw' set in. Based on nuclear strength, Stalin's successors worked towards a détente in the East–West conflict and a 'peaceful coexistence' of the two social systems; this was a departure from their previous ambitions for world revolution. In the economy there were discussions about the release of the potentials of socialism not only by plan discipline, but also by economic incentives. The Socialist Unity Party of Germany, too, followed the new policy and at the 3rd Party Conference in 1956 proclaimed the slogan of 'democratisation' in the state apparatus and in economic control. Such considerations, however, fell victim to Ulbricht's power politics. The uprising in Hungary was from his point of view an important warning: transformations of the system must on no account jeopardize the power of the Party.

At the same time the sociopolitical goal of construction socialism on German soil was to be further realised. The task, in view of the Party's policy of reuniting the German states under a socialist mantle, was to make the system attractive to people both in the East and the West. The most visible sign that this had not so far been accomplished was the *Republikflucht* (the flight from the German Democratic Republic) across the open frontier to the West. People voting with their feet was a constant challenge to the Party to decisively improve the economic situation and living conditions in the GDR. Towards the end of the fifties the Party launched another campaign to surpass the competitor in the West and to help socialism to be victorious. Living standards were to be raised by growing consumer goods production and the collectivisation of agriculture. At the same time the Soviet Union intended, in agreement with the Socialist Unity Party, to solve the Berlin problem and finally to secure the integration of the GDR in the Eastern Bloc by a separate peace treaty with the East German part-state. In consequence the East–West conflict once more became exacerbated. Simultaneously, owing to the forced socioeconomic transformation in the countryside and the acceleration of industrial growth – further intensified by systemic defects – there arose an acute economic and supply crisis. Both the internal crisis and the exacerbation of the East–West conflict resulted again in rising numbers of people escaping from the Republic, so that Moscow eventually yielded to Ulbricht's urgings to seal off West Berlin in order to safeguard the stability of the East German part-state.

Industrial and Structural Policy

The New Course represented a revision of the original targets of the first Five-Year Plan. The originally envisaged development of primary industry and of heavy engineering was toned down in the second half of 1953 in favour of the consumer goods industry. This also affected the biggest single investment of this Five-Year Plan, the EKO combine for the production of iron and steel. Construction of this plant had begun at Fürstenberg-on-Oder at the beginning of 1951, but because of the severe cutback of investments only six of the originally envisaged ten blast furnaces were completed while the steelworks, whose foundations had already been laid, was not built at all. In consequence only pig iron was produced at first. Even later, the much-needed steel and rolling-mill capacities were only partly constructed, because of a shortage of investments, so that the plant that was to have integrated the whole metallurgical cycle was never created. Nevertheless, the originally planned capacity was decidedly surpassed even with the existing six blast furnaces. Overall then the first Five-Year Plan was regarded as having been fulfilled – at least in respect of raised industrial production.

Admittedly however productivity was lagging; this was attributed chiefly to discontinuous production due to a shortage of materials and energy and the resulting stoppages. Contrary to the provisions of the Five-Year Plan, primary industry was not expanded.

Table 3.1: Shares of industrial branches in the gross production of all industry in 1950 and 1955 in per cent[1]

	1950	1955	
		Five-Year Plan Target	Actual
Primary industry	33.1	34.8	30.9
Metal-processing industry	24.4	26.0	27.8
Light industry	27.7	24.4	24.4
Foodstuffs industry	14.8	14.8	16.9

The second Five-Year Plan was to lay down the targets for the GDR's economic development from 1956 to 1960. Benchmark data were first worked out for this long-term plan: on their basis the production plans and the necessary goods exchange with the Soviet Union and the other Eastern Bloc countries were to be adjusted. This was formally done in the framework of the Council for Mutual Economic Assistance (Comecon) that had been set up at the beginning of 1949 in view of the common structural features of the Eastern European economies and of Stalin's prohibition on Eastern Europe's participation in the Marshall Plan. The GDR had joined the Council in September 1950. It also served the Soviet Union as an instrument for securing its sphere of control, which was why all plans in the fifties were in fact coordinated in the Soviet Planning Commission. In addition Comecon was intended to promote specialisation and cooperation among the industries of the member countries. These plans, however, failed in the fifties in view of the disparate interests of the individual countries; these differences resulted from their disparate levels of development, frequent changes to their national plans and a lack of multilateral coordinating institutions. After all, such adjustments were difficult enough even within the individual countries.

At the first adjustment in the spring of 1955 the Moscow planners asked the GDR to set its output targets higher in spite of limited resources and capacities. Consumption, too, was to be raised. However, because of the envisaged strong growth of the investment goods industry and the further development of the armed forces (a second rearmament programme) this was only partially possible. Moreover, the manpower reservoir was already exhausted. For this reason the drafts of the second Five-Year Plan envisaged a stronger increase of productivity and profitability through the introduction of new technology. The prioritisation of science and technology was the essential difference between the second and the first Five-Year Plans.

Under the draft of the Five-Year Plan approved by the 3rd Party Conference in March 1956, expansion investments were to be doubled. This was urgently necessary considering that they had been neglected for many years because of reparations. Moreover, investments were concentrated on primary industry and on engineering. With a target growth for industry as a whole of 52 per cent these two industries were to step up their production by about 60 per cent while the consumer goods industry was to increase by 40 per cent. Thus the priority of the capital goods industry was restored. Productivity of industry as a whole was to increase by 51 per cent. However, beyond the ambitious growth targets the figures contained contradictions between different parts of the plan, contradictions which the planners tried to even out by a mobilisation of all reserves.[2] The fact that the plans were being based on ever higher targets was a common phenomenon in the socialist economic system. On the one hand this was due to political pressure; on the other, the planners were hoping that by setting ever higher goals they would be able to mobilise the reserves they assumed to exist in the enterprises.

In 1956, however, what was decisive was the politically motivated idea of having to prove the superiority of the GDR's system over that of the West. In actual fact the premises of the policy with regard to Germany had changed since the Federal Republic had become a member of NATO in 1955 and the GDR had joined the Warsaw Pact in the same year. Since then the Soviet Union's actions were based on a Two-States Theory. This seemed to set the final seal on the partition of Germany. Although German unity continued to be the ostensible aim of the Socialist Unity Party's policy, the real issue now was the international recognition of the GDR as a second German state. But that also required evidence of economic potency and of an attractive living standard. For both these ends, as Ulbricht told the Soviet leaders, there was a need of economic stability and secure supplies for the population. For that reason the Party leaders asked for goods and foreign currency credits, pointing out that the high targets of the Plan – increase in gross industrial production by just under 9 per cent and of state investments by 40 per cent in 1956 – could only be more or less achieved with such help. However, it was only when the GDR leaders intimated that there was a danger of a 'serious food crisis' for the summer of that year and that, in view of the economic boom in Western Germany, there might therefore be 'very serious consequences' for the stability of the GDR, that the Soviet Union granted major assistance.[3] Nevertheless, supplies of raw materials and foodstuffs remained unsatisfactory throughout 1956 owing to defaulting deliveries. In the end the East German leaders had to confess to the Soviets that, in spite of all efforts, the West German level of productivity or of supplies could not be attained, let alone surpassed, in the foreseeable future. If the intention was to fulfil the plans at least formally, then it would be necessary either to lower the targets or to receive additional imports.[4] Thereupon the Soviet Union in July 1956 promised additional supplies and lowered the costs to be paid by the GDR for the stationing of Soviet troops in the GDR. This type of procedure became a regular feature of East-German–Soviet economic relations. With reference to its special position, the Socialist Unity Party attempted to receive help from the Soviet Union, in the form of reduced burdens, credits and additional deliveries; at the same time they spelled out the risks in the event of a Soviet refusal: weakening of the GDR, hence of the Eastern Bloc, and eventually also of the Soviet Union. Even though the GDR Party leaders were not always successful with their (quite realistic) warnings, they nevertheless succeeded in achieving a special status vis-à-vis Moscow and in Comecon, at least for the time being.

The economic results of 1956 were relatively poor, partly caused by the non-arrival of hard coal and hard-coal coke from Poland, where disturbances had broken out. In light of this, it seemed unrealistic to expect the economy to reach the Five-Year Plan targets set at the beginning of the year. Investments had to be cut back, and GDR exports which had been promised to the Eastern Bloc countries were cancelled. Finally, the Five-Year Plan had to be revised, 'elements of wishful thinking' eliminated, and the real economic capabilities as well as domestic and external economic interdependencies more accurately recalculated.[5] It was necessary to lower overall production considerably: the number of particularly prestigious cars, for instance, had to be virtually halved. According to the Law on the second Five-Year Plan, passed only in January 1958, when two years of the plan had already elapsed, industrial production was now only to be increased to 138 per cent between 1955 and 1960.[6]

In terms of structural policy, the second Five-Year Plan in industry prioritised the development of engineering and of the country's own raw material basis: the brown coal and potash industries, as well as basic chemicals. A (second) coal and energy programme was designed to close the discrepancy between industrial development and available energy amount. This gap was, on the one hand, historically conditioned: it was a result of the disproportion between the degree of industrialisation and domestic raw materials like fossil fuels that had arisen from the partition of Germany. On the other it was the result of wartime destruction, dismantling, outdated manufacturing plants and the lack of incentives for an economic use of energy. The programme envisaged an increase in coal production of 30 per cent by 1960 and in energy production of 33 per cent over 1956. Thus a large part of industrial investments was bound up in the energy and fuel industries: in 1958 it was 47 per cent, at the beginning of the sixties it was about 40 per cent.[7]

More ambitious still were the projects of the so-called chemical programme laid down on the Soviet model in 1958 with the slogan 'Chemistry gives bread – prosperity – beauty'. Under this programme production of chemicals was to be doubled by 1965. For this the traditional basic chemicals at the Leuna works and the production of coal-carbide basis at the Buna works were to be developed. It was also intended that the annual deliveries of 5 million tons of crude oil, promised by the Soviet Union, were to be utilised for the development of petrochemicals. The most important projects here were the Erdölverarbeitungskombinat Schwedt (a combine for the processing of crude oil in Schwedt) and the Chemiefaserkombinat Guben (a chemical fibre combine in Guben) that would serve as a road into synthetic chemicals. This double strategy – the development of petrochemicals and the enhancement of traditional coal chemicals, already in decline internationally – was a consequence of the raw materials situation in the GDR. With petrochemicals, the planners not only wanted to match the worldwide trend, but also expected cost advantages. Although these decisions were fundamentally reasonable, the coal, energy and chemical programme exceeded the available capabilities of engineering and plant construction, as well as of the building industry in general. In the end they claimed more than half of all industrial investments. For both areas large-scale enterprises were typical for technological reasons, which increased the share of investments that were committed but not yet producing an effective return.[8]

Beyond these priorities of structural policy, the second processing stage of metallurgy was to be developed by the mid sixties. Traditional measurement and process control engineering had been expanded ever since the mid fifties, but it was also intended that, in time, semiconductor elements should start to modernise the electronics industry.

Furthermore, the enterprises were expected to work out reconstruction plans after the summer of 1958 that should contain rationalisation projects and provide an impulse to specialise and concentrate production. This should lower costs and enhance quality. In order to increase piece numbers and reduce costs per unit, the fabrication of identical products by different manufacturers was to be stopped. The same purpose was served by unification of products, assemblies and spare parts in the framework of a standardisation campaign. Higher piece numbers and technological continuous flow processes were also the preconditions of the demanded mechanisation and automation of production, using, as was then customary, inflexible technical solutions. All these were elements of the Fordist production model by which the Party leaders were guided throughout their period of rule, right to the end. Undoubtedly considerable economies were possible in this way, since the production palette of enterprises in the postwar years had grown somewhat wild, without much rationalisation. However, behind the reconstruction programme there were also exaggerated ideas that called for the complete monopolisation of every single manufacturing process in one enterprise. At any rate it proved possible, by such reorganisation, to regain the pre-war level of manufacturing organisation in industry by the end of the fifties and the beginning of the sixties.

The Private Sector and Agriculture

Starting in 1956 a new policy was pursued vis-à-vis private enterprises. Although between 1950 and 1955 their share of industrial employment had declined from 24 per cent to just under 17 per cent, they accounted for 15 per cent of gross industrial production in 1955.[9] Since private firms supplied important inputs to the state's engineering industry and were making a crucial contribution to the population's supplies in the light and food-stuffs industries, new ways of involving this potential in the planned economy were being considered towards the end of 1955. The State Planning Commission now pointed out 'that the development of the private economy should be controlled not so much with purely administrative measures as with economic methods'.[10] As early as in the first half of the fifties the state had, now and again, financially supported private enterprises for macroeconomic reasons, since because of its restrictive price and taxation policy many of them had suffered from a shortage of capital and were unable either to enlarge or to modernise their production. In January 1956 the Council of Ministers decided not to grant any further credits to those enterprises but to let the state own a share in these firms. As a result these private enterprises had had a temporary guarantee of their existence, but the state's influence over them had grown. The state-owned enterprises (VEB) installed as partners were able, in practice, to make their 'cared for' enterprises dependent on themselves and to undermine the private control of these semi-state entrepreneurs even further. The Decree on the creation of enterprises with state participation (*Betriebe mit staatlicher Beteiligung*), dated 1959, eventually openly described them as 'a transitional form to a socialist enterprise'.[11]

In the eyes of the Party leaders the capacities of private industry were not insignificant for their growth targets, which was why the entrepreneurs had to be quickly convinced of the advantages of state participation. Following some 'help' with additional tax demands and other administrative measures the number of semi-state-owned enterprises in industry had risen from 144 in 1956 to 4,455 in 1960. Less than a third of all enterprises were now state-owned, fewer than a third were semi-state-owned and 40 per cent were privately owned; their share of production, however, was 89 per cent, 7 per cent and 4 per cent. Similar processes were taking place in domestic trade: private retail traders who had commission contracts with state trading enterprises already accounted for 7.5 per cent of the retail trade turnover in 1961.[12]

In agriculture, on the other hand, after a short pause in collectivisation because of the 1953 Uprising, the Party leaders were once more aiming at large-acreage farming. This, they believed, was in accord with the Soviet model as well as with the trend in Western Europe. Once the Agricultural Production Cooperatives (LPGs) had got over their teething troubles, the Party leaders believed, their superiority would soon be clearly seen. The Agricultural Production Cooperatives' share of the farmland rose initially mainly because of enterprises being given up by their proprietors. Simultaneously the quality of cooperative work further improved. In Agricultural Production Cooperatives of Type I, the fields only were cultivated jointly. Beyond that, in Type II, machines, equipment and draught animals passed into cooperative ownership, as did, in Type III, the breeding and working livestock as well as the pastureland. Until 1957 the proportion of Type III cooperatives increased. When, in the last third of the decade, cooperatives were forcibly set up, these often belonged to Types I and II, possibly because they facilitated more partial entry into cooperative work.

Table 3.2: Agricultural Production Cooperatives' share of total farmland and shares of areas worked by Types I and II and by Type III, 1952 to 1961 in per cent as of end of year[13]

	LPGs' share of total farmland	Worked by LPGs altogether by way of	
		Types I and II	Type III
1952	3.3	86.7	13.3
1953	11.6	41.3	58.7
1954	14.3	20.2	79.8
1955	19.7	10.0	90.0
1956	23.2	5.8	94.2
1957	25.2	5.3	94.7
1958	37.0	12.8	87.2
1959	43.5	12.7	87.3
1960	83.6	37.3	62.7
1961	84.4	34.9	65.1

Collectivisation and farmers' flight to the West drove each other forward: between 1952 and 1956 some 70,000 enterprises were abandoned through 'flight from the Republic' (*Republikflucht*), among which 30 per cent were enterprises of 20 to 100 hectares, classified as 'big farmers'. In 1950 such enterprises were still working 24 per cent of the farmland; in 1956 it was only 12 per cent.[14] However, not only 'big farmers', but also many small and medium farmers found themselves compelled to give up their enterprises. Transfer of the abandoned enterprises to the Agricultural Production Cooperatives in turn increased the proportion of cooperatives. At the same time, economically well-established individual farmers had been able, since the recall of the measures directed against them in 1953, to consolidate their enterprises for the time being. Their proceeds rose by 38 per cent from 1952 to 1955, mainly because of a substantial increase in purchases of surplus yields, whose prices exceeded the prices for the compulsory levies by anything between 150 and more than 400 per cent. According to an internal analysis in 1957, this price policy proved 'an important lever for agricultural policy'. Yet the performance of enterprises in the mid fifties was determined chiefly by the qualifications of the owners, their organisational skills, the size of an enterprise and, dependent on this, its supplies of agricultural equipment and resources. The different delivery quotas set by local authorities also played their part.[15]

The goal of the first Five-Year Plan, to surpass the per-hectare yields of the Western countries, was missed, even by the GDR's own calculations. According to State Planning Commission data the 1955 acreage productivity in agriculture lagged behind the Federal Republic by only 10 per cent.[16] It was thought that further collectivisation, the resulting concentration and possible specialisation, as well as a more intensive utilisation of machinery, would make it possible to catch up. But it was the Agricultural Production Cooperatives that acted as a brake: their performance, especially in livestock production, lagged behind those of the individual farmers. Despite all the benefits granted to them, their production declined in 1955 and again in 1956. Yet the weaknesses were structural: more than one-half of the land farmed by them came from abandoned properties, the bulk of the Agricultural Production Cooperatives members were former new farmers or farm workers, and the proportion of old-established and experienced farmers was declining. There was not only a lack of agricultural know-how, but also of fertile soil and high-performance livestock. One-third of the cooperatives of Type III had to be fully subsidised to make sure the Agricultural Production Cooperatives members received the state-guaranteed minimum income. Barely 7 per cent of Type III cooperatives managed without subsidies.[17]

In spite of this, the Agricultural Production Cooperatives' share of the farmland was to be doubled by 1960 from about one-quarter to one-half.[18] Pressure on the farmers was stepped up. Industrial workers sent on the land to help with the harvest were not only to make up for the manpower shortage but also try to enlist people for the cooperatives. So-called 'Propaganda Brigades' tried to win over first those farmers who were members of the Socialist Unity Party or the Peasant Party. In this way it proved possible, after the autumn of 1957, to create new cooperatives. Frequently, successful medium-size farmers formed cooperatives with well-situated neighbours, which improved their chances of achieving positive results. In addition to favourable weather conditions this was possibly a reason why agriculture and forestry, after years of stagnation and decline, were able, for the first time, to raise their value-added by 8 per cent and 9 per cent in 1957 and 1958. In this result the state-owned and cooperative enterprises had a disproportionately high share, which in turn enhanced the attraction of such enterprises and caused the number of Agricultural Production Cooperatives and their members to rise significantly by autumn 1958.[19]

Problems of the Control Mechanism

By the mid fifties the socialist economic system had almost assumed its 'classical' form. At the same time the Soviet Union still exerted strong influence. Until the end of the fifties Soviet advisers were working in the GDR ministries, three in the State Planning Commission and two in the Ministry of Finance alone; they were involved in the work on normative regulations and the basic outlines of the plans. Fundamental changes, however, in the GDR economy, changes that seemed advisable to the Soviets, were more often proposed in conversation or in writing at the leadership level.[20] The contacts between the East German Party leaders and Moscow were influential in the annual preparation of the plan too. Certain deliveries and other concessions were requested by word of mouth or in writing. With every acceptance or rejection of a request the Soviet Union exerted massive influence on the economic development of the GDR, even if it did not always consciously exploit this dependence. At any rate, the sovereignty of the GDR continued to be limited.

The most important instrument for controlling the economy in the fifties was the annual plan. Because of the various changes in economic policy the Five-Year Plans could only provide rough outlines of development. The central state plan covered production of about 850 items, the plans of the ministries and their Main Administrations covered some 2,500 items, that is products or product categories.[21] The contents of the plans were basically determined by the guidelines set by the centre. The influence of enterprises and their workforce remained severely limited. Even the State Planning Commission regarded the actual planning as over-centralised and criticised the fact that the responsibility of ministers, heads of Main Administrations and enterprise managers was being restricted, giving rise to 'bureaucratic excrescences'.[22] Capturing the various economic interdependencies in the plan and coordinating them proved an exceedingly complex problem. This was not changed by an overbrimming reporting system or the 'plan rounds'; these repeatedly handed targets and information on the plan down from the centre through the intermediate levels all the way down to the enterprises, to be subsequently summed up at the top and coordinated with each other. Both tied down considerable manpower and the plan became a 'fetish' in the State Planning Commission and the ministries: essentially they were always busy drawing up and revising the current and the following plans. Monitoring and analysis of the problems and difficulties underlying the plan, and hence feedback, were neglected.

By this point the disadvantages of the gross index numbers used for assessing goods and performances were becoming increasingly obvious:

production was reported at inflated figures and enterprises were rewarded if they produced their output even with the greatest possible inputs and costs. This gave rise to a so-called 'tonnage ideology' that militated against all efforts to be economical with resources. On the contrary, the proportion of material and energy in manufacturing costs was rising in the fifties. Added to this was the pricing problem: the creation of fixed prices, enacted in February 1953 by the Council of Ministers, was seen as a way of adjusting prices to the demands of the planned economy. However, the cost norms intended as the basis of fixed-price setting were often based on experiences only and not technologically or economically founded. In consequence they fulfilled their intended function only to a limited degree: they represented no incentive for either a lowering of costs or for increasing of production. Because of widespread persistent ignorance of economic categories the creation of fixed prices made only sluggish progress at first. However, by 1961 some 76 per cent of industrial production was regulated by fixed-price orders. These were unfortunately not internally consistent and, especially in the primary sector, no longer covered the real expenses resulting from meanwhile increased costs. Because they continued to exist alongside the partly still valid, modified 1944 prices and calculated prices (made in the previous years according to the real costs), they merely enhanced the inconsistency of the pricing system and the difficulties of controlling the economy centrally.[23]

Since the enterprises had had to surrender almost their complete depreciations and returns to the central authority by the beginning of 1955, questions of profitability, cost reduction and productivity did not receive the necessary attention. Enterprises concentrated on fulfilment of the production plan. There were only slight material incentives to steer economic action of the enterprises; plan directives were predominant. Admittedly in 1951/52 a contract system and the principle of economic accountancy had been introduced, under which the enterprises – legally independent and endowed with their own financial and material means – had to operate in a manner covering their costs. This basically self-evident economic principle was however constantly undermined by the certainty for the enterprises that in the end the state would invariably cover their financial needs; this was called soft budget constraint. Economic sanctions could only be applied to a limited degree since the enterprises, because of operational intervention from superior authorities, could not be held liable for infringements of contracts. This, too, reflected the primacy of politics over the economy.

Incentives for industrial employees continued to be a considerable problem too. After the June Uprising the political leaders avoided interference in matters of wages or the norms the wages were based on. Average norm fulfilment in industry was about 132 per cent in 1955. In the enterprises conflicts with the workers over the 'hot potato' of norms were avoided. Only a fraction of all norms had meanwhile been newly laid down on technological grounds. Thus actual wages increasingly exceeded standard wages.[24] However, a gradual wages reform, considered in 1957, seemed an incalculable risk to the Party leaders and was therefore only introduced in a rudimentary way that had scarcely any effect.

Although those responsible for the economy were aware of many of the problems listed above, they regarded them as imperfections that could be overcome. An overall critical examination only became possible after the Twentieth Congress of the Communist Party of the Soviet Union at the beginning of 1956. The partial opening-up in the Soviet Union following Stalin's death was by then official for the Communist world and could no longer be ignored by the East German Party leaders under Ulbricht. Eventually, at the Third Party Conference in the same year even he spoke, albeit in restrained terms, in favour of an improvement of the control and planning system. As a consequence the State Planning Commission began chiefly to work towards a critical examination of planning methods and the reduction of 'bureaucratic excrescences'.[25] Yet the proposals made by the economic hierarchy sometimes went further. The central question was to what degree and in what spheres of economic control decentralisation should be practised, and what rights should be conceded to subordinate levels, all the way down to the enterprises. The very principle of gross planning and accountancy was also questioned. Some of the proposals that came out of this process became effective before the end of 1957. Thus the targets in production planning were drastically reduced. Compared to 1955 the number of state plan items declined to less than one-half by 1957. A reduction was similarly made of central targets and nomenclatures for planning investments and manpower.[26] In addition, the economic incentives for enterprises were redefined: the existing *Direktorfonds* (directors' fund) was broken down into a *Betriebsprämienfonds* (enterprise bonus fund) and a *Kultur- und Sozialfonds* (cultural and social fund). While the enterprise bonus fund served as a direct financial incentive for the (over-)fulfilment of the production and profit plan, the cultural and social fund was used for social purposes benefiting the factory personnel. This included the operation of childcare and health facilities, as well as holiday homes and the financing of social events. The clear division between the two was to prove an advantage in the long term. Nevertheless 'decentralisation' continued to lack an economic basis as the subordinate levels had scarcely any more material or financial means than before.

Moreover, Ulbricht's demands provoked a discussion among economic theoreticians in 1956; discussions which, against the background of the disturbances and uprisings in Poland in June and October 1956 and in Hungary in October and November 1956, were viewed with suspicion by the Party leaders. Admittedly, Fritz Behrens – one of the best-known GDR economists of the day and Head of the State Central Administration for Statistics – observed with disappointment in October 1956 that the discussion about planning had been expected to produce 'rather more fundamental changes than have been proposed to date, so that the result is not fully satisfactory'.[27] This judgement is not surprising since Behrens was at the head of several scholars at the Institute for Economics of the Academy of Sciences who had begun to concern themselves with more fundamental issues of centralisation and decentralisation, as well as with the development of economic methods for controlling the economy by means of the plan. The debate mainly focused on two articles by Behrens and his co-worker Arne Benary. They sketched out the economic difficulties in the GDR: discontinuous production, the hoarding phenomenon, unsaleable products and surplus purchasing power, and blamed them all on the control of the economy, which they described as overcentralised, regimented, administrative and bureaucratic. This they countered by a plan-oriented coordination by economic means on the basis of economic self-management. In their view the central authority should only set a framework in order to steer the activities of enterprises and employees in the direction desired by the central authority. A minimum of central instructions and a maximum of initiative and independence 'from below' was what was needed, and these were to be achieved by the deliberate utilisation of economic instruments, i.e., individual market categories.[28] Although this draft by the two scholars did not actually depart from the foundation of Marxist theory, it certainly questioned its prevailing state-socialist version. At any rate their thesis anticipated conceptual ideas about economic reform in the sixties. However, their demands touched upon the Party's monopoly of rule, and thus the theoretical positions of Behrens and Benary were soon blackened by Ulbricht as 'revisionism'.[29]

Agrarian policy, too, was critically discussed in the GDR after the Twentieth Soviet Party Congress, as the economic situation of most Agricultural Production Cooperatives was precarious and cooperatives were being dissolved in Yugoslavia, Poland and Hungary. A few Party officials, such as Fred Oelßner, and a number of agricultural economists, gathered around Kurt Vieweg, pleaded for collectivisation to be slowed down, for uneconomical Agricultural Production Cooperatives to be dissolved instead of being further subsidised, for individual farmers and cooperatives to be allowed to coexist for some time, and for agriculture as a whole to be controlled solely with economic incentives, such as prices, taxes and credits.[30] For Ulbricht this was less of an economic than a political question. Considerations of profitability were of secondary importance to him. Erich Mückenberger, the responsible Central Committee Secretary, consoled himself: 'Building socialism in the countryside always costs money and no country has yet succeeded in achieving it on the cheap.'[31] In this respect these ideas were likewise condemned as revisionism. Yet it was not only economists and agricultural theoreticians who, after the Twentieth Party Congress and its criticism of Stalin's personality cult, wanted to set out on new roads of building socialism. Literary scholars, philosophers, legal scholars and historians were all discussing it. The East German Party leaders, altogether unconvinced by the politics of the Thaw and having their fears confirmed by developments in Poland and Hungary, noted that the intellectuals were having doubts about Marxism–Leninism.[32] At the beginning of 1957, therefore, Ulbricht directed his accusations not only against Behrens and Benary: the charges of 'revisionism' were directly and indirectly aimed against all reform-socialist ideas outside the Party line. Not until three years later did the 'revisionism debate', staged by the East German Party leaders, come to an end, with often enforced and humiliating self-criticism by the accused. Behrens by then had been relieved of his governmental functions and Benary had been transferred 'into production' in 1958.

In the autumn of 1956 disturbances broke out in the enterprises too and the Ministry for State Security reported that 'whenever there are disagreements and difficulties there is talk in the enterprises of a new 17 June or that strikes are being threatened'.[33] For this reason Ulbricht, at a Central Committee meeting a few days after the dramatic events in Hungary in November 1956, made the internally controversial proposal that workers' committees be set up in all enterprises. These were to judge the enterprise management, share in long-term planning, control whether notice had been taken of workers' suggestions, and have decisive influence on the distribution of bonuses and the setting of norms. By the autumn of 1957 this idea quietly fizzled out. The restabilised rule in the Eastern Bloc and the absence of serious internal workers' opposition rendered them superfluous. The fundamental problem, however, remained with the Party right to its end: on the one hand it needed employee participation in decision making in order to legitimise its rule, while on the other it could not really grant it because this would have eroded its power. Just as ambivalent as the workers' committees – hovering between crisis prevention and reformist efforts – were the production committees set up during the economic reform of the sixties.[34]

Given the country's economic problems the discussion on changes in economic control could not simply be cut short. Following the crushing of the uprising in Hungary emphasis was, in the interests of stability, put primarily on organisational changes. Apparently the administrative reform introduced in the Soviet Union in May 1957 provided an occasion for similar reflections in the GDR, even though different motives were decisive there. In 1958 the industrial ministries were abolished and planning and operational responsibility for industry was transferred to the State Planning Commission. At the same time another intermediate administrative level was created – the Association of People-Owned Enterprises, VVB in short. They were conceived as purely administrative authorities without economic autonomy. The 'economic cadres' were not too delighted with this 'reform', regarding it merely as another political campaign; the wider intention to get rid of bureaucratic methods fizzled out.

The attempt to remove previously discussed obstacles to innovation eventually also became largely characterised by purely administrative measures. The separate innovation phases were now increasingly to be planned, and in 1957 a GDR Research Council was set up that included well-known representatives of different scientific and technical fields. This was intended as a countermeasure to the failure by some responsible executives to understand the role of science and technology in a modern economy. The Research Council was to advise the Council of Ministers and was meant, in cooperation with the State Planning Commission, to work out new long-term plans for research and development of new technology, to adjust research capacities to economic requirements and to propose and coordinate fundamental steps towards the promotion of innovations.

The debates on changes in the economy had also been used by Ulbricht for squaring accounts with those who had not fully supported his hard political line since the Twentieth Soviet Communist Party Congress and thus for eliminating potential opponents among the SED leadership. Gerhard Ziller, Secretary for Economic Affairs in the SED Central Committee since July of 1953, committed suicide; Fritz Selbmann was recalled from his post of Deputy Head of Government and instead appointed deputy chairman for materials administration in the newly structured State Planning Commission – a dangerous post in which he could never fulfil all expectations. Meanwhile Erich Apel, a technocrat with a meteoric rise, assumed the direction of the newly created Economic Commission at the Politbüro in February 1958; Günter Mittag, previously a trade union and party official, became the new Commission's secretary. Both of them owed their rise to Ulbricht, which obliged them to display their loyalty. Alongside Ulbricht they significantly shaped the economic policy of the following years.

Growth, Structural Change and Standard of Living

According to Western estimates the East German gross domestic product per head of population did not reach the pre-war level until 1955/56. Industry succeeded in reaching pre-war levels as early as 1953, while agriculture was still more than 14 per cent below the 1936 figure even in 1958. Private consumption per head of population, similarly, according to more recent estimates, was still, in 1958, 12 per cent below the pre-war level, reaching only about 50 per cent of Western German consumption. Throughout the entire fifties the East German GDP per head was about two-thirds of that in the Federal Republic.[35] This means that consumption was lagging further behind the West German level than economic performance, which illustrates the distribution priorities in the GDR in the fifties. Apart from rising investments and hoarded stocks, the distributable domestic product was further diminished by the stationing costs of the Soviet troops, the expenses for the SAG Wismut and new rearmament efforts. In the mid fifties these expenses accounted for about one-fifth of the state's expenditure.[36] According to GDR statistics, value added per head of the population as an expression of the overall economic performance had risen by 1961 to 2.8 times the 1950 figure. Production of industry increased roughly to the same extent; the labour productivity (value added per employee) in this sector increased 2.4 times. By contrast, value added of agriculture and forestry had more or less stagnated since 1951. Accordingly the manufacturing industries' share of value added in the economy as a whole increased by nearly one-third to 54 per cent between 1950 and 1961, whereas the share of agriculture was nearly halved to 20 per cent. This was due, on the one hand, to the secular trend from the primary to the secondary economic sector, but, on the other, revealed the loss of efficiency in agriculture due to its restructuring by land reform and collectivisation. Even branches in the services sector were able slightly to extend their share, with transport, postal and telecommunication services losing a little and domestic trade gaining a little.[37]

Altogether the industrial structure changed less than might have been expected from the massive concentration of investments; the reason being that many sectors continued to work at less than full capacity. The sectors of electrical engineering, heavy machinery, general engineering, metal manufactures, vehicle production, metallurgy, clothing and needlework articles, as well as precision mechanics and the optical industry, increased their share of gross production during the fifties. The losers were energy production – despite its prioritisation since the middle of the decade – as well as the manufacturing of wooden and cultural articles, textiles, leather, footwear and fur articles, cellulose and paper, mining, the printing industry and glass and ceramics.[38] Generally speaking, the branches that gained, or maintained their levels, were in the area of the primary and the investment goods industries. The ready-made clothes and foodstuffs industries remained exceptions.

The part that innovations played in the structural change was slight. Although there were a number of new developments, these often failed to get into production because of obstacles from the control mechanism. If, in individual cases, they were nevertheless successful, then this was due as a rule to the commitment of individual scientists or engineers who stood their ground against the systemic obstacles put in their way. Moreover, the Cold War had its effect: Western embargoes prevented the necessary flow of information just as much as the East's sealing itself off. The technological level gradually began to lag behind, a circumstance which was initially camouflaged by the results of research and development from the thirties and forties. By the mid fifties, however, the poor quality and the inadequate technological level of the products made led to marketing difficulties both at home and in foreign trade. The failure in the spring of 1961 of the development of civil aircraft production – closely integrated though it was with military programmes – was a symptom of growing innovation problems. In the end the lack of manufacturers of qualitatively demanding semi-finished products prevented the success of this prestigious goal.

Generally speaking, industrial development in the fifties remained extensive, i.e., growth was achieved principally by an increasing input of production factors, mainly labour and capital. This was due chiefly to a planning method aiming at quantitative results, but also to the resultant scientific and technological shortfalls. Growth rates all declined in the course of the decade (see Figure 1 in Appendix). The originally available reconstruction potential, which for a time had made high growth rates possible, was exhausted.[39] Capacity reserves that might have been mobilised with relatively slight investments were nearing their end, which was reflected in declining investment efficiency. Their decline was moreover caused by an increase in long-term investment programmes as well as by the rising investment share of capital-intensive heavy industry. But it was also the frequent changes of medium-term production targets, inadequate preparation of projects and a lack of cost awareness that made the efficiency of investments decline during the fifties (see Figure 2 in Appendix). The result was all the more disastrous as the share of gross investments in value added had risen from 14 per cent (1950) through 17 per cent (1954) to nearly 26 per cent by 1960. An even greater increase was shown by the net investments in the 'producing' area, which had scarcely existed at the beginning of the fifties.[40] However, by comparison with the other Eastern Bloc countries, let alone the Federal Republic, the investments remained slight. The services sector only played a subordinate role in the industry-fixated Stalinist industrialisation model on which the Party relied. Just as with the infrastructure, it was being permanently neglected in investment terms. The transport system in particular, heavily afflicted as it was by dismantling, remained one of the major bottlenecks of the GDR economy.

Just as with the capacity reserves, so the manpower reserves, until then a substantial source of growth, were dwindling towards the mid fifties. The open unemployment of the postwar years had disappeared. In 1955, three-quarters of the population of working age were gainfully employed; by 1960 the figure was 80 per cent.[41] The growing labour-force participation rate was the result not only of the extensive development of certain industrial branches, but also of the system-immanent tendency of the enterprises to hoard manpower. Moreover, the development of the planning bureaucracy enlarged the number of administrative posts. Finally there was the emigration of some 940,000 persons who were lost to the economy between 1951 and 1955 (Table 3.3). A structural manpower shortage began to emerge. Since political reasons ruled out any legally binding workplace commitment, a de-facto labour market sprang up in which the enterprises competed with one another for the scarce manpower by means of arbitrary wage increases and other benefits not provided for by legislation. These improper methods were possible because the enterprises' wage policies were only inadequately controlled or limited by the central authorities. This in turn contributed to a situation where skilled workers were not always employed according to their qualifications, another reason why they emigrated to the West.

Table 3.3: Population loss of the GDR between 1949 and 1961[42]

Year	Refugees from the GDR registered in the West	Escaped gainfully employed recorded by GDR authorities	Balanced migration loss acc. to official statistics	Migration loss as a proportion of the population in per cent	Proportion of escapers of all those gainfully employed
1949	129,245				
1950	197,788				
1951	165,648	63,300	133,585	0.7	0.9
1952	182,393	73,190	159,291	0.9	1.0
1953	331,390	118,970	260,954	1.4	1.6
1954	184,198	67,720	145,644	0.8	0.9
1955	252,870	109,070	239,920	1.3	1.4
1956	279,189	130,480	284,826	1.6	1.7
1957	261,622	123,170	254,527	1.5	1.6
1958	204,092	72,300	150,130	0.9	0.9
1959	143,917	33,600	77,071	0.4	0.4
1960	199,188	84,380	157,841	0.9	1.1
1961	207,026	87,700	179,635	1.1	1.1
Sum total	2,738,566	963,880	2,043,424	11.1*	13.4*

* Proportion of those gainfully employed in 1950

In an investigation of the reasons for the *Republikflucht* ('flight from the [German Democratic] Republic') many of the respondents stated that 'they left because they would like to "work in an orderly manner"'. Other reasons given were 'economic difficulties and bottlenecks', the relatively low standard of living, inadequate organisation of work in the enterprises, and discontinuous production. To the Party leaders the main cause of the mass escape was Western 'enticement' – even Ulbricht had to concede the growing attraction of the West German economy and above all the living standard in the Federal Republic.[43] But there were additional causes such as arbitrariness and waves of repression against certain social groups, such as freelancers and farmers. As a result of university reform and threats against established physicians an increasing number of people with university degrees turned their backs on the GDR. Even though concessions to medical professionals reduced their emigration, medical care could not be provided everywhere – especially in rural areas – after 1960. Altogether some 15 per cent of the people who had lived in the GDR in 1950 had left the country by 1961. On balance, allowing for new arrivals, the country had lost about 11 per cent of its population. A problem for the economy was not only the number but also the social profile of the people escaping. About half of them were under twenty-five years of age and many of them had higher qualifications.[44]

The number of *Republikflüchtlingen* ('escapers from the [German Democratic] Republic') increased in inverse proportion to the growth of economic efficiency (see Figure 1 in Appendix). Whenever growth rates collapsed, the number of escapers rose, especially during the political crises of 1953, 1956 and 1960/61, which were always connected with the economy. As a result of the strikes in Poland and the uprising in Hungary, deliveries of coal, steel, non-ferrous metals and other raw materials failed to arrive in 1956, just as foodstuff imports from those countries declined. In consequence production came to a halt or had to be throttled back in the metallurgy, engineering, chemicals and light industry enterprises in the GDR. Supplies for the public continued to get worse. Although help from Moscow defused the situation, industry failed to fulfil the profit plans, channelled less money than planned into the state budget and demanded more subsidies: the result was a loss of some 8 per cent of state expenditure.[45] The deficit was made good by credit or cash emission (i.e., printing money) which in turn was a major cause of the large amount of money in circulation.

Another reason for money increases was that incomes were rising substantially faster than planned: in view of the consequences of the June Uprising and the open frontier no one now dared to tie wages rigorously to performance. In part, indeed, they had to be covered by printing money. Money in circulation rose by 31 per cent between 1953 and 1956, while the retail trade turnover during the same period rose by only 19 per cent. The purchasing power of the population in excess of goods on offer during that time has been estimated at 15 per cent.[46] During 1956/57, cash in circulation as well as money emission increased even more, so that an outstanding deficit was threatened in the state budget. Even the financial equipment of the economy was increasingly based on credits; those granted to the Agricultural Production Cooperatives were already being regarded as 'non-recoverable'.[47] Thereupon a money exchange without previous notification was effected on 13 October 1957, albeit with questionable success. The system-immanent causes of the money surplus could not be removed by a one-off exchange, and in 1958 the money in circulation was again rising.[48]

This renewed rise was partly due to the population's ambivalent supply situation, although the overall situation had markedly improved by the second half of the fifties and basic needs continued to be more or less satisfied. But subsequently the quality of the commodities on offer frequently failed to meet the increasing and more exacting demand of the population. With regard to many foodstuffs, such as pork, eggs and butter, consumption exceeded the pre-war level; this was due to the low prices and the improved, though still not sufficient, performance of agriculture as well as growing imports. Yields of cattle for slaughter and milk doubled between 1950 and 1960, and that of eggs nearly trebled.[49] For grain, oleagenous fruit, potatoes and fodder root crops the per-hectare yields in the second half of the fifties on average exceeded those of the first half. Consumption of clothing had increased by the mid fifties. The growing satisfaction of requirements was helped also by deliveries and credits from the Soviet Union. In May 1958 rationing of goods still rationed (meat, fat, sugar, milk) was eventually, after long pre-advertisement, abolished. This resulted in 1958/59 in a short-lived 'greedy eating wave', so that the now growing demand for meat and butter was not met by the weak agrarian economy. Despite the continuing vast gaps in supplies, demand became more differentiated: it ranged 'from dark rye bread to white milk bread, from lard and margarine to butter, and from pork to beef'.[50] Supplies of technical consumer goods also improved, but continued to fall short of demand both quantitatively and qualitatively. In 1960 nine out of ten households had a radio. Other high-grade consumer goods, such as washing machines, refrigerators, television sets, private cars or motorcycles could only be acquired by the few because of their high prices and the small quantities on offer. In consequence, saving deposits per head of the population and the savings quota (the proportion of savings of the net money income of the population) increased from 1.4 per cent to 7.2 per cent between 1950 and 1960.[51] This trend towards an increasing surplus purchasing power – especially if seen against the background of the goods on offer in the West – strengthened an 'impression of continuing shortages … even though the turnover of retail trade actually increased'.[52]

Why then was supply not able to meet demand? For one thing, production of consumer goods – with few exceptions – had no political priority. This meant a lack of investments, which left the sector unable to extend its capacities, and hence the number of pieces produced, to meet demand. Since enterprises had for a long time been rewarded for their pure production and not for the sale of their products, they had little interest in meeting the requirements of their customers. As a result there existed, ever since the early fifties, 'surplus-to-plan' stocks of commodities that, because of their quality and their inappropriate pricing, were not marketable. At the end of 1959 these stocks, in textiles and garments, amounted to more than 11 per cent of goods in that category sold during the same year.[53] Attempts to sell these goods in seasonal sales or at reduced prices in cheap-goods shops were only partially successful. Such sales also clashed with economic or ideological reservations on the part of the Party leaders, because of the loss of revenue implied and their demand for the greatest possible exclusion of such market-driven price movements. Therefore those efforts were the exception. Moreover it emerged, especially in clothing, that customers were increasingly attaching importance to quality, that they were more fashion-conscious and that they compared the GDR products to those of Western Germany.

Up to the beginning of the fifties the GDR population mostly compared their living standards to those before the war; but by 1954 they were comparing them to those of West Germany. In view of the similar nominal incomes in East and West the price level provided an immediate yardstick of comparison; indeed in Berlin one needed no more than an *S-Bahn* journey to make the comparison, a journey which was often also used for shopping in the West. In actual fact, after the end of food rationing in 1958, 20 per cent more on average had to be paid for retail goods or services in East than in Western Germany, according to GDR-internal data, or 20 to 30 per cent more according to data of the German Institute for Economic Research in [West] Berlin.[54] The Party leadership's pricing decisions gave rise to a curious price structure. The standard of living, which they believed they had to guarantee, was based on the needs of a working-class family during the Weimar era, i.e., a living standard under which most of them were themselves socialised. The battle against hunger, homelessness and rent sharks resulted in low foodstuff prices and low rents. Cheap transport connections ensured in their eyes the necessary manpower mobility and hence full employment. After the end of rationing, a bread roll in the GDR cost 5 Pfennig and half a pound of butter cost 2.50 Marks – and this is how matters remained until 1989.

Nevertheless these commodities, at the end of the fifties, were often no cheaper than in the West, where half a pound of butter cost 1.73 DM on average. Only after the subsequent price increases in the West did the GDR prices in this sector hang back and, by comparison, stay lower. The prices of industrial goods, such as petrol, motorcars, television sets, detergents, refrigerators and textiles, on the other hand, were frequently priced above their cost. East German consumers had to expend considerably more for qualitatively worse goods than those in the West, especially for coffee and tobacco and for clothing and footwear: one kilogram of bean coffee cost 19.40 DM in the West and 80.00 Marks in the East; the price of men's street shoes was, on average, 32 DM and 73.41 Marks respectively.[55] These relatively high prices in the GDR had dues imposed on them which were designed to finance the subsidies for basic needs. Foodstuff prices were kept low through this support and favoured an extremely high consumption. This was promoted also by low rents and service tariffs. Industrial goods, on the other hand, remained expensive. Admittedly this price structure militated against the changes in consumption structure typical for rising incomes, from foodstuffs to industrial and luxury goods, which was counterproductive both in economic and social terms. Although real wages in the fifties, according to more recent estimates, rose by more than 70 per cent, this had only a minimal effect on the lag of the GDR standard of living to that of the Federal Republic. There it was nearly twice as high.[56]

The 'Main Economic Task': 'Catch Up and Overtake'

The lagging of the GDR living standard behind that in the Federal Republic was a perpetual challenge to the East German Party leaders. It was logical therefore that the Party repeatedly made it its task to reach and surpass the living standard of the Federal Republic. In order to give a positive signal and to contain the *Republikflucht*, Ulbricht, at the Fifth Party Congress in mid-1958, announced the 'main economic task': by 1961 the per-capita consumption of the 'working population' was to reach and surpass 'the per-capita consumption of the total population of Western Germany in respect of all important foodstuffs and consumer goods'.[57] The basis of this optimism was belief in the potential of socialism, which finally seemed to unfold when the first artificial satellite, the Soviet Sputnik, went into orbit around the earth in October 1957. The Party leaders saw this as evidence of the superiority of their own system and the deputy head of government, Selbmann, declared: 'He who is first in sending an earth satellite into space will also be able to solve the economic main task – to outstrip capitalism in the production of meat and fat.'[58] In fact, economic results in 1957 had improved over the preceding years: the annual plan for gross industrial production was overfulfilled, whereas in 1956 the target had not been reached. The Party leaders saw themselves on the road to success. Moreover, the Federal Republic's temporary slowing down of the economy in 1958 was interpreted as the beginning of a profound economic crisis that would make catching up easier. That is why the Party leaders probably really believed they could manage this demanding task – even though they were counting on substantial help from the Soviet Union. This in turn explains the contradiction: the Federal Republic's level of consumption was to be reached and surpassed by the 'main economic task' as early as 1961, while its labour productivity would only be reached and surpassed in 1965 with the Seven-Year Plan (1959–65), which was decreed in 1959.[59]

The 'main task' was politically consistent, as only higher economic performance could make the system attractive enough, both at home and abroad, to secure the Socialist Unity Party's power in the long term. Economically, however, the Party leaders found themselves in a dilemma of their own making: on the one hand they realised that the investments were too small compared to the Federal Republic and even to the other Eastern Bloc countries. Yet the promised rise in consumption required higher investments in order to expand consumer goods production in the medium term. This, however, would restrict private consumption in the short term even further. In order to raise private consumption quickly and for a prolonged period funds had to be brought in from outside. And as, for political reasons, the Party leaders did not wish to be indebted to the Western countries, this meant that they depended on help from the Soviet Union.

The State Planning Commission's planning for this task proceeded on the basis of West German consumption levels in 1956/57; it was this level which was to be reached in the GDR by 1961, which seemed entirely possible according to East German statistics.[60] By this trick the planning commission evidently tried to escape the dilemma that, on the one hand, it was aware of the GDR's limited economic possibilities, while, on the other, it had to fulfil the unrealistic task set by the Party leadership. However, the Soviet Union was unwilling or unable to provide the necessary support. It was only prepared to exempt the GDR from the outstanding troop stationing costs, enabling it to use the sum thus saved for importing additional Soviet raw material supplies. The Soviet Union did not make any foreign currency available, which meant that the GDR lacked the means necessary for imports from the West, such as tropical fruit, cacao and coffee, which were urgently needed for a rapid rising of the per-capita consumption.

It was nevertheless possible to step up gross industrial production in 1958 and 1959 by a remarkable 11 and 13 per cent respectively, which in fact was more than the plan targets.[61] These results were due mainly to considerably higher investments and markedly increased, chiefly more continuous, imports. Thanks to these imports of raw materials and semi-finished goods the supplies to enterprises improved towards the end of the decade, helped additionally by an increase in domestic production. In some places, moreover, stocks and reserves were mobilised. In consequence the Party leaders at the end of 1959 and the beginning of 1960 viewed the future optimistically – apart from a few unsolved import questions. Inspired by a similar project in the Soviet Union they developed their ideas of the future until 1980 in a 'general perspective'. Its starting point was that the 'main economic task' would be fulfilled by 1965, i.e., that productivity and living standards would reach or surpass those in the Federal Republic. This should be followed by further rapid growth. Politically – Ulbricht left no doubts on this point – the realisation of the 'general perspective' should create the economic basis for the restoration of Germany's unity.[62] The dramatic developments in the autumn of 1960 meant that such exuberant planning died a natural death. Nevertheless it demonstrated, well into 1960, the Party leaders' fundamental optimism about the system's economic possibilities, even though those responsible were aware of its functional weaknesses.

One of these problems was the control of investments: in their pursuit of 'soft' plans the enterprises also 'hungered' for investments. The investments granted to them, in the fifties, hardly depended at all on their own economic results, i.e. they did not have to be 'paid for' by them. As a result the State Planning Commission found itself confronted with a multitude of demands for investments from which, in view of the economically limited possibilities, it had to choose. At the same time it lacked economic criteria for such a choice, as prices did not reflect scarcities and gave no indication of where resources were to be directed. This was an aspect of the above-mentioned information problem. The planners therefore based their decisions on investments on their own experience, on crude international comparisons and, above all, on political priorities. With this economically inadequate decision basis it was not surprising that investment projects were also chosen that were not economically efficient. An internal analysis in 1961 concluded that investment activity was determined, 'to a degree intolerable for the overall development, by subjectivism and spontaneity'.[63]

This fundamental difficulty was now increased by the central authority with its extravagant growth targets of the 'main economic task', while simultaneously the forced collectivisation of agriculture made even greater demands. Admittedly the State Planning Commission had generally increased the investments that, in line with the 'main task', were to primarily benefit the consumer goods industry. However, engineering – which had not been granted additional investments as this would have been at the expense of the consumer goods industry – was expected to produce the necessary machines and plants, thus increasing its own production. It was also impossible to increase overall investments any further, as this would have diminished the means available for private consumption and thus militated against the solution of the 'main task'. The result was therefore considerable imbalance between the demand for investment goods and the capacities of the engineering industry, evidence that the 'main task' was overstretching the economic potential.

Once a project was (financially) included in the plan, it was immediately tackled by the enterprises regardless of whether the necessary machinery was available; they were afraid that otherwise the money might again be withdrawn from them. This meant that many projects were begun without ever being brought to conclusion or yielding any output. In industry in 1960/61, this money tied up in unfinished projects roughly amounted to the sum that was annually invested, and they were tending to rise.[64] This was another reason why investment effectiveness drastically declined from 1960 onwards. In 1961 it amounted to only 25 per cent of the 1959 level (Figure 2 in Appendix).[65] This demonstrated, as did the stagnating number of those employed, that the extensive growth sources of the GDR's economy were exhausted.

The Seven-Year Plan took into consideration the declining number of persons of working age, a decline due to demographic development and emigration. Reality, however, vastly surpassed the estimates. The State Planning Commission calculated that 60,000 employed persons had 'fled the Republic' in 1960 and 40,000 in 1961. In reality the figures were about 84,000 and 88,000.[66] If only because of the resulting further increase of the system-induced manpower shortage, incomes were bound to rise by trend and average wages were unable to be guided by productivity increases to the expected extent. The main responsibility for this was the persistently inadequate quality of work norms and of the wages system. The fundamental problem of the Party leaders – their inability to motivate employees to higher performances due to fear of the political consequences – was made worse by the fact that the employees could also avoid any further performance demand by escape to the West. Hence the norm issue practically remained a taboo prior to the building of the Wall. As incomes rose more rapidly than planned, investments, which were anyway scarce in relation to the growth targets, were further reduced. Moreover, the increasingly growing money income of the population was confronted with a continuing inadequate supply of goods, the shortage being not least due to the collectivisation of agriculture.

Collectivisation and the Road into Crisis 1960/61

Under the 'main task' it was necessary to raise the plan targets for agriculture too, as the striven increase in consumption could not be met by imports alone. Once more, this time by the end of 1962, the Federal Republic was to be outstripped and full self-sufficiency achieved. In the eyes of the Party this meant a need to further speed up the collectivisation. In order to make the peasants more willing to join, Ulbricht had already, in May 1958, demanded a strengthening of the cooperatives so 'that the prosperous medium-size peasants should not, if at all possible, have to accept a lowering of their living standards as a result of joining an Agricultural Production Cooperative'.[67] But this was too much for the state budget, as in 1958 there were still more than 12 per cent of Type III Agricultural Production Cooperatives that were completely dependent on subsidies if their members were to be paid the minimum income. A further 71 per cent of these cooperatives required at least some finances from the state budget. Barely 17 per cent managed without subsidies. The difference between the incomes of cooperative members and those of efficient individual peasants was considerable. The latter made on average 5,000 Marks in 1957, whereas the cooperatives received 4,300 Marks; any cooperative member without his own small farm made only 3,700 Marks, with differentials on an individual basis often being considerably greater.[68] Under these circumstances Ulbricht's demand could only mean that the more efficient peasants should be quickly integrated into the cooperatives; when this did not work, pressure was exerted on them.

The state also supported the Agricultural Production Cooperatives in other respects. The new agrarian prices of 1957/58 favoured the cooperatives; their dues were reduced or scrapped and they received credits on special terms. The machine-and-tractor stations had to initially concentrate their work more on the Agricultural Production Cooperatives and eventually to hand over their machines to them altogether. This was accompanied by propaganda 'that combined general political and economic arguments in an increasingly militant manner, so that joining an Agricultural Production Cooperative was presented as a contribution to the strengthening of the peace-loving GDR, while refusal might, in doubtful cases, be interpreted as sabotage against peace and peace-making'.[69] Although in consequence the number of private agricultural enterprises halved between mid-1958 and mid-1959, they still farmed more than half of the farmland and, thanks to their higher productivity, were the main producers of agricultural products.[70]

In the first half of January 1960 the Party leaders decided in favour of complete collectivisation within the shortest possible time. Harvest yields of the principal crops in 1959 had lagged behind those of the preceding years and dramatic problems were expected in livestock production in 1960. The Party leadership saw the causes of this in the private agrarian sector and thus hoped that, with the collectivisation of the efficient individual farmers it would make a 'leap forward'.[71] Besides, the persons responsible wanted to switch the subsidies, manpower and imported goods, that until then had been provided for the cooperatives, to other areas of the generally exceedingly tight economy. The collectivisation campaign turned into a competition of Party functionaries on all levels. In the interest of their own careers everyone wanted to be the first to report plan fulfilment. Propaganda brigades swarmed through the villages, flooding the inhabitants with slogans and music. The peasants were threatened, some were even arrested. Persuasion and false promises played their part. The massive pressure was effective: by April all districts were able to report complete collectivisation. Some nine thousand new Agricultural Production Cooperatives were created, initially operating as the not fully collectivised Types I and II. The cooperatives' share of the farmland was almost doubled within six months, from the end of 1959 to mid-1960 (Table 3.2). About fifteen thousand farmers fled to the West in the course of this campaign, glorified by the Party as 'socialist springtime'. After complete collectivisation a mere 13,500 individual farmsteads operated on 8 per cent of the farmland, most of them as 'small producers'. Both their number and the acreage worked by them further declined over the next few years.[72] As a result, socialist relations of production, as understood by the Party, had been established in the countryside.

As cultivation in 1960 had still been performed by Agricultural Production Cooperatives established for some time as well as by individual farmers, a good harvest was brought home in this year. Livestock production, which was anyway practised individually in Type I cooperatives, also developed successfully. But even these good harvest results lagged behind the over-optimistic plan targets. Not until 1961 did the consequences of collectivisation appear: a substantial quantity of manpower had meanwhile left the villages so that labour for the harvest had to be brought in from other sectors of the economy. Plan targets for the Agricultural Production Cooperatives remained high and dissatisfaction was increasing among their members. Added to this were the unkept promises about improved working conditions. Moreover, there was a lack of finance to equip agriculture, in line with the requirements of a large-acreage economy, with machines and buildings. In consequence the degree of mechanisation of the grain harvest in 1960 dropped from 68 per cent in the previous year to 39 per cent, that for potatoes from 37 per cent to 21 per cent and for beets from 68 per cent to 46 per cent.[73] The situation did not improve in 1961 in spite of additional investments. After the end of 1960 attempts to leave the Agricultural Production Cooperatives became more frequent and the number of persons fleeing to the West increased, especially after the Berlin crisis became more acute. Some Agricultural Production Cooperatives were threatened with dissolution.

Unfavourable weather conditions, along with considerable organisational problems of the new form of enterprise, resulted in a disastrous harvest failure in 1961: per-hectare yields of grain declined by 21 per cent compared to the previous year, potatoes by 36 per cent, sugar beet by 26 per cent and fodder root crops by 25 per cent. This affected the feeding-stuff provision for livestock, so that production of slaughtering cattle declined by 13 per cent, of milk by 7 per cent and of eggs by 14 per cent in 1962.[74] This impaired supplies for the population; the situation was only stabilised on a low level by imports from the Soviet Union. All in all, the burdens resulting from collectivisation were estimated by the State Planning Commission at one billion Marks.[75] The cooperatives did not consolidate until some time after the erection of the Berlin Wall, about 1963/64. Although collectivisation represented a fundamental change in agrarian structures, from a longer-term perspective East German agriculture was following the overall trends of the twentieth century, with development across Europe tending towards a consolidation of acreages and the elimination of small farms, towards new cropping systems, the increased input of energy, chemicals and modern agricultural technology, as well as towards product diversification. This development had initially been delayed in the GDR by the land reform.[76]

It was not only the poor results of agriculture that prevented the realisation of the 'main economic task'. Imports were another weak point. In the inter-governmental negotiations in June 1959 the Soviet Union agreed only about one-half of the deliveries desired by the GDR for the period from 1960 to 1962. Bruno Leuschner, meanwhile promoted deputy head of government, estimated that on this basis the Seven-Year Plan target of increasing industrial production by just under 90 per cent by 1965 could be attained only 'by making a supreme effort'. Even then this meant that the quantity of products intended for private consumption would have to be reduced and, for the sake of balancing the plan, incomes would have to be allowed to rise more slowly than originally planned. Thus, of course, the West German per-capita consumption of motorcars, washing machines and refrigerators, tropical fruit, coffee and cocoa products, woollen articles and high-quality footwear was not attainable even by 1962.[77] As a result, the ambitious targets for 1961 were, after the beginning of 1960, no longer being talked about in government.

From the beginning of 1960 there had also been difficulties in the provision of the necessary input requirements for industry, in time and in the correct assortment. The GDR's Eastern Bloc partners either delivered nothing at all or products different from what had been contractually agreed. The GDR plans also included deliveries that had not been contractually agreed, mainly from the Soviet Union. In addition, promised deliveries of rolled steel from the Federal Republic arrived with delays because of lacking counter-deliveries from the GDR. Intra-German trade during the fifties, on the basis of the 1951 Berlin agreement, had been developing relatively reliably and with an upward trend. It soon became obvious however that intra-German trade was, on the side of the Federal Republic, governed more by political interests whereas in the GDR it was governed by economic motivations, a situation that was confirmed in the Berlin crisis. Because of the lack of rolled steel some enterprises came to a standstill. Compensating imports from other Western countries merely increased the GDR's debts. At the end of 1960 the GDR was in debt to the non-socialist economic area to the tune of 472 million Valutamark; by the end of 1961 this had risen to 670 million Valutamark. The Valutamark was an internal calculation unit which, for political reasons, was equated with the (West-)German Mark (DM). Subsequently this economically uncovered exchange rate was internally corrected by additional charges. Indebtedness to the West in 1960 corresponded to 21 per cent and in 1961 to 28 per cent of exports in the same direction.[78] In view of the exacerbated political situation and the fear of the Party, as also of the Soviet leadership, of being liable to extortion by the West, this indebtedness was considered alarming and was interpreted as a crisis symptom.

The supply of goods for the population also deteriorated noticeably in 1960/61. More and more often there was no meat, sausage, butter, cheese, footwear, various textiles or detergents. For certain products, such as butter, customer lists were sometimes compiled to ensure fairer distribution – a form of rationing by the backdoor. Many enterprises gave in to the wage demands of their employees to keep them from fleeing to the West. The imbalance between the population's rising money income and the lagging supply of goods became worse: more and more often customers faced empty shelves. Supplies even seemed to have got worse than at the end of the fifties. There could be no thought of a higher standard of living than in Western Germany.

When, because of the compulsory permits for West Germans visiting East Berlin, the Federal government, in September 1960, decided to terminate the agreement on intra-German trade at the end of the year, the situation was further exacerbated. The State Planning Commission concluded that if 'intra-German trade were to come to a halt entirely', then, without 'exceptional help' from the Soviet Union, 'the first quarter of 1961 … would perhaps witness production standstills in some 400 to 500 major enterprises of the engineering, textiles and building industries, as well as in the chemical industry'. Entire industrial branches might have to switch to short-time work.[79] Admittedly the authors of the report somewhat dramatised the situation because they wanted to convince the Moscow leadership of the urgency of their wishes; however, the situation was genuinely serious and the Party leaders repeatedly begged for help. Only after a conversation with Khrushchev at the end of November 1960 was Ulbricht finally successful. Henceforth the Soviet Union would support the GDR more strongly.

Yet even with these promises the targets of the Seven-Year Plan and of the 'main economic task' remained unattainable in 1961. At the beginning of 1961 Ulbricht informed the Moscow leadership:

> [T]he gap between us and Western Germany has not diminished in 1960. Internal difficulties, due to unpunctual and inadequate material-technical supplies have actually increased. Strong dissatisfaction among workers and the intelligentsia has been caused by the circumstance that in many enterprises the continuity of the production process is no longer assured. The cause of this is that numerous tasks of the national economic plan are not safeguarded in the material respect.[80]

The Seven-Year Plan targets were therefore lowered at the beginning of May 1961 or, in planners' language, 'rendered more precise'. Even Ulbricht realised that these corrections would not help. At a consultation in an 'intimate circle' he admitted that the *Republikflucht* would increase and the situation become more difficult.[81]

Ulbricht had every reason to give the migration to the West an economic interpretation. After all, in the economically favourable year 1959 'only' 143,917 persons had made their way to the West. Admittedly this was to some extent due to the 1958 citizenship law, which limited travel abroad. In contrast, collectivisation and supply shortages swelled the number to 199,188 in 1960 and to 207,026 in 1961 (Table 3.3). In view of the obvious economic problems, hardly anyone believed that the 'main economic task' could be fulfilled. Party propaganda greatly contributed to the rise of the *Republikflucht*: it demanded – following the 1958 Soviet ultimatum on Berlin – that West Berlin be converted into a 'free city' and that a peace treaty be concluded with Germany or its successor states. As a result people anticipated measures such as the blocking of escape routes to West Berlin. Many people therefore got ready to leave sooner rather than later. This in turn intensified the labour shortage and led to trouble in production; which caused new gaps in the supply of goods and thus new reasons for escape – a vicious circle. Until August 1961 planning in the GDR was always based on the assumption that people would remain in the GDR for the foreseeable future. For this reason alone every plan was unsafe. At the end of 1962 the State Planning Commission estimated that employed persons 'enticed away' in 1960/61 had caused a production loss of 3.9 billion Marks.[82]

In its search for a way out the Party leadership found itself in a dilemma since any short-term domestic-economy solutions, such as restriction of the surplus purchasing power among the population, through more consistently formulated working norms or through price increases, were bound to lead to more emigration. A rapid improvement of the supply of goods through imports – which in the circumstances could only come from Western countries – was something the Party leaders wished to avoid for political reasons because of increasing indebtedness. In the medium and long term the Party leaders – in a system-immanent view – might embark on a reform of the control mechanism, in order to improve economic results drastically. But they were aware of the risks involved, since reforms as a rule did not yield quick results but instead might create new readjustment problems and therefore intensify the flight to the West. Leuschner explained to his Soviet partners that 'given the conditions of the GDR with its open frontiers no experiments of any kind were possible'.[83] In the interests of maintaining their power the Party leaders were looking for an extra-economic way of throttling the escaping movement in order to make planning once more calculable. Not until then could they try to solve the economic problems. The shutting off of West Berlin was only the first step for Ulbricht towards the solution of the Berlin problem and the safeguarding of full sovereignty for the GDR. In August 1961 Ulbricht succeeded, mainly with economic arguments, in convincing the Party chiefs of the Soviet Union and the other Eastern Bloc countries of the need forcibly to stop the flight to the West and to erect the Wall. Internally this action was justified primarily economically, even though it was represented to the outside as intended to solve political problems, above all the Berlin crisis that had largely been fanned by the Party leadership itself.

Notes

1. Bericht über die Ergebnisse des 1. Fünfjahrplanes der DDR, 26.3.1956, BA Berlin DE1/31468.
2. Die Entwicklung der Volkswirtschaft der DDR in der Periode des 2. Fünfjahrplanes 1956 bis 1960, 16.2.1956, BA Berlin DE1/31014. Cf. *Direktive für den 2. Fünfjahrplan zur Entwicklung der Volkswirtschaft der DDR 1956 bis 1960. Beschluß der 3. Parteikonferenz der SED*, Berlin (East) 1956, pp. 7–12, 58.
3. Ulbricht to Bulganin and Khrushchev, 17.12.1955, SAPMO-BA DY30/3700; ZK der SED, Regierung der DDR to Bulganin, Khrushchev, 19.5.1956; ZK der

KPdSU to ZK der SED, 2.6.1956; Khrushchev to Schirdewan, Grotewohl, 9.6.1956; all SAPMO-BA DY30/3701.

4. Büro des Politbüro to Mitglieder und Kandidaten, 3.7.56, SAPMO-BA DY30/3701.

5. Kokurkin. 'Über das Tempo der wirtschaftlichen Entwicklung ...', 19.3.1957, SAPMO-BA DY30/3703.

6. Wolfgang Mühlfriedel and Klaus Wießner, *Die Geschichte der Industrie der DDR bis 1965*, Berlin (East) 1989, pp. 232 ff.; Cf. 'Gesetz über den 2. Fünfjahrplan zur Entwicklung der Volkswirtschaft ... vom 9.1.1958', *Gesetzblatt der DDR*, 1958, I, pp. 41 ff.

7. Cf. *Industriezweige in der DDR*, Berlin (East) 1989, pp. 14 f. Calculated according to: Lothar Baar, Uwe Müller and Frank Zschaler, 'Strukturveränderungen und Wachstumsschwankungen. Investitionen und Budget in der DDR 1949 bis 1989', *Jahrbuch für Wirtschaftsgeschichte* 1995, 2, pp. 47–74, here 68 f.

8. Informationen über die Erfüllung des Volkswirtschaftsplanes 1958, SAPMO-BA NY4090/331; Mühlfriedel, Wießner, *Geschichte der Industrie*, pp. 238–45.

9. *Statistisches Jahrbuch 1955*, p. 126.

10. SPK: Zu einigen wichtigen Problemen der Erfüllung des Volkswirtschaftsplanes 1956, 15.2.1957, SAPMO-BA NY4062/99.

11. 'Verordnung über die Bildung halbstaatlicher Betriebe vom 26.3.1959', *Gesetzblatt der DDR*. 1959, I, pp. 253 ff. Cf. Heinz Hoffmann, *Die Betriebe mit staatlicher Beteiligung im planwirtschaftlichen System der DDR 1956–1972*, Stuttgart 1999, pp. 54 ff.

12. *Statistisches Jahrbuch 1962*, pp. 241, 516. See also Frank Ebbinghaus, *Ausnutzung und Verdrängung. Steuerungsprobleme der SED-Mittelstandspolitik 1955–1972*, Berlin 2003, pp. 96 ff., 110 ff.

13. Calculated according to *Statistisches Jahrbuch 1962*, p. 405.

14. *Statistisches Jahrbuch 1956*, pp. 350 f. On the following see also Staritz, *Geschichte der DDR*, p. 133.

15. SZS: Zur wirtschaftlichen Lage der einzelbäuerlichen Betriebe in der DDR. Auswertung der Ergebnisse der repräsentativen Betriebsuntersuchungen in einzelbäuerlichen Betrieben 1955, Juni 1957, BA Berlin DE2/21678/0042804.

16. Dieter Schulz, *'Kapitalistische Länder überflügeln'. Die DDR-Bauern in der SED-Politik des ökonomischen Wettbewerbs mit der Bundesrepublik von 1956 bis 1961*, Berlin 1994, p. 7, fn. 10.

17. Schulz, *'Kapitalistische Länder überflügeln'*, pp. 7, 10 f., 27; Staritz, *Geschichte der DDR*, p. 133.

18. Schulz, *'Kapitalistische Länder überflügeln'*, p. 20.

19. Calculated according to Einheitliche Datenbasis. Cf. Schulz, *'Kapitalistische Länder überflügeln'*, p. 25.

20. André Steiner, 'Sowjetische Berater in den zentralen wirtschaftsleitenden Instanzen der DDR in der zweiten Hälfte der fünfziger Jahre', *Jahrbuch für Historische Kommunismusforschung* 1993, I, pp. 100–17.

21. Roesler, *Planwirtschaft*, p. 46.

22. SPK: Methodische Grundsätze für die Ausarbeitung des Volkswirtschaftsplanes in der Periode des 1. Fünfjahrplanes, 10.3.1956, BA Berlin DE1/417.
23. Vorlage über den Stand und Abschluß der Festpreisbildung ..., 23.9.1961, SAPMO-BA DY30 IV 2/608/51. Summing up: André Steiner, *Die DDR-Wirtschaftsreform der sechziger Jahre. Konflikt zwischen Effizienz und Machtkalkül*, Berlin 1999, pp. 187 ff.
24. Präsidium des Bundesvorstandes des FDGB, Komitee für Arbeit und Löhne. Vorlage für das Politbüro des ZK der SED: Konzeption für die Erhöhung der Wirksamkeit des Arbeitslohnes ..., 15.3.1960, SAPMO-BA DY30 IV 2/608/40.
25. Beschluß der SPK über die Durchführung von Untersuchungen zur Verbesserung der Methoden der Planung in der DDR, 1.6.1956, BA Berlin DE1/12901.
26. Roesler, *Planwirtschaft*, pp. 153 f.; Über die Verantwortung der Werkleiter der volkseigenen Industriebetriebe auf dem Gebiet der Planung, 10.1.1958, BA Berlin DE1/12903.
27. Behrens to Wittkowski, 5.10.1956: Verwirklichung des Beschlusses der SPK über die Durchführung von Untersuchungen zur Verbesserung ..., BA Berlin DE1/12901.
28. Fritz Behrens, 'Zum Problem der Ausnutzung ökonomischer Gesetze in der Übergangsperiode', *Wirtschaftswissenschaft* 5, 1957, (3rd special issue) pp. 105–40; Arne Benary, 'Zu Grundproblemen der politischen Ökonomie des Sozialismus in der Übergangsperiode', ibid., pp. 60-94.
29. 'Grundfragen der Politik der SED. Referat auf der 30. Tagung des ZK der SED vom 30.1.1957', in Walter Ulbricht, *Zur Geschichte der deutschen Arbeiterbewegung. Aus Reden und Aufsätzen*, Vol. IV, Berlin (East) 1962, pp. 305 ff.
30. 'Ein alternatives Agrarprogramm für die DDR 1956', in Judt, *DDR-Geschichte*, pp. 117 f.
31. BA Berlin DE1/11683, quoted according to Schulz, '*Kapitalistische Länder überflügeln*', pp. 13 ff.; Bauerkämper, *Ländliche Gesellschaft*, pp. 176–81.
32. Büro Hager: Information über die ideologischen Unklarheiten in der Partei und bei der Bevölkerung (1956), SAPMO-BA NY4062/107.
33. Quoted according to Stefan Wolle, 'Das MfS und die Arbeiterproteste im Herbst 1956 in der DDR', *Aus Politik und Zeitgeschichte* B5/91, 25.1.1991, pp. 42–51, here 48. Cf. Büro Hager: Information über die ideologischen Unklarheiten in der Partei und bei der Bevölkerung, (1956), SAPMO-BA NY4062/107.
34. Dietrich Staritz, 'Die "Arbeiterkomitees" der Jahre 1956/58. Fallstudie zur Partizipations-Problematik in der DDR', in *Der X. Parteitag der SED. 35 Jahre SED-Politik – Versuch einer Bilanz*, Cologne 1981, pp. 63–74; Thomas Reichel, 'Konfliktprävention. Die Episode der "Arbeiterkomitees" 1956/58', in Peter Hübner and Klaus Tenfelde (eds), *Arbeiter in der SBZ-DDR*, Essen 1999, pp. 439–52.
35. Stolper, *Structure*, pp. 417 f., 440. The data on private consumption have been corrected with the aid of a more recent estimate. On the basis, see Jennifer Schevardo, *Vom Wert des Notwendigen. Preispolitik und Lebensstandard in der DDR der fünfziger Jahre*, Stuttgart 2006, pp. 281–86. On the estimate, see André

Steiner, 'Preispolitik und ihre Folgen unter den Bedingungen von Diktatur und Demokratie in Deutschland im Vergleich', in idem (ed.), *Preispolitik und Lebensstandard. Nationalsozialismus, DDR und Bundesrepublik im Vergleich*, Cologne 2006, pp.171–203, here 196 f.

36. Calculated according to Rainer Karlsch, 'Wirtschaftliche Belastungen durch bewaffnete Organe', in Deutscher Bundestag (ed.), *Materialien der Enquete-Kommission, 'Überwindung der Folgen der SED-Diktatur im Prozeß der deutschen Einheit'*, Baden-Baden 1999, Vol. III/2, pp. 1500–84, here 1569 ff.; Diedrich and Wenzke, *Die getarnte Armee*, p. 679; Steiner et al., *Statistische Übersichten*, Table 0.2.01.
37. Calculated according to *Einheitliche Datenbasis*.
38. Calculated according to Manfred Melzer, *Anlagevermögen, Produktion und Beschäftigung der Industrie im Gebiet der DDR von 1936 bis 1978 sowie Schätzung des künftigen Angebotspotentials*, Berlin (West) 1980, p. 183 (Table 20).
39. Buchheim, 'Wirtschaftsordnung', p. 194.
40. Calculated according to *Einheitliche Datenbasis*.
41. Cf. Steiner et al., *Statistische Übersichten*, Tables 3.1.1.1., 3.2.1. and 3.2.2.
42. The balanced migration loss refers to all emigration and immigration across the GDR frontiers. Compiled and calculated according to H.-H. Hertle, K.H. Jarausch and C. Kleßmann (eds), *Mauerbau und Mauerfall. Ursachen – Verlauf – Auswirkungen*, Berlin 2002, p. 312; [presumably SPK:] Einschätzung der Verluste, die der Volkswirtschaft durch Abwerbung von Arbeitskräften entstanden sind, SAPMO-BA NY4182/972; Steiner et al., *Statistische Übersichten*, Tables 0.1.1.1., 0.1.1.4., and 3.1.2.1.
43. Bericht der Kommission zu Fragen der Republik-Flucht, 25.5.1956; Auszug aus dem Protokoll Nr. 29/56 des Politbüro vom 19.6.1956; Stellvertreter des Vorsitzenden to Leuschner: Republik-Flucht, 25.9.1956; all BA Berlin DE1/6109; Entwurf [of a letter from Ulbricht to Khrushchev], 3.5.1958, SAPMO-BA DY30/3704.
44. Percentages calculated according to the following table. On the whole section cf., among others, Patrick Major, 'Innenpolitische Aspekte der zweiten Berlinkrise (1958–1961)', in Hans-Hermann Hertle, Konrad H. Jarausch and Christoph Kleßmann (eds), *Mauerbau und Mauerfall. Ursachen – Verlauf – Auswirkungen*, Berlin 2002, pp. 97–110.
45. Rumpf to Ulbricht, 22.3.1957: N. Zapkin, Einige Überlegungen über die Lage und weitere Verbesserung der Staatsfinanzen der Deutschen Demokratischen Republik vom 15.3.57, SAPMO-BA DY30/3702; Steiner et al., *Statistische Übersichten*, Table 0.2.0.1.
46. Partly calculated according to Ermer, *Von der Reichsmark*, pp. 185, 190; *Statistisches Jahrbuch 1990*, p. 55.
47. Zapkin, Einige Überlegungen über die Lage und weitere Verbesserung der Staatsfinanzen … 15.3.1957, SAPMO-BA DY30/3702; Kuckhoff to Grotewohl, 6.6.1957, SAPMO-BA NY4090/336.
48. Ermer, *Von der Reichsmark*, pp. 188–200.
49. *Statistisches Jahrbuch 1990*, pp. 39, 42 f.

50. Jörg Roesler, 'Privater Konsum in Ostdeutschland 1950–1960', in Axel Schildt and Arnold Sywottek (eds), *Modernisierung im Wiederaufbau. Die westdeutsche Gesellschaft der 50er Jahre*, Bonn 1993, pp. 290–303.

51. Steiner et al., *Statistische Übersichten*, Table 0.4.2.0.a.

52. Hübner, *Konsens*, p. 156.

53. Calculated according to Judd Stitziel, *Fashioning Socialism: Clothing, Politics and Consumer Culture in East Germany*, Oxford 2005, p. 110; *Statistisches Jahrbuch 1990*, p. 55.

54. [SPK:] Preisvergleich DDR – Westzone, 1.12.1958, BA Berlin DE1/9891. The DIW figures compiled in Bruno Gleitze, *Sowjetzonenwirtschaft in der Krise*, Cologne 1962, p. 29. The two sets of data are based on different methods, which explains their discrepancy.

55. All prices according to *Statistisches Jahrbuch 1962*, pp. 212 ff.; Statistisches Bundesamt (ed.), *Statistisches Jahrbuch für die BRD 1970*, Wiesbaden 1970, p. 432.

56. Estimated on the basis of data in Schevardo, *Vom Wert des Notwendigen*, pp. 281–86. On the estimate see Steiner, 'Preispolitik', pp. 196 f.

57. Cf. *Protokoll der Verhandlungen des V. Parteitages der Sozialistischen Einheitspartei Deutschlands, 10. bis 16. Juli 1958*. Berlin (East) 1959, pp. 68, 70.

58. Stenografische Niederschrift des wissenschaftlichen Gesprächs der Redaktion der 'Einheit' über die Bedeutung des Starts des sowjetischen Erdsatelliten ... , 10.10.1957, SAPMO-BA NY4113/11.

59. *Gesetzblatt der DDR* 1959, I, p. 705. This discrepancy already has been pointed out by Staritz, *Geschichte der DDR*, pp. 175 f.

60. Bemerkungen zum überarbeiteten Projekt ..., 1.7.1958, SAPMO-BA NY4062/99; *Statistisches Jahrbuch 1962*, p. 573.

61. Information über die Erfüllung des Volkswirtschaftsplanes 1958, SAPMO-BA NY4090/331; SPK: Übersicht über die Erfüllung wichtiger Kennziffern des Siebenjahrplanes der DDR 1959–1965, 24.3.1966, SAPMO-BA, DY30 IV A2/2021/260.

62. HA Perspektivplanung: Protokollarische Notizen zur ersten Sitzung der zentralen Parteikommission ..., 3.6.1960, BA Berlin DE1/49121.

63. Bericht der Arbeitsgruppe Investitionen über die notwendigen Maßnahmen ..., September 1961, SAPMO-BA NY4097/21.

64. Calculated according to SZS: *Statistisches Jahrbuch über Grundfondsökonomie, Investitionen ... 1970*, BA Berlin DE2/22949/0910976.

65. Calculated according to *Einheitliche Datenbasis*.

66. Cf. Probleme für Arbeitskräfteplan 1962 und Arbeit der Abteilung Arbeitskräfte, 12.7.1961, SAPMO-BA DY30 IV 2/608/46; Arbeitsmaterial. Einschätzung der sich aus der Entwicklung bis 1961 ergebenden Auswirkungen ..., 18.1.1961, BA Berlin DE1/49122; *Statistisches Jahrbuch 1976*, p. 31.

67. Quoted according to Staritz, *Geschichte der DDR*, p. 182.

68. Schulz, '*Kapitalistische Länder überflügeln*', pp. 26 f., 30.

69. Staritz, *Geschichte der DDR*, p. 183.

70. Calculated according to *Statistisches Jahrbuch 1962*, p. 403.

71. BA Berlin DE1/1254, quoted according to Schulz, *'Kapitalistische Länder über-flügeln'*, p. 34. Cf. Schöne, *Frühling*, pp. 202–6.

72. Calculations according to Statistisches Bundesamt, *Ausgewählte Zahlen zur Agrarwirtschaft 1949 bis 1989 (Sonderreihe mit Beiträgen für das Gebiet der ehemaligen DDR, No. 8)*, Wiesbaden 1993, pp. 11 ff. On what preceded cf. Staritz, *Geschichte der DDR*, pp. 189 f.; Schulz, *'Kapitalistische Länder überflügeln'*, pp. 34 f.; Bauerkämper, *Ländliche Gesellschaft*, p. 186.

73. Schulz, *'Kapitalistische Länder überflügeln'*, p. 35.

74. Calculated according to *Statistisches Jahrbuch 1990*, pp. 39, 42.

75. Schulz, *'Kapitalistische Länder überflügeln'*, pp. 36 f.

76. Cf. Kluge, *'Verhinderte Rebellion'*, p. 319; Bauerkämper, *Ländliche Gesellschaft*, passim.

77. Leuschner: Ergebnis der Beratungen über die ökonomischen Fragen, 17.6.1959, SAPMO-BA DY30/3705.

78. Leuschner: Politbürovorlage (Entwurf). Probleme des Außenhandels der DDR. Information …, April 1962, SAPMO-BA DY30 IV A2/2021/67; *Statistisches Jahrbuch 1962*, p. 547.

79. Zusammenfassende Übersicht über die Hauptprobleme der wirtschaftlichen Entwicklung, October 1960, SAPMO-BA NY4113/19.

80. Ulbricht to Khrushchev (russ.), 19.1.1961, SAPMO-BA DY30/3708, published in André Steiner, 'Politische Vorstellungen und ökonomische Probleme im Vorfeld der Errichtung der Berliner Mauer. Briefe Walter Ulbrichts an Nikita Chruschtschow', in Hartmut Mehringer (ed.), *Von der SBZ zur DDR: Studien zum Herrschaftssystem in der Sowjetischen Besatzungszone und in der Deutschen Demokratischen Republik*, Munich 1995, pp. 233–68, here 248 f.

81. Vermerk über die Besprechung bei Gen. Walter Ulbricht am 3.5.1961, SAPMO-BA DY30/3709.

82. Einschätzung der Verluste, die der Volkswirtschaft durch Abwerbung von Arbeitskräften entstanden sind, SAPMO-BA NY4182/972.

83. Niederschrift über die Wirtschaftsverhandlungen … am 22.4.1961, 23.4.1961, SAPMO-BA DY30/3708.

Chapter 4

The 'Golden' Sixties? Economic Reform between Dawn and Crisis 1961–1971

The construction of the Wall marked the GDR's 'undeclared foundation day'.[1] The Party, moreover, gained a new freedom of action vis-à-vis the population because it no longer had to ask, at every measure it took, how many people would flee to the West as a result. With the completion of total collectivisation in the countryside 'socialist relations of production', as the Party understood them, had been victorious. Henceforth socialism should be able to develop on its own basis – with a closed frontier but still in competition with the Federal Republic. After a short-term stabilisation the economy would now therefore require fundamental modernisation. Some ideas that had long been in the air were now taken up, favoured by appropriate discussions in the Soviet Union, and a reform of the economic system was embarked upon. This was intended to create new incentives for performance and innovation.

If the Party surrendered a few responsibilities in the economic area, the question arose whether it would also do so in other areas. After an initial euphoria, however, the scope for more freedom within the political system remained relatively slight. In all considerations of reform the Party leadership was careful not to jeopardise its own power. Accordingly certain ideological and Marxist premises were never abandoned, causing the whole concept of reform to be contradictory and inconsistent. Since initial success was limited, the concept was further developed as innovations and structural changes were forcibly introduced using centralised instruments in the final third of the sixties.

For this technological and growth offensive, through which Ulbricht intended to win the competition with the Federal Republic, Western technology was imported on a growing scale. This meant, of course, getting into debt to the West. In this connection Ulbricht endeavoured to intensify economic relations with the Federal Republic and other Western countries. He had come to realise that the comparatively slight division of labour in the Eastern Bloc did not provide a basis for the implementation of his ambitious modernisation plans; it was only collaboration with the

West that would make it possible to realise his plan of 'overtaking' them. This may sound paradoxical, but was probably based on a dialectical argument. For the Soviet leaders, however, who viewed the development of reform and Ulbricht's insistence on technological progress with growing detachment, he seemed to be pushing his policy on Germany too far. When another economic crisis arose in 1969/70, this was presented by the opponents of the reform as the result of his transformations. The precarious economic situation was attributed to Ulbricht and 'his' reform and, with Moscow's approval, he was deposed by his opponents among the Party leadership. The new Party boss, Erich Honecker, turned back to the Soviet course. However, the starting point for East German economic development ever since the closure of the frontiers in 1961 remained: the problem of making socialism attractive to the people in the GDR.

Störfreimachung and *Produktionsaufgebot* 1961/62

The construction of the Wall did not solve the crisis of 1960/61. Indeed, it was at first exacerbated, as construction costs, including the costs of re-routing of railway tracks, telephone, water and power lines necessary for the success of the project, amounted to about two billion Marks.[2] Nevertheless, the Wall provided protection to those in power who, for the time being, opted for short-term solutions to the crisis. One of their projects was *Störfreimachung* (the policy of 'elimination of disturbances') in the GDR economy, practised since the turn of 1960/61; this was intended to reduce dependence on imports from the Federal Republic and other NATO states. Something like that had been demanded from the enterprises before, but now it was formulated programmatically. The Federal government's threat that it might give notice of termination to the intra-German trade agreement had demonstrated to those responsible in East Berlin and in Moscow the degree to which the West might politicise the deliveries required from it. Dependence was especially marked with regard to specialised products for the metal-processing, chemical and metallurgical industries. Even sporadic delivery failures could impede production in entire manufacturing areas. Most vulnerable to interference, i.e. most dependant on imports from the Federal Republic and other NATO states, were 'mainly the key positions of technological progress and the production of high-quality consumer goods'.[3] Some 30 per cent of the funds available for research and development in 1962 were to be spent on finding substitutes for and replacing these imports. The investment costs for ensuring independence from Western Germany were estimated in the *Volkswirtschaftsrat* (National Economic Council, which from 1961was the operational control institution for industry) at about 550 million Marks for 1962 alone; revenue losses in industry of some 300 million Marks as a result of production conversions, substitute materials and parts were furthermore taken into account.[4] Moreover, the technical norms were changed from the German DIN system to the Soviet GOST, which supported the tendency by which innovation activity was shuttered off from the world markets. All in all, 'elimination of disturbances' probably burdened the GDR to the tune of one billion Marks.

Nonetheless the policy seemed to be a necessity so long as the Party felt itself to be under pressure from the West. In mid-1963 Apel, who had meanwhile risen to the post of chairman of the State Planning Commission, observed that 'in the present international political situation' no 'rupture of trade relations need be expected'. The action was therefore terminated, as it was thought that 'disturbances in the economy to a degree that might still have been possible in 1960 in the event of a trade rupture' could now be ruled out.[5] If there were to be a rupture nevertheless, then it seemed certain that goods until then imported from the Federal Republic could also be obtained from other countries. By taking this step, the GDR renounced at least some development potential resulting from international trade. It became more firmly tied into the Eastern Bloc, principally into economic relations with the Soviet Union, and in consequence imports from the Federal Republic and other Western industrialised countries stagnated between 1961 and 1963 at a relatively low level.[6] It was not until 1964, when the Eastern Bloc countries and especially the Soviet Union had shown themselves unable to deliver raw materials and foodstuffs to a sufficient degree, that Western imports once more increased suddenly. From the mid sixties the GDR also allowed itself to become more dependent on Western technologies for modernising its industries. Nonetheless the East German leadership never entirely gave up the idea that it had to be independent of the system adversary and of worldwide economic imponderables.

At the end of May 1961 Ulbricht agreed with Khrushchev a 'close merging of the economies of the GDR and the USSR'.[7] Admittedly the two sides had different ideas about the solution of the 'main question of how and by when it will be possible to put the GDR on its own feet'. While the GDR was attempting to modernise its economic structure with temporarily greater support from Moscow, the Soviet Union insisted that the East German economy should develop without contributions from anyone else.[8] The Soviets were evidently not aware that they had been indirectly subsidising the GDR since the end of the fifties and the beginning of the sixties. They delivered their raw materials at prices below those in the world market, but received East German industrial products at prices above those that the GDR might have achieved elsewhere in the world market. The East German persons responsible, on the other hand, believed at the beginning of the sixties that they were being disadvantaged by the USSR with respect to prices.[9] Eventually, though, when

Moscow declined more direct support, they became dependent on exhausting their own economic potentials more thoroughly.

At least the construction of the Wall stabilised the manpower situation and provided the State Planning Commission with 'new preconditions for exact planning'.[10] This did not, however, solve the problem of the declining employment potential: plans by the GDR leadership to employ a major number of workers from other Eastern Bloc countries were not realisable immediately after the construction of the Wall. Only from the second half of the sixties did employment of foreign 'contract workers' – the East German equivalent of West Germany's 'guest workers' – increase in the GDR. At the same time the employment of women was to be increased by various qualification offers and by the development of childcare facilities. Whereas there was only one nursery place for every hundred children of appropriate age (under 3) in 1950, there were places for 15 per cent in 1961 and for 30 per cent at the beginning of the seventies. Kindergarten places for children of relevant age (usually from 3 to 6) were available for 20 per cent, 49 per cent and 69 per cent respectively. As a result, 66 per cent of women of working age were gainfully employed in 1960, as against 52 per cent in 1950. By 1970 the number had risen to 82 per cent.[11]

At the beginning of the sixties the Party tried to reduce the continuing imbalance between purchasing power and goods on offer by adopting two measures. First, the shortcomings in wages policy was to be abolished by means of a *Produktionsaufgebot* ('production mobilisation'). Officially a brigade from Berlin demanded: 'More to be produced in the same time and for the same money!' This campaign raised norms and throttled wage development. The workers often reacted to this with performance restraint and also with strikes. Although in 1962, the year of the 'production mobilisation', industrial productivity was actually increased by more than the average wage, the old conditions returned the following year.

Secondly, however, the Party leaders decided to increase prices for a whole range of foodstuffs and industrial consumption goods, as well as for some services. After the construction of the Wall they evidently believed that they need no longer be politically considerate towards the population. Economically this was entirely justified since, owing to the harvest failure in 1961 and the persistent difficulties of collectivised agriculture the supply of foodstuffs had shrunk. The same was true of industrial consumption products, which were increasingly exported in order to finance imports. However, such price reactions ran counter to the system and to the Party leaders' promise to keep consumer prices stable or to lower them. Instead, in line with the system, customer cards were introduced, thus practically reintroducing the rationing of meat and butter. Although additional foodstuffs were imported from Western countries in the autumn of 1962, these were not sufficient to relax the situation. In 1962 the same amount of butter was available to the public as in 1958, which meant that consumption declined markedly compared to the preceding years. The extent to which supplies declined was shown by the fact that the retail turnover in 1962 dropped in absolute terms for the only time in GDR history – in spite of rising prices.[12] Losses in real incomes (3 per cent lower in 1962 compared to 1961), a shortage of goods, and rationing, all fanned dissatisfaction, giving rise to the popular formula: 'No food improvement – just like the Movement' (*Wie die Verpflegung so die Bewegung*). The workers reminded the functionaries of the trauma of the Uprising: 'Communists, give us more to eat soon – or have you forgotten the 17 June?'[13] (*Kommunisten, gebt uns mehr zu fressen, oder habt ihr den 17. Juni schon vergessen?*) All this was happening against the background of a rising standard of living in the Federal Republic, which, as the Party realised and emphasised to Khrushchev, was still 'very strongly' influencing the public mood after the building of the Wall.[14]

The situation was critical. The State Planning Commission's chairman believed that the moment had come when 'the stability of socialism would have to prove itself'.[15] Wage freezes and price increases did not contribute to securing the system and hence the power of the Party. What was needed was a dynamic development of the economy as a whole, free from crises, with appropriate welfare effects. But this seemed to require a modification of the economic control system. Ideas for such a reform had been about since the fifties, but it probably needed the crisis of 1961 for the Party leaders to realise the threat to their system and to start experimenting with them. The fact that Moscow in 1962 declined to grant credits for the modernisation of the GDR economy was the final incentive for embarking on a reform. It is against this background of economic crisis and Moscow's refusal that we have to understand Ulbricht finally speaking in favour of reforming the economic system which he himself had significantly moulded. This attitude was facilitated by the fact that a discussion of reforms was going on in the Soviet Union at the same time. Even though Moscow eventually did without any reforms, the Soviet leadership – particularly considering its refusal to support the GDR to a greater extent – had to agree to the reforms in Eastern Germany, especially as these did not actually touch upon the foundations of the system.

A 'New Economic System'?

Ulbricht placed himself at the head of the reformers, since his overriding intention was to safeguard the power of the Party. Alongside him Apel and Mittag represented the reform ideas in the Party leadership. The real 'fathers' of the reforms, however, were, above all, Walter Halbritter, a graduate economist and long-time economic official in the state and Party apparatus, and Herbert Wolf, professor of political economy, who, 'banished' to an enterprise in 1960, rose with the economic reform to become the deputy director of the Research Institute of the State Planning Commission and later deputy State Planning Commission chief. The other members of the Party leadership followed Ulbricht, even though they were sceptical about the idea of granting more rights to economic units. The most important representatives of this group among the leading economic officials were Alfred Neumann, chief of the *Volkswirtschaftsrat* (National Economic Council), and Willy Rumpf, who, as Minister of Finance, held a key position in the reform, as financial categories were to acquire greater importance in the control of the economy. Subsequently, when the reform failed to produce the quick results hoped for, the sceptics turned into opponents of change. However, they were all anxious to safeguard the existence of socialism and to increase its attractiveness. Their differences were merely about the path to be followed.

After tedious discussions and first experiments, a concept for the changes of the control mechanism was adopted in the summer of 1963. The reform – initially described as the 'New Economic System of Planning and Management of the Economy' – aimed above all at modernising the economy and increasing productivity. The basic ideas were: the Associations of People-Owned Enterprises, the VVBs, until then more like administrative authorities for the various branches of industry, were to become economic units with greater autonomy, just as were the enterprises placed under them. The plans were to focus on important key data and medium-term targets. In this way it was hoped to make better use of the economic interests of the VVBs and enterprises, as well as of the 'creative activities of the working people', in order to stimulate and carry out innovations and structural changes. The reformers proceeded from the view that the interests of the central authorities and of the economic units were not a priori identical, but had to be harmonised by economic mechanisms. Economic incentives should be so fashioned that they served those interests of the VVBs and enterprises that harmonised with those of the central authorities. The main target of the reform, the aim which the Party leadership could not ignore in the given domestic and intra-German situation, continued to be the presentation of their system as a competitive alternative to the Western system of capitalism.

Under the new system, the central performance benchmark of the enterprises would not any longer be gross production, but profit. This required conditions in which 'development and full application of new technology, an increase of labour productivity, a lowering of costs, achievement of high quality, demand-oriented production and marketing activities … would lead to high profit, while the violation of these social necessities would lead to profit setback(loss)'.[16] Profit represented the core of a 'system of economic levers', which meant that a basis would have to be created for an undistorted cost accounting. Industrial prices were to be newly fixed according to uniform principles. Branches and enterprises would have to do more to earn their own finances, especially investments (*Eigenerwirtschaftung der Mittel*); this would limit waste and defuse the problem of soft budget constraint. Moreover, a kind of 'interest on capital' was being considered for enterprises in the form of a production fund charge: they would have to hand over a percentage charge for the buildings and plants made available to them by the state, and this would compel them to achieve at least a minimum profit. Additionally to these economic incentives at the level of VVBs and enterprises it was intended to link wages and bonuses more firmly to the individual performance of the workers.

The framework within which the independent economic operation of the VVBs and enterprises was to take place was set by the medium-term perspective plan as the decisive central control instrument. Within this plan the State Planning Commission only had to lay down the essential targets and principal economic proportions. Goods considered indispensable for the control of the overall economy continued to be dealt out by the central authority; all other distribution plans were to be worked out for their products by the VVBs and enterprises themselves. Planning therefore continued to be the main instrument of economic control. The 'economic levers' – prices, costs, wages and bonuses, interests, profits, credits, charges and monetary funds – were to complement it and make it more efficient. But even these monetary categories were predominantly planned: only when it was known whether the enterprises or VVBs had, for instance, fulfilled their profit plan or failed to do so, was the amount of their bonuses and other benefits calculated. Incentives therefore continued to be tied to plan fulfilment – and this once again favoured 'soft' plans. Efforts were made to counteract this by complicated regulations, but these proved ultimately rather ineffective.

Basically the reformers were trying to simulate market mechanisms without, however, introducing the foundations of a market economy. Neither the dominance of 'people's ownership' nor the power of the Party were questioned. Dogmatised Marxism as the theoretical basis was not abandoned. This contradiction marked the introduction and realisation of the economic reform and inevitably resulted in inconsistencies. This was especially far-reaching in the creation of the new prices, which were, as before, set on the basis of costs and only in exceptional cases reflected supply and demand; in no way were market prices intended. For that reason they were unable, alongside their measuring and incentive functions, to provide any guidance on where the use of the scarce resources would be most efficient. In the distribution of economic resources in the economy – a matter that the central authority continued to claim for itself – there was still the problem of what information should be used in decision making. One advantage of the concept of the new mechanism was that the VVBs and the enterprises were compelled to make better use of their resources. But incentives for innovations continued to be slight, as enterprises were unable to realise extra profits from them – a clear contradiction of the goal of the reform, which was the modernisation of the economy.

The inconsistency of the reform resulted from the fact that the Party leaders' decisive motivation for this (not quite risk-free) reshaping was the realisation that this was the only way of safeguarding their own power. And it was this intention of preserving their power that limited the degree of autonomy permitted in the economy. The economy – and only the economy – was granted its own rationality criteria. The political and ideological foundations of this society, the centralistic one-party rule and Marxism–Leninism, were not to be revised. Thus the social policy pursued by the Party with the economic reform was marked by a conflict of aims: on the one hand the autonomy of economic units was to be recognised and strengthened and its interests thereby instrumentalised. On the other hand there was no economic or political framework for the articulation of new interests or for evening out any contradictions that arose.

The reformers tried a multiplicity of economic experiments to find practicable solutions for individual control problems. This trend, along with a new openness in public discussion of economic, but also of wider, questions changed the social atmosphere in 1963/64. What favoured this change was that, after the construction of the Wall, many people saw more promising conditions for the building of socialism and new opportunities. Others felt 'walled in' and thus compelled to come to terms with the system. Much as these attitudes differed, they were both favourable to the acceptance of the reform. The cautious new societal awakening was permitted by the Party leadership and stage-managed by it; it was wooing for acceptance and wished to utilise the competences of more people for its aims. Among the public the sense of impending change appealed chiefly to the intelligentsia. The workers viewed the economic reform with rather mixed feelings: in view of the now more consistently applied performance demands they feared their wages might be cut. But they also realised the opportunities offered by the reform, when Ulbricht demanded 'good work for good money', at the same time 'making the shop windows the magnet of material interest'.[17] Employees should be assured that for the money they made they would really be able to buy the required consumer goods of appropriate quality. As it seemed that matters were improving with the economic reform, not only those who supported the system but also those sections of the population that were indifferent were ready to cooperate with it. However, the Party wanted, as before, to control the limits of 'opening up', which meant that in cases of doubt they remained tight. Thus, towards the end of 1965, the 11th Central Committee plenary session – the so called *Kahlschlag* (clear-cutting) session – publicly reprimanded artists who, in the eyes of the Party leadership, had ventured too far. This effectively put an end to the trends of political liberalisation, timid as they were, and the reform period continued to be characterised by the contradiction between permitted economic 'obstinacy' and the Party's power interests.

Implementation of the Reform

A start was made on introducing the reform at the beginning of 1964. The core of the reshaping and the basic condition for its functioning, which was the reform of industrial prices, was to be implemented in three stages. In order to keep the price system free from internal contradictions, the first stage covered the new prices for raw materials and basic materials, as well as energy and transport tariffs; the second covered semi-finished goods and the third covered the prices of finished articles. Introduction of the last step was the most difficult, if only because of the multiplicity of products affected and their interconnections; the price reform was therefore not concluded until 1967. As a result, prices of goods in the first phase rose by 70 per cent on average, in the second by 40 per cent and in the third by 4 to 5 per cent. The first two steps regulated one-third, and the final phase regulated the remaining two-thirds of industrial production. On average, industrial prices rose by 12 per cent from 1963 to 1967.[18] The newly created industrial price system represented progress compared with the pre-reform status, even though the goal of doing away with subsidies was not reached. Moreover, political considerations demanded that consumer prices should not rise because of the reform of industrial prices: in consequence the former had to be even further subsidised. The crucial disadvantage of the new prices was that they largely continued to be static. Although there were considerations of and first attempts at a price dynamisation, they were only rudimentarily realised in the final phase of the reform.

Just as with the industrial price reform, so the overall reform was to be carried out in stages. The Party leaders wanted to make sure that this process was controlled and directed from above. Because of the step-by-step implementation of the industrial price reform many of the new incentives at first produced no effect and could only be made effective by modification. Hard budget constraints, i.e., the absolute dependence of earnings on economic results, had not been put in force for the enterprises. It was therefore consistent that, regardless of their accumulated money, they continued to receive material goods only if provided for in the plan. The plan continued to be at the centre of the enterprises' activities, although there was a lot of argument about economic levers and profit. Because of the confusing coexistence of the old and the new, the behaviour of the enterprises hardly changed: thus they continued to wish for 'soft' plans.

Nevertheless, the economic units now had more scope than before. Thus the VVBs planned the distribution of their products themselves, even though they lacked the information that would enable them to decide which of the orders received were important in terms of the overall economy and which were not. At the same time the enterprises, in the absence of hard budget constraints, demanded as many resources of every kind as possible. The consequence was that the resources allocation provided in the 1965 plan was inefficient and thus nearly all VVBs struggled throughout the year to meet their needs for materials and semi-finished goods. Several of them, admittedly, exploited their 'monopoly position' by enforcing price surcharges for certain products, if only with the justification that they were making their deliveries within the legal ordering times. Manufacturers of goods in short supply also tried to gain advantages by demanding manpower or bonuses from their customers. Getting hold of their inputs continued to require major efforts from the finishing producers. At the Warnow shipyard in Rostock, for instance, it was pointed out that the Blohm & Voss shipyard in Hamburg employed six buyers and three office employees for securing its required inputs, while their own enterprise employed ninety-five persons for that purpose.[19]

At the same time a number of VVBs were able to make use of gaps in the calculation regulations for the industrial price reform, thus achieving exorbitant increases in their profits, which in turn earned them big bonuses, without actually improving their performances. This marked the failure of one of the pivotal points of the reform: creating conditions in which enterprise interests and the macroeconomic interest would coincide. The responsible departmental chief in the Central Committee made no secret of his scepticism about these reform instruments: 'These so-called levers appeal to immoral instincts, closely related to profit seeking and must therefore be stopped.'[20] Although the bonuses paid to the employees went up, they still remained relatively small: the average annual bonus between 1964 and 1967 amounted to 58 per cent to 70 per cent of the average monthly wage.[21] In addition to the bonuses the reform concept demanded that wages themselves should be productivity-oriented to provide individual incentives. In this connection, enterprise management now set new work norms, and with their new authority strengthened by the reform, acted as 'masters of the house'. This not only contradicted the legitimising emphasis on 'people's ownership', but also worked against consensus within the enterprises. As often in such circumstances, the workers thereupon held back with their performances or, in extreme cases, downed tools. The fact that so much public emphasis was put on 'economic levers' encouraged the workers to demand higher wages – as a rule successfully. Not until 1966/67 did it prove possible to throttle down wage developments, up to a point. In relation to productivity, the average wages in industry once more moved faster than in the years immediately after the construction of the Wall, when wage sacrifice had been demanded.[22] All in all, wages and bonuses could scarcely become more effective individual incentives for the workers, as the above-mentioned underlying dilemma was insoluble for the Party leadership.

The reaction of the central authorities to the problems resulting from the implementation of the reform was once again interference from 'above' into the planning and the economic process. Mittag therefore complained in the summer of 1965: 'We see once more a stronger tendency to manage plan fulfilment with purely administrative means, with decrees and directives, etc., with a huge amount of paper for daily dispatcher reports … Meanwhile the correct control with economic means is pushed into the background.'[23] The 'reform sceptics' now seemed to get the upper hand. They blamed the problems mainly on the 'one-sided seeking for profit' of the VVBs and the enterprises, which was not really true but sounded a little like 'capitalist profit seeking' and therefore was something clearly politically objectionable. But although the position of the reformers was becoming more difficult, the experiments and implementation of various reformist steps were driven further forward.

Moreover, the Soviet Union, because of its own economic problems, asserted its interests more strongly in 1964/65: deliveries of agricultural products were cut and rising raw materials deliveries made increasingly dependent on return favours. The shortfall in rolled steel and grain now had to be imported from the West. Moscow moreover reduced the number of chemical plants to be delivered, even though these production capacities had been developed at Soviet request and then, lacking purchasers, worked at a loss. This, along with the low competitiveness of GDR products in the international markets, worsened the foreign-trade conditions for the reform and complicated the work on a new medium-term plan which had been being drawn up since mid-1962.

This plan was now even more urgent since, according to the reform concept, it was to have an even stronger position in economic control than before. As the Seven-Year Plan had not been fulfilled after 1960 and had been de facto abandoned in 1961, the economy was now directed by annual plans. The new *Perspektivplan* (medium-term plan) was to promote a speedier development of science and technology and to allow for a transition to intensive growth, to be achieved mainly through increased productivity. The guidelines of the *'Perspektivplan* until 1970', enacted in 1963, therefore envisaged a high annual growth of labour productivity of 7.4 per cent. For that purpose investments were to be increased and to be focused on the sectors that promised well for the future. Priority was to be given to the chemical industry, more especially to petrochemicals, as well as to second-stage metallurgical processing in order to develop rolled-steel production in line with the demands of the engineering industry, and also to electronics and the modern branches of engineering, such as machinetool production.[24]

However, it proved extremely difficult to fund these targets materially and to balance the plan with domestic and foreign interrelations, especially in view of the Soviet delivery cuts. The State Planning Commission was unable to submit a balanced medium-term plan with realistic targets running until 1970. In spite of the new incentive system the enterprises and VVBs continued to strive for high inputs and the lowest possible output targets, whereas the central authority wanted to attain the highest possible targets with strict observance of the priorities in resource allocation. The employees in the enterprises debated about the sense of working on a long-term plan when it was 'unclear which variant applied at the moment and when the next variant will be worked out'.[25] More important to them were working and income conditions. With an eye to the Federal Republic, there were more and more demands for a five-day week, an increase in basic leave, wages and pensions. It seemed that in the enterprises the initially cautious agreement with the New Economic System was increasingly giving way to a scepticism that had been subliminally present from the start.

In the autumn of 1965 the difficulties multiplied: for one thing the results of the new economic negotiations with the Soviet Union were rather unfavourable from the GDR's point of view. For another the State Planning Commission had no clear concept of how the discrepancies in investments and foreign-trade demands and possibilities were to be balanced out. On the basis of the guideline for the *Perspektivplan*, publicly issued in 1963, investments had begun to be made, foreign-trade agreements had been concluded and thus, according to Apel, 'the flexibility of the *Perspektivplan* greatly restricted'.[26] However, the growth rates aimed at in 1963 were no longer attainable within the parameters of the actual plan. At the beginning of December 1965 the basic outlines of the submitted *Perspektivplan* draft and the State Planning Commission's work were severely criticised at a Politbüro meeting. Apel now found himself under heavy pressure in his most special domain, planning. However, the proceedings at this Politbüro meeting were probably only the trigger for Apel committing suicide the following day. He had been losing influence and power even before these controversies: he had no longer been closely involved in the preparation of further reform steps, and had not participated in the negotiations for the long-term trade agreement with the Soviet Union. Ever since the beginning of the year the State Planning Commission and Apel had been repeatedly in the cross-fire about the *Perspektivplan* and the annual plan, with Mittag playing a particular role. The two had, moreover, fallen out on various informal occasions. His loss of power and his realisation that Mittag was stepping into the limelight at his expense are likely to have hit Apel severely; these were probably the decisive reasons for his suicide. Added to this was the possibility that – as was being speculated in the West – he really saw the terms of the long-term agreement with the Soviet Union as unfavourable and jeopardising the realisability of the *Perspektivplan*. He was possibly also concerned that his past as a rocket specialist working with Wernher von Braun in the external camp Dora of Buchenwald concentration camp might become public, though it was already known to the Party.

Apel's death significantly weakened the position of the reformers within the Party leadership. Gerhard Schürer, until then Apel's second-in-command, moved up into the position of State Planning Commission chief. He was one of those men who obeyed the valid decisions on the reform, but tended to be rather hesitant. He saw himself more as a 'calculator' than as a creator and, in consequence, never became a fully-fledged member of the Politbüro.

The multiplicity of difficulties encountered in 1965 was blamed by the reform sceptics mainly on the reform itself, and more and more of them became opponents of change. That was why Ulbricht, at the 11th Central Committee meeting in mid-December 1965, regarded it as necessary to defend the economic reform against those who saw it mainly as a risk. Simultaneously the Party leadership sharply rejected an 'opening up' in society by massively attacking several artists and works of art. The public was to realise from this that the Party had no intention of lessening its control over society. At the same time a 'second phase of the New Economic System' was proclaimed at the end of 1965. Its most striking aspect was that the *Volkswirtschaftsrat* (National Economic Council), created in 1961 and responsible for the operational direction of industry, was dissolved and replaced by eight industrial ministries set up on the Soviet model. These industrial ministries were to devote themselves to fundamental issues within their sectors and to resolve and coordinate overarching questions that could not be settled among the VVBs. The State Planning Commission interlinked the plans of the industrial ministries with one another, enforcing the state's overall interests and allowing long-term anticipation by economic forecasts. Basic knowledge on future scientific and technological trends and the requirements resulting from them were to be passed on to the State Planning Commission by the Ministry for Science and Technology. The Council of Ministers and de facto its presidium had to take decisions on the main tasks and basic proportions of economic development. In all this the prerogatives of the Party leadership were invariably preserved. This institutional structure of the central control level, created at the beginning of 1966, continued to exist, with slight modifications, to the end of the GDR.

Compared to expectations, the tangible results of the reform in the mid sixties were modest. In industry, where the reshaping was most advanced, the growth rates of production and productivity were, admittedly, steadily rising, but this was largely due to the fact that investments had been increased and a number of major projects had become effective in 1964. A role may also have been played by the initially widespread 'new dawn' atmosphere, but this gave way to a sobering-up as early as 1965. Enterprises continued to hoard resources and did not trouble enough about innovations. These inadequate results, however, were not only due to the reform itself; the lagging division of labour within the Eastern alliance also had a negative effect. Ulbricht had long been demanding that this should be intensified. In his, entirely correct, opinion the efficiency of the GDR's economy could only be ensured by a higher number of pieces of manufactured products with assured sales within Comecon in prospect. This, however, presumed division of labour and specialisation, as the GDR was not in the position to develop all technology areas. In order not to be dependent on imports from the West, Ulbricht urged a fundamentally open-minded Khrushchev and the other Soviet Party leaders towards more intensive cooperation. When Brezhnev succeeded Khrushchev, Ulbricht tried indefatigably to convince him, too, that scientific-technological cooperation was urgently needed within Comecon. The Soviet Union, however, was careful, if only for security reasons, not to grant any deeper insights into essential areas of its own research and development, even to its allies, with the result that scientific-technological cooperation remained slight. Added to this were the disparate development levels of the Eastern Bloc countries and the institutional shape of Comecon. Although Comecon enjoyed greater importance in the sixties, specialisations were agreed with only a limited, if not indeed questionable, benefit.

Because of the insufficient results of the reform, the reform protagonists found themselves under increasing pressure. Among the competent experts discussions began in 1965/66, which eventually led in 1967/68 to a change in the reform concept. These new reflections aimed at getting a limited number of fundamental innovations and structural changes controlled centrally. The bulk of the enterprises were to be given more scope for autonomy by the reformers. It was a question of balancing central and subordinate competences. This was in line with the system and, within this framework, rational. Any ideas beyond this, such as greater price flexibility or the rudimentary creation of a capital market, were seen by the reformers as transcending the boundaries of the system. Ulbricht was not prepared to permit any developments that would excessively limit the control competence of the central authorities. Since the end of 1965, moreover, the climate for more far-reaching considerations had deteriorated. In view of the risks and the uncertain prospect of success the opponents of reform in the East German Party leadership would not be convinced by such ideas and the Moscow leadership under Brezhnev reacted to experiments more suspiciously than before. The reduced scope became manifest domestically in the GDR's new 1968 constitution and in foreign politics in the crushing of the Prague Spring in the same year.

'Overtake without Catching Up'

'Overtake without catching up' was the formula with which Ulbricht, in the last third of the sixties, hoped to inspire scientists and engineers, as well as economic officials and workers, to 'maximum performances' in the competition of the systems, while convincing the public of the potentials for the future. This slogan was born when the State Planning Commission chief's deputy for forecasts in November 1968, in the presence of Ulbricht, quoted this sentence from an *Izvestiya* article by the Soviet cybernetics expert Glushkov.[27] Glushkov had written his article with an eye to existing and future generations of dataprocessing equipment, evidently thinking of a technology not yet being worked on in the West: in other words, a leap that might place the Soviet Union at the head of technological progress. Ulbricht liked this idea so much that he expanded it and, with an eye to the competition between the two systems, more and more often spoke of 'overtaking without catching up'. The motto became a key idea of further reform steps – steps that were taken from 1967/68 onwards under the banner of the 'Economic system of socialism', which in concept and contents supplanted the New Economic System. The future outlooks in science and technology, in production and consumption, were now to be determined by means of long-term forecasts. On this basis the 'structure-determining principal products and product groups' were to be laid down and summed up for the economy in an appropriate concept. There would be concentration on those branches and disciplines that formed the basis for technological change, the so-called scientific–technological revolution: the modern sectors of chemicals (petrochemicals, artificial fibres, etc.) and of engineering (machinetool production, construction of chemical plants, etc.), electronics, manufacturing of dataprocessing equipment and automation of the economy. These processes were to be driven forward, controlled and prioritised by central structure-determining planning; in other words, these sectors were to be given priority in the granting of resources and finance. Those parts of the economy that did not come under the central heading of 'structure-determining planning' were to be set a framework by overall economic planning; within this framework enterprises would themselves organise their economic activity through market-like relations, but in accordance with central targets. The framework targets contained economic norms to be kept constant in the medium term; these would regulate payments into the state budget and hence the minimum profitability to be achieved, as well as the bonuses available to enterprises.

From the final third of the sixties onwards foreign trade was moreover intended not only to perform a supply function, but to become effective as a productive factor. The foreign trade monopoly would be modified, but by no means abolished. For the producers, the foreign-currency income from their exported products was to be shown in their profit and thereby become an incentive for foreign trade. In this connection the traditional price adjustment between domestic economy and foreign trade was – at least partially – abandoned. The enterprises, thanks to the improved competitiveness of their products and the resulting higher export profits, were able to increase their profit and in the same way their bonuses. Nevertheless, the resulting exogenous impulses for a structural change remained limited. They were politically distorted by state-set (and corrected) rates of exchange. Export losses continued to be subsidised by the state, provided the exports were regarded as necessary for trade-policy reasons. The results produced by these new rules reflected their half-heartedness: although manufacturing enterprises were now paying more attention to export matters and contributed to the increasing profitability of exports, the immediate 'pressure' of the foreign markets was too slight for them to be concerned about the international competitiveness of their products.

Generally speaking, the 'Economic System of Socialism' created a two-stage mechanism: innovation processes and the resulting structural changes were to be forced by direct intervention from 'above'. 'Down below', the economic units – unless they were subject to 'structure-determining planning' – were given greater scope to raise their efficiency. Admittedly it was clear from the start that the sphere covered by 'structure-determining planning' would expand and would tend to require ever more resources. The chance of receiving priority treatment by inclusion in this circle and the overall shortages led to attempts by many VVBs and enterprises to be included in the circle of the 'structure-determining'. The selection of projects to be supported was to be objectivized through consultation with experts, and founded on forecasts, but the results of the many forecasts were simply not included in the plans because they often hardly hung together and were poorly founded economically. In many instances the national economic conditions were inadequately allowed for; instead the forecasts were guided by international trends. Frequently it was not the feasible but the desired that stood in the foreground. There were no economic criteria for deriving the key aspects of structural policy from the forecasts; they were replaced by political considerations.

Eventually the interests of the economic units resulted in a state of affairs when the total volume of projects regarded as important exceeded economic possibilities. And as the central authority was aiming at major growth and rapid structural change, it tended, in its planning, to increase investments at the expense of consumption. Between 1962 and 1967 the share of gross investments in terms of economic value added was raised from 25 to 28 per cent; subsequently, up to 1970, in a new growth offensive, it was increased to not quite 33 per cent.[28] Even this was not enough with regard to the goals aimed for, but in view of the direct confrontation with the Federal Republic consumption could not be cut any further. Thus resource hunger from 'below' and growth fetishism from 'above' repeatedly led to the national economic potential being overstretched.

The lists of 'structure-determining' products, investments and scientific–technological tasks got longer and longer and claimed an ever growing share of economic resources. The structure-political concept of the summer of 1968 envisaged about one hundred 'structure-determining' tasks. They comprised individual products or product groups, processes and technologies; assigned to them were appropriate tasks for science and technology, investments and supported export enterprises. Moreover, in the branches designated as 'structure-determining', combines and large-scale scientific research centres were set up; these were thought to be suitable for promoting the selected innovation processes because their capacities and potentials could be bunched together. The share of 'structure-determining' products laid down in July 1968 as a proportion of total industrial goods production was to rise to 16 per cent by 1970 and to 21 per cent by 1975; the funds employed for this purpose in science and technology were to amount to 54 per cent and 61 per cent of their total volume respectively. Between 1967 and 1970 altogether 23 per cent of industrial investments were envisaged for the production of 'structure-determining' products.[29] This meant that far more investments and, above all, means for science and technology, were employed for the selected products than the industrial average.

At the end of 1968 and the beginning of 1969 the SED centre became convinced that the structural changes envisaged so far and the growth generated by them were insufficient for overtaking the West. The economic policy departments of the Party Central Committee therefore believed that:

> [S]ome things must be done more quickly than in the USA or other countries in order to reach the world top position. This means: we must attain a leap-type development of technology and our production basis in some areas. After all – contrary to whole-society development – leaps are allowed in technology.[30]

This was a reference to the policy of the 'Great leap forward' in China at the end of the fifties, when 'after three years of intensive work ten thousand years of happiness' had been promised; eventually it suffered total shipwreck.[31] The responsible Party leaders already seemed to have forgotten their own experiences with the 'main economic task'. The idea of the greatest possible development leap became increasingly radical in 1968/69. This revealed, for one thing, the pressure on the Party to show some success, but was possibly also a result of the reflection that the Soviet leaders, who were once more conservatively minded after the Prague Spring, would have to be shown the efficiency of the GDR national economy and the functioning of the GDR reforms. It appeared moreover that some movement might be possible in German–German relations and would therefore be desirable to demonstrate a prosperous economy.

Internally it was believed that it would be possible to catch up with and surpass the Federal Republic's productivity level and living standard by 1980. For that reason the long-term plan for 1971 to 1975, drawn up in 1968, envisaged an annual growth rate of industrial productivity of 'only' 8.5 per cent on average. In the eyes of the State Planning Commission's chairman this was a realistic, if 'gigantic task', especially as simultaneously 'world peak performances in crucial areas' was to be achieved, automation speeded up, the living standard improved and, moreover, the country's readiness for defence enhanced.[32] In the Party headquarters, on the other hand, the general growth targets were thought to be insufficient. With a temporary productivity growth of 9 per cent it was convinced that an average of 10 per cent was possible in the long term. Ulbricht therefore called for a new plan, according to which productivity in industry would rise by between 10 per cent and 12.5 per cent annually, thereby reaching the level of the Federal Republic by 1975 or 1977/78. After negotiations in Moscow about the raw materials necessary for this growth it was 'only' possible to aim at an average productivity increase of 9 per cent.[33] Yet even this figure was too much for the economic potentials.

Among the Party leaders Ulbricht also encountered doubts about his concept, chiefly because of his orientation to the Western productivity level. His conservatively minded critics realised that one could not at the same time maintain the alternative character of one's own system and chase after an 'outdated' system without abandoning one's own claims. Ulbricht, on the other hand, realised that his socialism would only survive and become attractive if it proved more efficient than the capitalism of the Federal Republic.

The unrealistic growth targets thus, on the one hand, followed Ulbricht's political calculations and, on the other, were the consequence of the control mechanism: the extent of the burden placed on the national economy by 'structure-determining' tasks is shown by the share of these 'structure-determining' investments as proportions of total investments. According to the plans of October 1969 this share, in the same year, was to be 31 per cent in the centrally controlled industry and in construction. Accordingly the 'structure-determining' spheres in 1969 – measured by their production share – invested about three times the industrial average.[34] In 1970 the plan targets were once again raised. The share of 'structure-determining' tasks as a proportion of the total investments in industry and construction was to rise from the originally envisaged 38 per cent to 57 per cent.[35] This shows the extent to which central intervention again dominated the economy. Moreover, towards the end of the sixties expenditure on the military and security sphere also increased. At the beginning of the decade it had claimed about 10 per cent of budgetary expenditure; by the mid-1960s its share had declined, but between 1968 and 1970 it rose to over 14 per cent – a not inconsiderable strain on the budget and, by available data, probably the greatest in GDR history.[36]

All this limited the funds for the part of the economy that was not covered by 'structure-determining planning', where economic units enjoyed *de jure* incomparably greater scope for their own dispositions than before. As, however, they received too few resources, they were unable to make use of that scope. Instead, enterprises and VVBs exploited the gaps in the regulations for acquiring additional means, mainly through credits. Between 1966 and 1970 the volume of investment credits taken up by industry multiplied by eight.[37] As a result the demand for material resources – already overstretched by the plan – rose even further. Admittedly the greater scope given to enterprises in the non-structure-determining sectors, and the high growth targets for the 'structure-determining' products, also had the result, towards the end of the sixties, that enterprises began to employ their reserves and 'cushions' – often in direct exchange with other enterprises. In 1970, however, this disposability came to an end. The economic units again tried to increase their stocks. In this situation – as the head of government Willi Stoph complained – the investing enterprises in particular resorted to compensation deals, unlawful target bonuses, and 'so-called expense allowances for the provision of materials' with individual amounts of up to 2,000 Marks, in order to get the materials or capacities they required.[38] Even the import of scarce required inputs hardly relieved the tense situation.

Imports of Western technologies and raw materials were in fact considered necessary for the exacting structural and automation projects. In this context intra-German trade was playing an increasing role. But the GDR's products were not very competitive internationally and therefore did not earn sufficient foreign currency to finance the imports. The result was that the GDR slipped deeper into debt with the non-socialist economic area, and the amount of debt regarded as politically acceptable was limiting imports. That is why the resource shortfall could not be fully compensated for in this way in the 1970 plan. The more growth and structural change were pushed forward, the more difficult it became to safeguard industrial interrelations. In 1970, therefore, the high growth rates achieved in industrial production and productivity during the two preceding years slightly declined again. Because of the shortfalls the central authorities were continually intervening in economic activity, without, however, being able to close the gaps. In this way the plan was not implemented, which tore new gaps in the plan's interrelations. In view of the high growth targets this vicious circle accelerated. Moreover, owing to the enforced structural policy, producers of semi-finished goods and energy had been granted too few investments 'according to plan'. The hard winter of 1969/70 further threw back industrial production and disrupted transport and the power supply. Added to this there were harvest losses in 1969, causing in 1970 appreciable shortages of feeding stuffs and bread grain, with negative consequences for livestock production and supplies for the population. The economic situation, tense as it was already, deteriorated further.

The agricultural losses were a severe setback; after all there had been an attempt in agriculture, after the production collapse due to collectivisation in the early sixties, to stabilise the situation. Through support measures as well as through economic pressure the number of cooperatives requiring bridging credits had declined by 1964 to one-quarter of the 1962 figure.[39] Simultaneously the Agricultural Production Cooperatives' own share of investments had risen. But incentives continued to be a crucial obstacle to development. The 'economic levers' of the reform were intended to become effective also for agricultural enterprises. In addition – as for industry – the Agricultural Production Cooperatives were to take a greater part in planning, their plan indicators were to be reduced, and they were to be given more autonomy. In crop production the compulsory deliveries were abolished in 1963, the double price level of acquisition and purchasing prices abolished within the framework of an agrarian price reform and uniform prices were laid down. These were one-quarter to one-third above the previous average price. In order to create further production incentives various surcharges on top of the unified producer prices were imposed on crop products from 1964 onwards. Because a substantial part of animal products were still produced privately, with the higher prices functioning as production incentives, the dual price system was kept here until 1969.[40] The additional income resulting from the higher prices was predominantly used by the Agricultural Production Cooperatives for offsetting their revenue losses due to the abolition of subsidies or else for financing additional expenses such as tractor driver wages and repair costs resulting from the takeover of agricultural machinery.

The aim, pursued since 1963 and more intensively in the last third of the sixties, of introducing 'industrial production methods' in agriculture led to more intensive arable farming and stockbreeding. Particular importance was attached to the concentration of production and to cooperation. Agricultural cooperation enterprises were formed, such as the *Kooperative Abteilungen Pflanzenproduktion* ('Cooperative Department Crop Production'), which were intended to specialise further. Integration was horizontal and vertical. Cooperation associations were formed for individual products and inter-enterprise organisations set up; these undertook services such as fertiliser application, crop protection and repair work for several Agricultural Production Cooperatives and People-Owned Estates. Even greater specialisation was called for: in livestock production there were first of all eleven Industrial Fattening Combines, whose poultry fattening and laying-hen enterprises were to follow Western trends in producing meat and eggs. The fattened chickens produced there were marketed as 'Gold broilers'. These enterprises came into being after the Soviet Union had considerably cut its supplies of grain, meat, butter and wool in the mid sixties, because of a serious harvest failure. From the seventies onwards the GDR was eventually able to do entirely without imports of poultry for slaughtering. In view of this success similar pig fattening and cattle fattening enterprises were set up. Admittedly however these mega-enterprises caused considerable ecological problems because of their large accumulations of liquid manure and excrement.

Once the Party had begun, in 1967, to promote cooperation among agrarian enterprises, officials vied with one another to set up new enterprises and develop their links with the foodstuffs industry. Ever greater units sprang up; at times there were attempts, just as shortly after collectivisation, to establish mega-Agricultural Production Cooperatives, though the development potential of such mergers was overestimated. At the end of 1968, 23 per cent of Type III Agricultural Production Cooperatives, 7 per cent of Types I and II, as well as 24 per cent of People-Owned Estates participated in cooperation associations that tended to develop into large enterprises. In view of the increasing production targets, however, attempts to create ever larger enterprises were in latent contradiction to the desired autonomy of agricultural units during the economic reform.[41] The growing size of the enterprises made high demands on the managing personnel, who found it difficult to keep an overview. Moreover, the concentration process and the specialisation of individual agricultural enterprises had reached a degree that could no longer be economically controlled and therefore resulted in efficiency losses. The fact that the Party repeatedly 'back-pedalled' was probably due less to the realisation that enterprise size could lead to inefficiency than to fear of new unrest among the farmers.

All in all, conditions in agriculture were consolidated by the mid sixties, largely thanks to better technological supplies: farming then reached its pre-war performance again and per-hectare yields in 1968 surpassed the pre-collectivisation levels. Altogether agriculture in the course of the sixties made an increasing contribution to food supplies. However, at the end of the decade production once more broke down owing to unfavourable weather conditions and possibly also because of excessive concentration on size.

Economic Results and Living Standards in the Reform Period

In spite of all difficulties and inconsistencies economic results improved in the sixties. According to GDR statistics the growth rate of macroeconomic productivity (value added per head of population) rose from its low point of less than 3 per cent in 1961 to over 5 per cent in 1967 and in 1970 climbed to above 6 per cent. This growth was primarily due to investments, which had gone up since 1963; in particular the share of net investments in the 'producing' sphere as a proportion of value added was increased from 11 per cent in 1963 to just under 17 per cent in 1970.[42] The efficiency of investments also steadily increased from its low point in 1961 to 1964, after which, admittedly, it stagnated until 1970 (cf. Figure 2). In other words: the greater investments also yielded a higher return. The renewed crisis of the late sixties and early seventies was reflected chiefly in a lack of intermediate inputs and in the conspicuously worsened supply of the population. The growth rate, on the other hand, remained high and in 1971 only declined to under 5 per cent. The GDR's productivity lag behind the Federal Republic, however, increased drastically during the acute crisis of the early sixties. In the further course of the decade the growth of this difference in standards – even allowing for the uncertainty of the data – was at best slowed down but never reversed.

The economic structure in the sixties continued to develop with similar trends as in the fifties. As a result of the Party's industry-focused economic policy the share of industry in gross value added rose from 52 per cent to 57 per cent between 1960 and 1971, while the share of industry in the Federal Republic over the same period was stagnating or possibly even declining. Such a development is generally understood as a modernisation process of the economic structure; the fact that the GDR did not follow the same course was a result of the hypertrophic industrialisation model of socialist origin. Agriculture, on the other hand, produced less than 16 per cent of the total value added in 1971, after having accounted for 23 per cent in 1960. Here the development followed the secular trend in Germany.[43]

In the structural policy of the early sixties the energy and fuel industries continued to be prioritised. In the second third of the decade metallurgy – especially its secondary processing stage – and the chemical industry moved centre stage. As the chemical programme of the end of the fifties had failed in 1961, a second programme was decided upon in 1964; this was intended to drive the change in the chemical industry forward. Coal-based chemicals were to be pushed back, whereas petrochemicals, internationally already well advanced, were to be further developed. Thus the Leuna plant II, the chemical fibre combine Guben, and the crude-oil processing plant Schwedt were created with funds from this programme. The withdrawal from coal-based chemicals, however, had its limits since the quantity of available crude oil could only be slightly increased. The search for native oil deposits had remained just as unsuccessful as attempts to receive major quantities of crude oil from the Arab countries. For its crude oil supplies the GDR therefore continued to be dependent on the Soviet Union, whose oil was now reaching Schwedt by the 'Friendship' oil pipeline in greater quantities, though not sufficiently to replace coal-based chemicals altogether. Since the middle of the decade the engineering and vehicle-building industries had also been receiving more considerable quantities of means of expansion. In the final third of the decade, eventually, electrical engineering and electronics moved to the fore. Measured by their fixed assets they received almost double the industrial average in investments, which gave rise, above all, to capacities for electronic components and data processing equipment. The light, textiles and foodstuffs industries, on the other hand, those closest to the consumer, remained below average virtually throughout the decade. At the end of the sixties expansion even in the primary industry remained overall far below requirements, as revealed in the growth crisis of 1969/70.[44]

The structural change of the sixties, then, mainly favoured the electrical engineering and electronic industries, chemicals, engineering and vehicle production. Net production increases during the sixties were particularly marked in the share of chemical fibres, data processing and office machines, electronics and traditional measurement and process control engineering, chemical plant construction and plastics. The greatest loser of the structural change in industry was hard-coal mining. Deposits in the GDR, anyway slight, were running out. A crucial reason for the shortage of electrical energy in 1970/71, however, was the fact that, relying on Soviet crude oil, the brown-coal industry and energy generation had been neglected. Among the winners in the structural change were also branches regarded as particularly innovative by international comparison. But this did not mean that significant innovations had a major impact on industrial structure. Nevertheless, there were a few internationally noted outstanding developments, such as the flexible manufacturing systems 'Rota F' and 'Prisma 2', which had been objects of 'structure-determining planning'. With this prioritising instrument, support was mainly given to developments that were well advanced and whose possible application and potential economic effects would be so obvious that the risk seemed calculable.

Other growth branches were the manufacturing of agricultural machinery, road vehicles and tractors. The growth spurts of agricultural machine engineering were due to the programme, enacted after the agrarian collectivisation, for equipping agriculture more generously with machinery. The increases of output in the manufacture of road vehicles and tractors resulted from a thorough product renewal in the sixties. At that time the bulk of the motorcars and lorries dominating the GDR's street picture right to its end (Trabant, Wartburg and W50) went into serial production. At that time they were still, in many respects, up to the international state of the art.

The dynamic branches, therefore, predominantly belonged to the investment goods industries. This structural trend derived mainly from the above-mentioned ideology which demanded that the production of the means of production must always grow faster than that of consumption goods. But it also resulted from the tendency to limit trade in the world market to the most necessary items. That is why the 'smokestack industries' remained structure-determining in the GDR, while the Western countries were beginning to turn away from them. In consequence of the technology and structure offensive it proved possible, in the final third of the sixties, by means of structural change, slightly to increase industrial productivity above the years preceding and following, but this remained at a very low level. From the beginning of the sixties growth was stabilised and speeded up, which was chiefly due to an expansion of fixed assets. Innovations and structural change primarily resulted from pressure from the central authorities and was not generated from the economic process itself. Besides, the persons in charge shrank from closing down enterprises, let alone industrial branches: while this might have assisted structural change it would have led to temporary local unemployment, and that was a political and ideological taboo just as much as the bankruptcy of an enterprise under socialist conditions. Operating losses of the enterprises were ultimately always borne by the state. In this way any economically induced structural change was almost impossible and growth and productivity effects remained slight. In spite of improved results it had therefore not been possible, even with the reform, to create the basis of a thorough modernisation of the economy.

The improved economic results were also reflected in the living standard of the population. While the net money income per head of the population had only been rising on average by 1 per cent annually between 1960 and 1963, by 1967, in the first reform phase, it had risen by more than 4 per cent annually over the 1963 figure. In 1968 and 1969 the net income rose even faster, each year by nearly 5 per cent. As, however, prices also rose very considerably during those years, real income development lagged behind the growth of productivity. In 1970/71 the growth of net income by 3 per cent annually was again lower, as in the previous years of reform,[45] ultimately as a consequence of higher investments, the resulting overstretching of the economy and, above all, the decline of agricultural production.

Gradually, however, there were more goods on offer. Foodstuffs consumption hardly increased at the beginning of the sixties because of the unfavourable development of agriculture after collectivisation. But from 1963 onwards there was considerable change until the end of the decade: the 'Gold broilers' offered from the final third of the sixties onwards in a restaurant chain of its own, as well as the greater supply of fish, provided by the restaurants' association as *Gastmahl des Meeres* ('Banquet of the sea'), enriched the public's food supply. Moreover, the broiler and fish production made it possible to reduce the still necessary foodstuffs imports. But the hoped for self-sufficiency continued to be beyond the reach of agriculture.

Since 1964/65 the investments were beginning to show an effect: the trade was able to offer more consumer goods than in the past years. Even so there were, time and again, local and temporary gaps in supplies, especially with regard to high-value and, increasingly, status-determining consumer goods, such as television sets, refrigerators, washing machines and motorcars, where supply lagged behind demand. Moreover, many industrial goods were nowhere near Western standards, technically, in consumer-friendliness, in design or in packaging. The result was that, side by side with supply gaps, there continued to be considerable above-plan stocks of unsaleable goods. Admittedly, within the framework of the reform, there had been attempts to conduct consumer goods market research. However, the idea that consumers should be educated to adjust their needs to available supplies continued to dominate. Consumer demand could not be satisfied in many respects, qualitatively or quantitatively. In the sixties the 'mismatch between the quality, fashionableness and price ... on the one hand and consumers' expectations on the other remained one of the most common explanations for surpluses' of unsaleable goods.[46] Yet in spite of these structural flaws there was an improvement in supplies and part of the excess demand was 'absorbed'. This demand was partly also served by the 'Exquisit' shops, first opened in 1961, which offered fashionable clothes made in the GDR or imported at the highest possible prices. These were complemented in 1966 by the 'Delikat' shops, which sold 'delicacies', i.e., special foodstuffs, drinks and tobacco, at twice or three times the price in the regular shops. These shops, popularly known as 'Ulbricht's profiteering kiosks', built on the experience gained from the foundation of state-owned HO stores. The move was a successful one: in 1970 the 'Exquisit' shops were already realising 3 per cent of the total turnover of textiles and footwear, and in 1982 it was 15 per cent.[47]

As a result of better supplies, more and more households began to be equipped with technical consumer goods (Table 4.1).

Table 4.1: Number of selected industrial consumer goods per 100 households in 1960, 1965 and 1970[48]

	1960	1965	1970
Motorcars	3.2	8.2	15.6
TV sets	18.5	53.7	73.6
Refrigerators	6.1	25.9	56.4
Washing machines	6.2	27.7	53.6

This increase is the more remarkable as the prices for industrial consumer goods were considerable compared to average incomes: a television set cost 2,050 Marks in 1965, a refrigerator 1,350 Marks and a washing machine 1,200 Marks at a time when the average net monthly income of workers and employees was 491 Marks.[49] About 40 per cent of the consumer price of television sets and refrigerators went to the state budget.[50] This was intended to fund the subsidies for the prices of goods for basic needs. Admittedly there was repeated discussion, in connection with the price reforms, whether it would not be a better idea to use these sums for raising incomes at the lower end, and at the same time to moderately increase the prices of goods for basic needs and lower those for industrial goods. But this was politically too explosive an idea for those responsible in the state and party hierarchy; besides, it would have required a sufficient supply of industrial goods. The subsidies were therefore kept and indeed needed to be increased as, with the excess purchasing power and the poor supply and high prices of industrial goods, public demand concentrated on foodstuffs, drink and tobacco. The imbalance between supply and demand therefore remained undiminished even during the second half of the sixties: retail turnover from 1960 to 1971 rose annually by just under 4 per cent on average, with the population's net money income rising by just over 3 per cent. Thus the increase in surplus money among the population was only slightly slowed down.[51]

A considerable part of the growth of retail turnover, however – nearly one-half in 1970 – was due to higher prices.[52] Although for a large part of the goods on offer the average prices remained constant, or were even reduced, the prices of new products were nearly always fixed higher than the old ones and state surcharges increasingly imposed on them. As the enterprises made less profit with their cheaper goods, these disappeared from the shops and average prices rose substantially. Even an SED work group had to admit that 'despite stable single retail prices there can be no talk of stability of the price level'.[53] Prices of industrial goods rose by 2.5 per cent between 1962 and 1967 altogether and then, in 1968 alone, by more than 3 per cent. These price increases continued until 1970, embracing nearly all groups of industrial products and even some foodstuffs. By the beginning of 1970 the price of men's overcoats had risen by 65 per cent over the 1967 figure and that of refrigerators by 10 per cent. These higher prices should really have pleased those responsible for the economy, seeing that they reduced the excess purchasing power. But because this development was being seen as hidden inflation and as a breach of promise it worried the leaders.[54]

The cost-of-living index rose roughly by an estimated 1 per cent on average annually from 1960 to 1971, with the rate of inflation, after its peak in 1962, probably at first slowing down but accelerating again towards the end of the decade.[55] From the nominal annual growth of the population's net money income of 3 per cent in the sixties there probably remained, after price adjustment, a little more than 2 per cent. These values, however, make no allowance for the availability or the quality of goods. In the Federal Republic – according to what calculation basis is used – real wages over the same period rose by 5 to 6 per cent annually.[56] The development of living standards in the GDR thus lagged ever further behind that in Western Germany.

Even so, conditions had improved: the five-day week, often already in use, was gradually legalised and generally introduced in 1965 and 1967.[57] The minimum wage rose from 220 to 300 Marks in 1967, child benefit was increased, old-age pensions slightly improved and a voluntary additional-pension scheme introduced in 1968. The additional contributions for the latter were also intended to reduce the excess purchasing power of the population.[58] The higher living standard and the intention to change demonstrated by the economic reform were probably the reasons why the sixties in the GDR were remembered rather positively. New problems, however, appeared in 1970.

The Growth Crisis of 1969/70 and its Political Consequences

The year 1970 once more began with high growth targets and further showpiece projects, even though it had already been difficult in 1969 to provide adequate amounts of electrical energy, gas, solid fuels, metallurgical products and transport space. Investments were to be raised even further than in the preceding years. Projects with a total cost of just under ten billion Marks were additionally included in the plan: 179 automation projects, a polyester and polyurethane programme, the development of scientific instrument making, an intensified search for native natural gas deposits, as well as the development of light metal construction and cement production. This represented more than 60 per cent of the investments planned in the centrally controlled industries and in construction. Added to these were the costs of converting the railways from coal to diesel and a container system, of additional measures in agriculture and the foodstuffs industry, the creation of a second television programme and of colour television, and new autobahn construction. Some of these projects were only decided upon when the 1970 plan had already been confirmed and without checking whether sufficient funds and resources were available for 1970 and the following years. As a result, the plan was very unbalanced and had so many gaps that it was illusionary right from the beginning.

The real cost of the investment projects turned out eventually to be higher than planned and imports reached the limit of the GDR's export strength and its debt capacity. Producers did not implement their plans or contracts either in range and quality or in time, which led to further stoppages in industry and to gaps in domestic supplies. The structural policy that was forced through was focused on final products and neglected investments in the energy and construction industries, in ancillary industries and in transport. Since 1968 producers of semi-finished goods had been developing more slowly than final producers. In the autumn of 1970 many enterprises still did not know from where they would receive the required inputs laid down in the 1970 plan. Even in the Central Committee Department for Planning and Finance there were resigned moans: 'No one is saying how things will continue.'[59] In October 1970 the delivery arrears in industry eventually reached a peak with arrears amounting to 6.6 days of production.[60]

From the beginning of 1970 the government and the industrial ministers issued a multitude of directives and resolutions to increase the pressure on economic units. However, this 'well-tried' crisis management failed to resolve the problems; at best it defused them. Besides, these interventions from 'above' progressively overrode the economic rules and standards of the reform, so that it was eroded long before its actual end. Directives at first aimed to try and catch up with the plan arrears by working extra weekend shifts in the concerning enterprises, which, in the course of the year, aroused considerable resentment among the workers. To them the disrupted interdependencies became very manifest when, having been unable to work during their working hours because of a lack of material, they were then made to catch up with the arrears over the weekend. This situation was counter-motivating even for the executives in enterprises, combines and Associations of People-Owned Enterprises. Because of the 'minor material incentives with, at the same time, the high degree of physical and psychological stress and moral pressure' more and more of these executives wanted to give up their jobs. Resignation and indifference were gaining ground.[61] Although the 'cadres' were still functioning, there was no longer the élan or the keenness that had characterised the first few years of the reform.

The enterprises were feeling the crisis not only in the missing required inputs but also in power cuts. The production arrears led to growing supply deficits in retail trade and thus hit the population. There was a shortage, above all, of warm underwear, children's wear and track suits, winter footwear, batteries, pressing irons, modular furniture, household chemicals, toothbrushes and spark plugs. Due to extra shifts and overtime the incomes of industrial employees rose rapidly in 1970, which further increased demand. Because of the harvest failure in 1969/70 it was necessary to import additional agricultural produce; to this end more industrial consumer goods were exported. Thus the supply of foodstuffs remained stable, but there was a shortage of industrial consumer goods.

In spite of the serious disturbances in the economic process, 1970 saw a growth of production and of labour productivity in industry, each of 6 per cent. But this went hand in hand with considerable costs and an efficiency loss in the shape of declining productivity of the plants and stocks; it was therefore bought at the expense of substance. Such a course could not be kept up for long; it was only thinkable for a short period, and moreover with growing imbalances being caused. Besides, results were not based only on domestic performance. In 1969 one-third and in 1970 two-thirds of the increase of the used national income came from excess of imports. Thus the potential of the economy was overstretched by the ambitious, ever more forced, growth and technology offensive.[62]

This is not to say that this strategy was mistaken from the start. In view of the GDR's state of development and the system premises it was a promising option. To be successful, however, the targets would have had to be lowered and a few basic problems of system designing resolved. When Ulbricht in the Politbüro began to sense an 'atmosphere of subversion' towards the reform, he addressed one of the structural problems in November 1970. If more was consumed than produced in the GDR, 'there should have been a signal through the system: Stop, comrades, we can't go on like that! This stop, which we decided upon a few weeks ago, should have come at the beginning of 1970. Instead we just carried on ...'[63] But that 'signal' was just what the system was unable to do; this would have needed a market mechanism (regulated in whatever way), which was neither considered nor desired. The socialist-market models then occasionally considered possible were rejected by the Party on political grounds and would probably not have been tolerated by Moscow in the long run. It therefore seemed more logical – especially for the reform opponents in the Politbüro – to control the economy again more strongly by way of individual goods and from the centre.

The Party leaders had been aware of the crisis symptoms ever since the first half of 1970. Nevertheless they clung to the excessive targets for 1971, still believing in the technological leap forward and hoping to make the GDR attractive to its citizens. To that end the productivity of the Federal Republic was to be caught up with in the foreseeable future. This was one reason why Ulbricht was now striving for closer economic cooperation with the Federal Republic. Although Brezhnev warned him in May 1970 that Western Germany was endeavouring to penetrate the GDR economically, he stuck to his strategy and explained to the Soviet deputy head of government:

> We are making debts with the capitalists to the limit of the possible in order to get through one way or another. Some of the products of our new plants must therefore be exported to where we bought our machines and made our debts. In a short time these new plants must be redeemed ... We are now correcting the arrears from the days of the open frontier. We are making a leap forward, albeit with exact calculations. We realise that this upsets the plan. ... But in the interest of structural policy it was necessary to act in this way.[64]

Economically it was sounding plausible to import modern equipment, financed by credits from the West, and to repay the credits from production by this equipment and from its profits. Its successful realisation, however, presumed that within the country enough incentives could be mobilised to utilise the advantages of the imported technology. Converting its higher technical efficiency into economic efficiency required an appropriate background. An understanding with the Federal Republic offered a chance, in Ulbricht's view, to create, with more flexible politics, a framework for more economic cooperation with it and the conditions for an improvement of trade relations with other Western countries. All the more so as the Soviet Union in the summer of 1969 had rejected providing a greater volume of supplies of raw materials. However, Ulbricht invariably believed that, in the medium term, the superiority of the 'socialist' part of Germany must prove itself.

Since the summer of 1970 these questions had been leading to conflicts within the Politbüro, with the amount and the structure of indebtedness to the West playing a particular role. Total indebtedness to the non-socialist world amounted to 45 per cent of 1970 exports to the non-socialist world.[65] The debts, moreover, had an unfavourable structure: liabilities were predominantly short and medium-term, while demands were long-term and their redeemability often questionable. Ulbricht did not let this put him off and stuck to his course of 'overtaking without catching up'. In consequence, however, his opponents, grouped around Erich Honecker, became increasingly active, with some help from Moscow, and in September 1970 brought about Politbüro decisions by which the policies enforced since the beginning of the year by economic necessity, which had been until then piecemeal, became policies shaped programmatically and approved by the supreme authority. With 'structure-determining planning', the plan had effectively become the dominant control instrument long before, while the money-oriented rules and incentive mechanisms of the reform had already lost their power of control at the beginning of 1970. This turn-away from the reform however took place gradually at first. Not until the beginning of December 1970 did resolutions on the rules of running the economy in 1971 turn noticeably away from the reform idea; once more it was intended to strengthen the centralistic control instruments, orienting them furthermore to a steering by concrete goods and not by financial instruments. Thus the dismantling of essential elements of the economic reform was completed. When Ulbricht tried to resist, a part of the Party leadership turned to Brezhnev in January 1971 with the request that he persuade Ulbricht to resign, which he did officially at the beginning of May 1971 in favour of Honecker. His rebellion against the end of the reform and his own loss of power were in vain.

The reformers in the GDR – just as other first-generation reformers in Poland, Hungary, the Czechoslovak Socialist Republic and the Soviet Union – had believed that plan and market could be so combined that they would complement and correct one another. The market was to be a control instrument of the central economic authorities; hiding behind this was the idea that those responsible in the central authority could 'pull all the strings of indirect control and the profit-maximising agents [will] respond like obedient puppets'.[66] The 'market-oriented economic activity of enterprises' remained constricted in the planned-economy corset because even the reformers were unwilling or unable to overcome certain theoretical and ideological limits, such as cost-oriented prices. Crossing these lines in the direction of the market would have ultimately questioned the control claim of the central authorities and hence the hegemony of the Party and its right to the formulation of overall economic plan targets; eventually it could have questioned even Marxism–Leninism as the dominant ideology. But that was something not even the reformers dared to think about.

Notes

1. Staritz, *Geschichte der DDR*, p. 196.
2. André Steiner, 'Eine wirtschaftliche Bilanz der Berliner Mauer', in Hertle et al. (eds), *Mauerbau und Mauerfall*, pp. 189–202.
3. Abt. Planung und Finanzen, Arbeitsgruppe Industrieökonomik: Bericht über den Instrukteureinsatz der wirtschaftspolitischen Abteilungen zur Untersuchung des Standes der Arbeit zur Sicherung unserer Wirtschaft, 8.9.1961, SAPMO-BA DY30 IV2/2029/115.
4. Informationsbericht des Volkswirtschaftsrates an das Politbüro …, 29.1.1962, SAPMO-BA DY30/3712.
5. Apel to Ulbricht, 4.7.1963: Analytische Einschätzung des Standes der Abhängigkeit der DDR …27.6.1963; both SAPMO-BA NY4182/969.
6. Statistisches Bundesamt: Fachserie 6, Reihe 6: Warenverkehr mit der DDR und Berlin (Ost); *Statistisches Jahrbuch 1990*, p. 33.
7. Ulbricht to Khrushchev, 19.1.1961, SAPMO-BA DY30/3708; Kommuniqué über Verhandlungen und Unterzeichnung eines Protokolls am 30.5.1961 …, in *Dokumente zur Außenpolitik der Regierung der DDR*, Vol. IX, Berlin (East) 1962, p. 418.
8. Mewis to Ulbricht: Niederschrift über eine Beratung … am 25.5.1962, SAPMO-BA NY4182/1207.
9. Buchheim, 'Wirtschaftliche Folgen', pp. 357 ff.; Ahrens, *Gegenseitige Wirtschaftshilfe?*, pp. 82 f.
10. SPK, Abt. Arbeitskräfte: Analyse über die Durchführung des Arbeitskräfteplanes in der Zeit von Januar bis September 1961, 14.10.1961, SAPMO-BA DY30 IV2/608/46.
11. Steiner et al., *Statistische Übersichten*, Tables 3.1.1.1., 8.1.3., 9.1.1.
12. *Statistisches Jahrbuch 1990*, p. 55.

13. Abt. Organisation und Kader: Kurzinformation über Stimmungen und Meinungen …, 7.6.1962, SAPMO-BA NY4182/968; Patrice G. Poutrus: *Die Erfindung des Goldbroilers. Über den Zusammenhang zwischen Herrschaftssicherung und Konsumentwicklung in der DDR*, Cologne 2002, pp. 65 f.

14. Probleme der Versorgung der Bevölkerung, Anlage (zum Brief an Khrushchev, 21.6.1963), SAPMO-BA DY30/3712.

15. Information über die Stellvertreterberatung der SPK vom 14.3.1962, SAPMO-BA DY30 IV A2/2021/247.

16. *Richtlinie für das neue ökonomische System der Planung und Leitung der Volkswirtschaft*, Berlin (East) 1963, p. 54.

17. Walter Ulbricht: Das neue ökonomische System der Planung und Leitung der Volkswirtschaft in der Praxis, Berlin (East) 1963, pp. 78, 103 f.

18. On the concept and implementation of the price reform cf. Steiner, *DDR-Wirtschaftsreform*, pp. 198–267, figures 219.

19. SPK: Informationen über Aussprachen mit leitenden Genossen aus VVB und Betrieben über Fragen der Durchführung des NÖS …, 13.11.1965, BA DE1/45454.

20. Abt. Planung und Finanzen: Information über die Arbeitstagung der Leitung des VWR …, 7.7.1965, SAPMO-BA DY30 IV A2/2021/274.

21. Calculated according to Steiner, *DDR-Wirtschaftsreform*, appendix tables A12, A13.

22. Steiner, *DDR-Wirtschaftsreform*, p. 313.

23. Protokoll über die am 13.8.1965 durchgeführte Beratung des Gen. Dr. Mittag mit den Sekretären der Bezirksleitungen …, SAPMO-BA DY30 IV A2/601/8.

24. Protokoll der Verhandlungen des VI. Parteitages der SED, 15. bis 21. Januar 1963, Vol. 1, Berlin (East) 1963, pp. 71 ff.

25. VWR: 2. Information der Leitung und Probleme bei der Ausarbeitung des Planvorschlags 1966, 14.8.1965, BA Berlin DE4-S/18-8-65. On working hour demands cf. Hübner, *Konsens*, pp. 120 ff.

26. Abt. Planung und Finanzen: Information über eine Beratung der Stellvertreter des Vorsitzenden der SPK vom 20.11.1965 …, am 22.11.1965, SAPMO-BA DY30 IV A2/2021/252.

27. Beratung zur Weiterführung und Qualifizierung der prognostischen Arbeit … am 28.11.1968, SAPMO-BA DY30 IV A2/2021/441.

28. Calculated according to *Einheitliche Datenbasis*.

29. Beschlußprotokoll der Ministerratssitzung am 26.6.1968: SPK: Strukturpolitische Konzeption der Volkswirtschaft der DDR, Juli 1968, BA Berlin DC20-I/3-672, 673.

30. Material [der wirtschaftspolitischen ZK-Abteilungen] zur Vorbereitung der 1. Beratung der Perspektivplankommission [am 26./27.9.1968], SAPMO-BA DY30 IV A2/2021/450.

31. David Bachman: *Bureaucracy, Economy, and Leadership in China. The Institutional Origins of the Great Leap Forward*, New York 1991.

32. Schürer: Bericht des Vorsitzenden der SPK über den Stand der Vorbereitung des Perspektivplanes, 25.9.1968, SAPMO-BA DY30 IV A2/2021/449.

33. SPK, Schürer: Grundkonzeption des Planes für die Entwicklung der Volkswirtschaft 1971–1975, [März 1970], BA Berlin DE1/56076.
34. SPK/Arbeitsgruppe für die Gestaltung des ÖSS: Analyse über die Wirkungsweise der Maßnahmen zur weiteren Gestaltung des ÖSS … , 10.10.1969, BA Berlin DE1/51172.
35. SPK: Zusammengefaßte Einschätzung zu den Hauptaufgaben des Volkswirtschaftsplanes 1970, 27.11.1969, BA Berlin DE1/53993; SPK: Vorschlag für die Festlegung der volkswirtschaftlich strukturbestimmenden Investitionen 1970, 29.12.1969, BA Berlin DE1/51168/4.
36. Included in these data are the budgetary contributions to the expenditure of the Defence, State Security and Interior ministries. Calculated according to Karlsch, 'Wirtschaftliche Belastungen'; *Einheitliche Datenbasis*; Steiner et al., *Statistische Übersichten*, Table 0.2.0.1.
37. Steiner, *DDR-Wirtschaftsreform*, p. 486.
38. Referat des … Gen. Willi Stoph vor den ersten Sekretären der Bezirksleitungen der SED und des Vorsitzenden der Räte der Bezirke über Probleme der Plandurchführung 1970 … am 21.9.1970, SAPMO-BA DY30 IV A2/2021/474.
39. Calculated according to Jörg Roesler: *Zwischen Plan und Markt. Die Wirtschaftsreform 1963–1970 in der DDR*, Berlin 1990, p. 131.
40. Prices according to Edgar Tümmler, 'Die Agrarpolitik in Mitteldeutschland', in idem et al. (eds), *Die Agrarpolitik in Mitteldeutschland und ihre Auswirkungen auf Produktion und Verbrauch landwirtschaftlicher Erzeugnisse*, Berlin (West) 1969, pp. 1–167, here 133–42.
41. On the preceding cf. Roesler, *Plan und Markt*, pp. 138 ff., 148; Bauerkämper, *Ländliche Gesellschaft*, pp. 196 ff.; *Statistisches Jahrbuch 1976*, pp. 176 f., 184.
42. Calculated according to *Einheitliche Datenbasis*.
43. Calculated according to *Einheitliche Datenbasis*.
44. See the data in Steiner, *DDR-Wirtschaftsreform*, p. 567.
45. Calculated according to Steiner et al., *Statistische Übersichten*, Table 0.4.1.0.
46. Stitziel, *Fashioning Socialism*, p. 97.
47. Ina Merkel, *Utopie und Bedürfnis. Die Geschichte der Konsumkultur in der DDR*, Cologne 1999, pp. 251–71.
48. *Statistisches Jahrbuch 1990*, p. 325.
49. *Statistisches Jahrbuch 1968*, p. 433; SZS: Sammelband ausgewählter Kennziffern über die Entwicklung der Volkswirtschaft 1960–1971, BA Berlin DE2/30191/0014157.
50. Untergruppe Konsumgüterpreise, Zum Problem: 'Konsumgüterpreise im neuen ökonomischen System', 6.1.1967, SAPMO-BA DY30/3318; Ministerium der Finanzen, Standpunkt und Vorstellungen über die Konzeption …, 28.1.1969, SAPMO-BA DY30 IV A2/2021/428.
51. Calculated according to *Statistisches Jahrbuch 1990*, p. 55; Steiner et al., *Statistische Übersichten*, Table 0.4.1.0.
52. SZS: Bericht über die Produktion und Verwendung des Nationaleinkommens …, 28.2.1971, BA Berlin DC20-I/3-844.
53. Untergruppe Konsumgüterpreise, Zum Problem: 'Konsumgüterpreise im neuen ökonomischen System', 6.1.1967, SAPMO-BA DY30/3318.

54. Abt. Planung und Finanzen, Information über die Entwicklung ..., 23.6.1969, SAPMO-BA DY30 IV A2/2021/678; Beschlußprotokoll der 58. Sitzung des Ministerrates am 19.8.1970. Anlage 2: Analyse der Entwicklung der Einzelverkaufspreise ..., BA Berlin DC20-I/3-807.

55. Estimated according to the data quoted for the prices of industrial goods, the indices for other goods and services, as well as the consumption structure of 1968, in *Statistisches Jahrbuch 1970*, p. 357; *Statistisches Jahrbuch* 1976, p. 308. This value can only be taken as a first approximation and is probably a little too high.

56. Calculated according to Bundesministerium für Arbeit und Sozialordnung (ed.), *Statistisches Taschenbuch 1998: Arbeits- und Sozialstatistik*, Bonn 1998, Table 5.4.

57. Hübner, *Konsens*, pp. 128 f.

58. Manfred G. Schmidt. 'Grundlagen der Sozialpolitik in der Deutschen Demokratischen Republik', in Bundesministerium für Arbeit und Sozialordnung und Bundesarchiv (ed.), *Geschichte der Sozialpolitik in Deutschland seit 1945*, Vol. 1: *Grundlagen der Sozialpolitik*, Baden-Baden 2001, pp. 685–798, here 730 f.

59. Abt. Planung und Finanzen to Mittag: Zur Beratung Stand der Planerfüllung 1970 im Politbüro am 20.10.1970, 16.10.1970, SAPMO-BA DY30 IV A2/2021/475.

60. SZS: Bericht über die Produktion ..., 28.2.1971, BA Berlin DC20-I/3-844.

61. Zentralinstitut für sozialistische Wirtschaftsführung beim ZK der SED: Bericht über Besuche von Kombinaten und VVB ..., 10.3.1971, SAPMO-BA DY30 IV A2/612/6.

62. Steiner, *DDR-Wirtschaftsreform*, pp. 518 f.

63. SPK, Staatssekretär: Persönliche Notizen über die Beratung der Grundfragen zur Ausarbeitung des Volkswirtschaftsplanes 1971 im Politbüro des ZK der SED am 3.11.1970, 4.11.1970, BA Berlin DE1/56118.

64. Niederschrift über die Beratung des Gen. Walter Ulbricht mit Gen. Tichonow am 25.6.1970, BA Berlin DE1/56128.

65. Calculated according to [SPK:] Disposition: Grundlinie der Ausarbeitung des Volkswirtschaftsplanes 1972, 4.11.1971: Anlage 3. Entwicklung der Salden ..., BA Berlin DE1/56121; *Statistisches Jahrbuch 1990*, p. 32.

66. Janos Kornai: 'The Hungarian Reform Process: Visions, Hopes, and Reality', *Journal of Economic Literature*, XXIV, 1986, pp. 1728 f.

Chapter 5

'Unity of Economic and Social Policy' 1971–1982

Ulbricht's growth and technology offensive of the late sixties had resulted in a growth crisis that was also a supply crisis for the population, as the forced development of high-tech areas had led to the neglect of consumption-related economic sectors. Similar phenomena were observed in other Eastern Bloc countries that had experimented with reforms in the sixties. In December 1970 the Polish workers reacted to the attempt of an austerity policy with strikes and protest actions, which were brutally crushed; it was therefore decided in 1970/71, in all the Eastern Bloc countries except Romania, to perform an about-turn in economic and social policy. The East German Party was also anxious, in the interest of its power, to consolidate the situation and, instead of its modernisation drive, was now following an appeasement policy: the workers were to be pacified with better supplies of food and other consumer goods at stable prices and an expanded social welfare policy. This should motivate them for higher performances. The control mechanism, as in all other reform countries, was again more closely oriented along the Soviet model and its centralistic structures and instruments. Relations with the Federal Republic were governed at the beginning of the seventies by the Basic Treaty; both German states became members of the United Nations and the GDR was now internationally recognised and respected. Contacts and the number of visits – mainly from West to East – increased. At the same time the Party made more determined attempts to differentiate itself from the Federal Republic politically and ideologically, emphasising, more than under Ulbricht, its solid alliance with the Soviet Union. It seemed therefore all the more important to improve the living conditions of the population and thereby to also give the differentiation a material basis.

The economic situation was eventually stabilised in the first third of the seventies, but this had required additional imports already. The far-reaching consumption and social welfare programme that was now embarked upon demanded further extensive funds and imports. As GDR products continued to be insufficiently competitive in the world markets, it was not possible to step up exports to a scale where their earnings might have financed those imports. When, in the second half of the seventies, a programme for the forced development of microelectronics was set in motion, this failed to produce the expected results, despite immense expense, because of inadequate division of labour within Comecon. Efforts were therefore made to remedy the lacking competitiveness of GDR products. However, along with a housing programme, expanded in the second half of the seventies, this tied down a considerable proportion of the means of the national economy.

When, after 1973/74, the GDR was also – with some delay due to the principles of Comecon price setting – affected by the raw material prices exploding in the world markets, economic scope was narrowed down. Various factors meant that indebtedness was bound to increase further: the rising raw material prices not being passed on to the consumers; the social appeasement policy continuing; the pushing forward of technological progress for the sake of the economy's future; and the lack of mobilisation of additional exports. At the end of the seventies, when rates of interest rose worldwide and raw material prices once more multiplied, this problem became even more acute. The Soviet Union, moreover, found itself under growing economic and political pressure: due to its stationing of missiles, the discussion about counter-armament beginning in the West and, above all, due to its invasion of Afghanistan in 1979. Hence less and less economic support could be expected from the Soviets. Politically, however, Moscow complained that the GDR was running up growing debts in the West and economically leaning more strongly on the Federal Republic. But in view of the renewed disturbances and strikes in Poland at the turn of the next decade any austerity policy with a reduction of welfare benefits was out of the question for the East German Party; it was anxious to avoid conflicts. When Poland declared itself unable to pay, when West–East relations once more became tense and when the West imposed a de facto credit boycott on the Eastern Bloc, reality caught up with the GDR: it was in an indebtedness trap. A decade earlier no one had expected such a dramatic development, even though there had been no shortage of warnings of the economic consequences the new policy would have.

Honecker's 'Main Task'

Following the replacement of Ulbricht by Honecker at the top of the Party the fundamental lines of economic policy were redefined. After similar resolutions by the XXIVth Soviet Communist Party's Congress in April

1971 Honecker, at the VIIIth East German Party's Congress in June 1971, proclaimed the new 'main task': this would aim at 'raising the people's material and cultural standard of living on the basis of a fast developmental pace of socialist production, of higher efficiency, of scientific-technological progress and the growth of the productivity of labour'.[1] Economic development was now to adjust to sociopolitics 'that would overcome existing social inequality, improve the condition of the socially weak and, above all, focus on the material interests of "the employed", especially the workers'.[2] These had, in the final Ulbricht years, fallen behind the 'intelligentsia' in income and prestige and should now receive more justice in line with the legitimating models of socialism. Social (advance) benefits, under this political concept, should be reflected in improved work motivation and higher productivity of labour. At the same time Ulbricht's technology offensive was stopped because funds had to be freed for the consumer and social welfare programmes.

This change of direction in economic policy was also a reaction to the imponderables and waywardness of the people-owned enterprises and their associations that had come to light during the final years of Ulbricht's reform. Because the economic difficulties were believed by those in power to be due mainly to a shortage of goods, this was to be remedied by product-oriented economic instruments. And because the autonomous economic activity of enterprises had often been in conflict with the guidelines set by the central authorities, the goods-oriented economic direction was to be centralised. With this return to old models it was hoped that a growth path would be found that guaranteed the 'proportionality of the economy as a whole' which Ulbricht, in the interest of its dynamics, had done without.

Such an economic policy was implemented in nearly all the Eastern Bloc countries in 1970/71. Two alternatives had offered themselves. One option was to continue, as before, to increase efficiency and hence the living standard by enormous efforts, as Ulbricht had urged. Such a policy followed an economic logic aimed at an internationally competitive economy and a resulting improvement in the living standard of the population. Or else one attempted – like Honecker – to draw a cheque on the future by first improving the material conditions of the population by extensive consumer and social welfare measures in the hope that this would provide an incentive for a corresponding economic performance. The decisive triggers for adopting the second option throughout the Eastern Bloc were the demonstrations, strikes and riots in Poland in December 1970 by which the workers had reacted to price increases for a whole series of basic necessities. In order to calm the situation, to pacify the workers and to safeguard the leaders' own power the standard of living was to be raised in the short term. It is possible that a role was also played by the experience of the Hungarian 'goulash Communism', where a barter trade of 'political calm against relative affluence and social security' had been practised for some time.[3]

In view of the disturbances in Poland, the East German Party leaders were greatly alarmed by the fact that the number of strikes in the GDR had also risen between the autumn of 1970 and the spring of 1971. In many cases the workers had downed tools because they feared that the increasingly frequent production breaks might lower their incomes and drive up prices. Against the background of the high living standard in the Federal Republic this situation was particularly explosive for the East German Party in comparison to its sister parties. In March 1971 Honecker demanded in the Politbüro that 'a number of phenomena, which threaten to spread to us from other countries, must be prevented'. 'Up to a point the Polish school comes to mind. These are signals that we must take notice of.'[4] The about-turn to the policy of the 'main task' was ultimately due to the same motive as the initiation of the economic reform at the beginning of the sixties: concern about power.

The concept championed by Honecker – praised from 1975 onwards as the 'unity of economic and social policy' – was intended, by means of an expanded consumer and welfare policy, to win over the population for the system and, at the same time, to pacify it. With it the Party leadership created for itself, and even more so for the population, the illusion of a realised modern industrial welfare state. However, the economic policy pursued, unlike Ulbricht's, was bound to be at the expense of the country's economic substance. At the same time the Party, with this course, was once more in step with the Soviet Union and most of the other Eastern Bloc countries.

All in all the new economic policy seemed more unpretentious and more realistic. In the spring of 1971 Honecker called on the Politbüro to create an atmosphere 'where matters are realistically assessed and soberly calculated'.[5] And at the Party Congress he pointed out that the economy could not 'cope with too many "additional" miracles'.[6] After turning away from Ulbricht's policy, with its continuous demands and complicated rules, the economic officials felt unburdened and relieved. The short-term simple and calculable solutions, which were now in the foreground, were more in line with the ideas in the bureaucratic apparatus; utopian and visionary aspects of the socialist project were sidelined. The new line was structure-conservative. Structural change and innovation were now only regarded as secondary goals. The promise of greater and earlier affluence was intended to create stability and loyalty. This promise, along with an ideologically less rigid attitude among the new Party leaders gave rise, from the beginning of the seventies until the mid seventies, to a kind of new-dawn atmosphere.

The Party leaders however made demands on the economy with this policy that the State Planning Commission could hardly expect to bring into balance: the supply of consumer goods and the living standard were to be improved, continuous balanced growth was to be guaranteed, and the prerequisites for all this were to be created in the ancillary industry, the raw material and power basis of the economy – but this demanded appropriate investments. Furthermore foreign debts were to be reduced, which required increased exports. As early as spring 1971, when the State Planning Commission submitted a first concept to the Politbüro of how the new 'main task' was to be implemented, it had to point out that neither the foreign-trade targets nor the social welfare measures were sufficiently ensured and that the plan concept as a whole could not be balanced. Yet Honecker demanded that concentration on the raising of the living standard must 'absolutely be kept' and that 'higher productivity ... should be attained through the development of consciousness'.[7] In the summer of 1971, the Minister of Finance and the president of the State Bank both pointed out at an early stage that increased imports were envisaged for the shortfalls in the plan, although no additional exports could be secured to finance them.[8]

The discrepancy between political aims and economic possibilities increasingly widened in the eyes of the State Planning Commission in the autumn of 1971. The state of the payment balance and the endowment of the economy with raw materials and semi-finished goods, as the planners put it, do 'not really make it possible to envisage improvements in working and living conditions in the near future'. Sporadically the comment was heard: 'In the past we had an overstretched structural policy and now consumption is overstretched'.[9] That was why, in January 1972, the State Planning Commission was not only massively criticised by the Politbüro, but the reduction of indebtedness in the West that had previously been striven for was put aside because, as Honecker put it, 'that would be directed against the resolutions of the Party Congress ... and mean the torpedoing of the main task'. Instead 'a substantial part of these debts to the capitalist states should be converted into long-term loans in order to ensure appropriate growth of the economy'.[10] But the State Planning Commission insisted that the social welfare programme exceeded the possibilities of the GDR, whereupon Stoph, the head of government, declared in the spring of 1972, rather as Honecker had a year earlier: 'If we appeal to the working class with the announcement of the social welfare measures, this will yield such results in production as are not yet contained in the calculations of the State Planning Commission'.[11] This argumentation reflected the faith in the omnipotence of politics over the economy and had little to do with the reality principle emphasised by Honecker on his assumption of power. For such certainties the structure of incentives provided no kind of guarantee and the new expanded social welfare policy could ultimately only be financed by even bigger debts. That way was bound to lead to economic ruin.

Social welfare policy in the GDR was not a new invention by Honecker. It had been practised pragmatically from the start, even if not called by this name. Even in the sixties, when social process was increasingly viewed through an economic lens, it had been extended. With Honecker's assumption of power, however, the function of social welfare policy changed, while at the same time it was greatly expanded.[12] As early as at the beginning of 1971 minimum wages and low incomes had been increased; the same was done again in 1976. The number of leave days was increased several times. Old-age pensions rose a few times but still remained low by comparison with other incomes. Working hours for employed mothers with several children were shortened, their holidays were prolonged and paid maternity leave was extended; maternity grants were also paid. Young married couples were granted interest-free credits of up to 5,000 Marks; these were partly remitted when the couple had children. Childcare institutions were further developed, so that by 1980 a crèche vacancy was available for 60 per cent of children in the appropriate age group and kindergarten places for more than 90 per cent of appropriate children.[13] These social welfare measures were designed not only to encourage women's employment, but also to act against the declining birth rate. Finally the measures also met the socialist claim of promoting the emancipation of women. By their participation in working life women did in fact become economically independent. At the same time, however, the social-political measures confirmed the traditional role assignment: only women, not both parents, benefited from the shorter working hours and the longer holidays. Ultimately this was intended to check the manpower shortage caused by manpower hoarding. However, in 1970, 89 per cent of the population of working age, including 82 per cent of women of working age, were employed. Further incentives were therefore needed to encourage, above all, more women to take up work. By 1980, 87 per cent and in 1989, 91 per cent of women of working age were employed.[14]

In addition, an ambitious residential building programme was embarked upon, designed to solve the housing problem as a 'social problem' by 1990. Between 1971 and 1975 some 500,000 residential units, and after that, until 1990, about 3 million units, were to be built. During the preceding years housing construction had lagged behind demand, the stock of old buildings was only scantily maintained and the equipment of homes was mostly far below modern standards. In this area therefore there was a real need to catch up. Admittedly this programme was not as new as it seemed: it was possible to go back to concepts worked out in the

State Planning Commission in the sixties. To ensure that the satisfaction of basic needs was within the reach of everybody, the prices for basic foodstuffs and children's clothing, energy rates, transport charges and rents were frozen at a low level. It was very obvious that the contents and standards of these social welfare measures were essentially based on the needs of working-class families between the wars, when most members of the Party leadership became politically socialised, while the population had long judged standards in lifestyle by the standards reached in the West. This discrepancy was bound to give rise to new discontent.

Whether or not this social welfare programme was economically feasible depended crucially on the extent to which the incentives for the employees worked. Since the Party's old dilemma of having to act simultaneously as 'overall entrepreneur' and as the representative of the workers was insoluble, the Party was essentially facing the same problem as before. From 1972 onwards the entire wage structure and the underlying work norms were to be revised and the existing 'levelling' overcome by strengthening individual incentives.[15] Next, an ambitious 'project of standard rates' was established. All the long-raised demands of wages and norm policy, i.e., new standard wages staggered according to the economic importance of the branches, technologically founded work norms and the re-grading of workers into wage brackets, were to be introduced step by step in order to bring about 'better relations of wages according to qualification, responsibility and performance' and 'deliberately to reduce wage differentials not justified by performance'. But since wages were not allowed to be lowered,[16] the project could not be paid for when, in the mid seventies, considerable additional costs arose from the first explosion of raw material prices and the changes in Comecon price setting.[17]

From 1976 onwards, all that was left of the project was the attempt to create a stronger incentive for the workers by new basic wages. That payment of basic wages, which included the former standard wage and part of the wage for increased performances, was now directly linked to the fulfilment of certain indicators, which could be influenced individually or collectively. As a result of the higher calculation basis both overfulfilment and underfulfilment of the norms had a greater bearing on the effective wage. As, however, wages were still not to be lowered and as available funds for their increase were severely limited, the scope for the creation of new wage structures remained slight. This fact, along with the continuing high labour shortage, was used by the workers for negotiating their wages individually. The same applied to the 'special salaries' for executive personnel, who could not be recruited for these jobs without them. All in all incentives for the employees remained insufficient and were in no way linked to the growing social benefits.

As a result of the increasingly centralised and product-oriented alignment of the control mechanism, even the slight potentials for increasing efficiency of the earlier reform were no longer working. Whereas in the last years of the reform only 200 to 250 distributional balances had been made out at the highest level, from 1972 onwards some 800 raw materials, other materials, equipment and consumer goods were balanced by the State Planning Commission and the ministries.[18] Moreover, since 1971 the State Planning Commission controlled individual investment projects by 'title lists', which continued the registers of 'structure-determining' investment projects. The use of investment funds by the enterprises was now also strictly tied to the plan.

A particular focus of control, according to the goal of the 'main task', was consumer goods. From 1971 onwards, about 230 'vital supply' goods and product groups were centrally planned according to quantity and value, and sometimes according to price categories, where previously it had only been 140. From 1973 on these were to be supported by about 900 'assortment balances', so that about 90 per cent of goods on offer to the population were 'planned and balanced in a product-specific and per-value and quantity' manner.[19] As a result the highest degree of penetration of product-oriented control for consumer goods was reached.

Simultaneously the financial instruments and incentive mechanisms were losing the importance originally intended for them, even though they were not entirely abolished. In contrast to the reform period, profit was no longer the principal indicator by which the performance of enterprises was measured, but 'commodity production'. Everything else was subordinated to the growth of this 'commodity production'. Thus the old gross principle was once more valid: the more costly an enterprise's production, the more it could bring to account. The remaining indirect control instruments were again consistently tied to the plan and its fulfilment. At the same time, however, there were some continuities from the reform period. Thus greater use was already being made of centralist control instruments in the final reform phase with its 'structure-determining planning'. And a few instruments developed during the reform, such as the production fund charge, were kept on. However, the overall character of the control mechanism had fundamentally changed.

Enterprises tended more, as in the sixties, to hoard manpower and material resources of all kinds again. Managements took the view that it was 'better to have a little more stock than shutting down production for lack of material once more'. Another argument heard was: 'We sometimes buy in larger stocks in order to have something to barter with'.[20] Because of the rigid rules on the planning and use of funds, the enterprises were unable to react purposefully and flexibly to new demands within the annual plan. Economic activity closely oriented on the annual plan contradicted the long-term character of investments and impeded innovation. The rigidity and pervasiveness of central control further increased in the course of the decade. Towards the end of the seventies some chief executives of the combines pointed out that 'with the regulations issued on planning the tendency has grown over the past few years more and more to saddle the combines with detailed tasks, tasks which should preferably be within their own discretion'.[21] This inflexibility in the economic system was further enhanced when, after Honecker's assumption of power in 1972, the remaining small and medium-sized private and semi-state enterprises, as well as bigger craft cooperatives, were expropriated. This meant the removal of relatively flexible economic units that had lent the economy a little adaptive elasticity.

Between 1960 – the end of the previous socialisation campaign in industry – and 1970, the number of private industrial enterprises was halved from 6,476 to 3,184. The share of industrial workers in these enterprises diminished from 6 per cent to less than 3 per cent. Simultaneously the number of enterprises with state participation rose from 4,455 to 5,632 and the share of their workers rose slightly from 10.5 per cent to 12.5 per cent.[22] The private sector had also – as earlier – been impeded and pressurised in the sixties. Above all, it was still disadvantaged in the allocation of resources. Moreover, private and semi-state enterprises were increasingly pressured to provide input requirements for state enterprises. Without touching ownership, relationships of dependence were thus created. In December 1970 a package of measures was introduced designed to diminish the incomes of private entrepreneurs and of partners of semi-state enterprises. At the same time it was intended forcibly to bring about higher performance through higher taxes, for instance by introducing the production fund charge (essentially a tax on capital and previously only applicable to the state sector) in the non-state sector. Payments for adjustment of profits, which had been introduced with the industrial price reform in the sixties in order not to raise consumer prices and to avoid production stoppages, were now abolished. These and other measures – given a formally equal treatment – were a greater burden for private and semi-state enterprises than for those in the state sector, which received more resources and funds. As a result, in the spring of 1971, a growing number of private partners threatened to recall their shares, which would have resulted in the shutdown of the enterprises. This had to be prevented if only because of the feared production losses, though it seems that this was not possible everywhere.

These problems with private enterprises led, after the spring and summer of 1971, to the East German Party leaders considering ridding themselves of this headache for good by transferring these enterprises into state ownership. These plans were driven forward by the growing difficulties of basing Honecker's new political course on a solid economic foundation. However, 'the impression must absolutely be blurred that the middle-class enterprises are urgently needed to fill the gaps in the plan'.[23] For this reason the takeover into state ownership was ideologically justified to the public, but could also be understood as calculated social policy in a negative sense: with his dictum about the 'former small capitalists … who have … blossomed into millionaires',[24] Honecker fed a social envy that was present in the population. The last private and semi-state entrepreneurs had, in 1971, on average about three-and-a-half times the net income of workers and employees after all.[25] Despite the economic background this class-struggle impetus played the decisive part, as the nationalisation campaign, based as it was on central decisions of February 1972, became increasingly radical. Some 11,000 industrially producing craft cooperatives, semi-state and private enterprises were eventually affected: in 1971 they had produced 11 per cent of gross industrial output and employed just under 15 per cent of industrial manpower.[26] In semi-state enterprises the shares of the private general partners were paid out by the state, while private enterprises were formally purchased by the state and transferred into People's ownership. The purchasing price represented a small compensation. As a result of this step private property was very nearly suppressed in the sphere of production, even though certain forms were to be revitalised in the late seventies and eighties in order to increase the supply of consumer goods. The Party had thus brought to an end a special development in the Eastern Bloc. In most of the other countries 'social' ownership of the means of production had been completed in the early transformation phases. The GDR's peculiarity was probably chiefly due to the situation of a divided Germany.

The Party leadership, however, had not considered the consequences of this adoption in the medium term. Many of the enterprises affected had, until then, also manufactured final products, especially in the area of small everyday consumer goods. After their inclusion in major state enterprises they were often reduced to subcontracting enterprises. As a result many consumer goods disappeared from the market and new 'supply gaps' were created. Consumer policy had been dealt a blow.

Nevertheless, the economic situation was stabilised again by 1973 after the 1969/70 crisis. With generally lowered growth targets ancillary industries had received more funds and resources and were thus better able to satisfy the demand of their customers. Even the investments of Ulbricht's technology offensive now gradually became effective in production. Productivity in 1973/74 again increased by 6 per cent to 7 per cent, though this was to remain the peak figure in the Honecker era.[27] However the attained stability was in part bought through foreign trade: the trade deficit vis-à-vis the non-socialist economy area continued to grow.

Fewer Investments and Innovations?

Under Honecker the Party leadership only slightly reduced the proportion of gross investments in the economic product (value added) compared with the high values during Ulbricht's final phase. At just under 33 per cent the investment quota in 1976/77 was even higher before it began to decline steadily after 1979. What was more decisive, however, was the fact that, due to Honecker's economic strategy, the proportion of 'productively' used net investments as a proportion of value added was lowered in the course of the seventies: from just under 17 per cent in 1969/70 to 14 per cent in 1978 and just under 10 per cent in 1982. Instead, more investments went into the consumer sphere, especially into house building. In 1970 it had required only 7 per cent of the gross investments, in 1978 it was already 11 per cent and in 1982 eventually 12 per cent.[28] Within industry the central authority reassigned investments in the early seventies. To begin with, the projects of Ulbricht's structural policy were essentially completed. As a result, the share of uncompleted projects as a proportion of industrial investments rose steadily from 61 per cent to 79 per cent between 1969 and 1972.[29] Alongside these projects yet to be completed, new large-scale projects in the sectors of energetics and fuel industries were started in order to do away with the deficits in electric power supply. The same applied to consumer goods production and the ancillary industry. The relatively greatest investments between 1971 and 1973 were nevertheless in the branches which had already been in the forefront of the structural policy in the late sixties and had been considered to have a promising future: with plastic and elastic-processing engineering, machine tool manufacture, electronics, data processing and office machines.

The growing number of new projects at the time of a reduced increase in overall investments caused the percentage of unfinished investments to rise ever more until the beginning of the eighties. This development was further encouraged by centralistic control: in order to get their projects included in the plan, enterprises initially set the volume of their projects as low as possible. During realisation the started projects became steadily more expensive; additional equipment was demanded, but this could often not be provided in time or on demand. Although the efficiency of the investments rose between 1971 and 1974, afterwards it declined again until 1978 and after a temporary improvement collapsed in 1982, again nearly reaching its low point of 1961 (cf. Figure 2). Capital productivity in the economy as a whole also initially declined only slightly until 1978 and then massively until 1982. Admittedly, about one-third of all machines and equipment in 1980 was no older than five years. At the same time the replacement rate – the proportion of written-off equipment of the total equipment – was above 50 per cent.[30] This stock of outdated equipment reflected the imbalance between performed expansion investments and omitted replacement investments, the result of the declining proportion of 'productive' investments.

These trends were the subject of an analysis that was prepared in the State Planning Commission and submitted to the Party leadership in the autumn of 1979. It observed critically that these trends were increasing the costs of repairs and maintenance. Besides, it was impossible to react speedily and flexibly to new developments in science and technology, i.e., innovations, because too many funds were tied up for too long in large-scale projects. The State Planning Commission proposed that investments in the 'productive' areas should be markedly raised, that in the consumption sphere they should be concentrated on house building and that they should not be allowed to grow any further in education, health and social welfare. The problems revealed in this analysis were in fact acknowledged in the Politbüro; Honecker demanded: 'Here the course must really be altered.' But the meeting did not wish to follow the structural-political proposals. In the end, the resolution concluded: '[T]he analysis was merely taken note of, but not circulated'. The measures decided upon were largely confined to stricter control over the use of funds. But this was not enough in itself to cope effectively with the problematic investment developments.[31]

At the same time expenditures in the military and security sphere rose disproportionately between 1976 and 1978, reaching a proportion of nearly 13 per cent of budgetary expenditure. In spite of the détente between the superpowers the Warsaw Pact continued to rely on military superiority. A new round of an arms race was evolving, which is why the armaments industry in the GDR was expanded after 1975. Because of the escalating debts at the end of the seventies expenditure on the military and on security could no longer be driven up, so that its share in the state budget declined to 11 per cent by 1982.[32]

These expenses and, even more so, those on the consumer and social welfare programme, had, since the early seventies, limited the money that could be made available for the development of science and technology. For that reason research and development were now concentrated on the short and medium term and on what was feasible in the GDR. Expressions such as 'forecasts' and 'science and technology', which under Ulbricht were keywords in the Party language, were for the time being not among the standard formulas under the new Party chief. Likewise, the originally planned development of large-scale science centres (*Großforschungseinrichtungen*) was halted. In consequence hundreds of university graduates, mainly mathematicians, information scientists, physicists and chemists, had difficulty finding a job, and often had to take one that did not correspond to their qualifications. It was no great novelty that scientific-technological problems had to take a back seat in the economic bureaucracy and in the enterprises, but this ignorance right up to the top levels of the economic hierarchy acquired a new level at the beginning of the Honecker era.

The foreign market shares achieved by research-intensive GDR products, such as machine tools, data processing and accountancy machines, optical and precision mechanical products, as well as printing machinery, was usually below 5 per cent in the early seventies and not infrequently below 1 per cent.[33] The breakdown of a number of innovative developments further widened the existing gap between GDR products and international development. The increasing sales problems in export were a major reason why attempts were made again to close the technological gap with the West. From 1973 onwards the Party apparatus once more demanded that the credit-financed imports of modern technology from Western countries be stepped up for the use of export-intensive branches. With the export of products manufactured with these investments the credits should later be redeemed. This strategy, originally propagated by Ulbricht, had initially been rejected after his replacement, but was now being justified by a similar policy in the Soviet Union.[34] At the same time intensive growth factors were to be mobilised, in other words production increased through a better use of the production factors employed. As consumption could not be lowered for political reasons, and because foreign indebtedness – especially with worldwide rising interest rates at the end of the seventies and the beginning of the eighties – must have its limits, investments could only be redistributed and concentrated on key sectors. They had to increase the competitiveness of GDR products, as well as render the economic process itself more efficient.

In 1977 the Party leadership therefore decided to concentrate efforts on the development of microelectronics, which had increasingly emerged worldwide as the new basic innovation. In this way the GDR's export potential could be strengthened and production intensified. At that point in time, according to an internal report, 'the GDR's lag behind the international peak amounted from four to eight years for analogue circuits, to six or seven years for digital semiconductor memories and microprocessors, and anything up to nine years for equipment for the manufacture of semiconductor materials and other crucial procedures'.[35] Ironically, when such developments had been cut short in the GDR with Honecker's political about-turn in the early seventies, it seemed that the GDR was close on the heels of the 'world level'. The intention now was to cooperate in this task with the Soviet Union, but this proved difficult in view of its notorious secretiveness even towards its own partner countries. In consequence, know-how was to be acquired at great cost chiefly in the West, 'partially by conspiratorial means ... because most of the equipment is under embargo', as Alexander Schalck-Golodkowski, head of the division Kommerzielle Koordinierung ('Commercial Coordination'), informed Mittag.[36] This division had a share in the fact that from 1977/78 the first microprocessors were available: these were either 'purchases' in the West or clones of Western circuit elements. In the final third of the seventies it is thought that about 2 billion Marks was spent on the microelectronics programme, which corresponded to roughly 12 per cent of the then annual net investments in the 'producing' sector.[37] However, the lag behind the West did not diminish and industrial production was technologically increasingly lagging behind the world market standard. As a result, export earnings declined. Whereas in 1970 the GDR still achieved 0.54 Valutamark of exports to the non-socialist economic area for every Mark spent domestically, in 1980 it was a mere 0.45 Valutamark.[38]

The division Kommerzielle Koordinierung (KoKo) had been created in 1966 in the Foreign Trade Ministry, in response to the GDR's chronic shortage of Western foreign currency. It was charged with the task of gaining as much convertible foreign currency as possible by dealing outside the plan. Its initiator and chief Schalck-Golodkowski extended the division from the beginning of the seventies and thereby also strengthened his own position within the GDR ruling structure. This organisation very quickly managed to obtain, illegally or semi-legally, technological products listed on Western embargo lists for export to the Eastern Bloc states (COCOM-list). This kind of economic espionage had already been demanded by Ulbricht: 'Where you get it from, where you steal it, is a matter of complete indifference to me ...', he had told leading scientists and technicians in 1962.[39] If only because of this illegal activity KoKo was personally and institutionally closely linked to the Ministry for State Security. To enable it to perform its tasks, KoKo was given the status of a non-resident person in the early seventies and thus a special position in the GDR's economic cycle, beyond the valid legal order and the plan bureaucracy. Thus it freed itself, in practice, from government control. From 1976 onwards KoKo was subordinated only to Mittag and Honecker. They alone could dispose the Western currency obtained, which lent them additional power. Similarly Schalck-Golodkowski and the division were directly assigned to the Ministry for State Security and its chief Erich Mielke.

With this position KoKo was intended to make the most of the special status of German–German economic relations in the interests of the GDR. This special status arose from the legal concept of the Federal Republic under which the GDR was not a foreign country, so that GDR products could be imported free from customs duty and with taxation benefits. In practice the GDR – as laid down in a special protocol of the 1957 Treaties of Rome – belonged to the European Single Market. Koko was expected, in the seventies, to earn a maximum of Western currency in order to finance the imports of capital goods. It is thought that four-fifths of KoKo imports of supplies for the economy were accounted for by modern technologies.[40] It is difficult to assess the importance of the technology imports performed by KoKo. Purely quantitatively they amounted in the second half of the seventies, at a cautious estimate, to 8 per cent (probably a little less) of the investments in machines and equipments made by the economy over the same period. Yet this form of technology transfer only provided isolated applications and was unable to abolish the system's restraints on innovations. In consequence the efficiency gains achieved by it were bound to remain limited. The remaining one-fifth of KoKo imports also included consumer goods for the East German Party leaders and other top officials, as well as for the population. Supplies to the leading officials probably came to less than 1 per cent of the Western currency earned by KoKo, which was economically negligible but politically explosive. Admittedly, KoKo's contribution to the population's consumer goods supply, according to a judgment made for the investigating commission of the Bundestag in 1994, 'hardly came to more than some sweets of the political leaders on certain occasions, as well as imports to bridge oppressing shortages'. Besides, Honecker and Mittag, in the seventies, made about 1 billion D-Marks available every year from the KoKo-earned foreign currency in order to relieve the payments balance.[41]

KoKo consistently used the possibilities deriving from its special position on the frontline of the two systems. However, it could only serve as a 'fire brigade' to solve individual problems. As the difficulties were growing all round, this special division's importance for the Party leadership increased in the Honecker era. It is probably one of the ironies of GDR economic history that the stability of the system had to be buttressed by an instrument standing outside the system.

Concentration in Industry and Agriculture

Towards the end of the seventies all industrial enterprises were to be concentrated into combines. These conglomerates were to include all enterprises with identical products, manufacturing processes or raw materials to be processed (horizontal integration) or else enterprises with linked manufacturing steps (vertical integration); a conglomerate was to cover the entire value-added chain from research and development to sales. These combines, Mittag hoped, would ensure a faster application of innovations, improved interlinking, more efficient use of machinery and other cost advantages – in short synergy effects. It was also expected that coordination between sectors would be simplified and planning made more flexible. To concentrate enterprises in this way was not in itself a bad idea. The idea of combining consecutive processes was not an invention of socialist planners, but with appropriate prerequisites it reflected a rational organisation of production, of which sensible concepts and positive examples existed also in the GDR. But already during the first great waves of combine foundation, in the final third of the sixties, decisions were taken on technocratic grounds and without proper economic calculation. It was obvious even then that the Fordist model of production had a lot of attraction for the GDR leaders because with ever larger (and hence fewer) production units the control process became less complex. That such an organisation also meant a loss of flexibility in the economy, and the fact that by the seventies it was already beginning to be abandoned in Western developed countries, evidently escaped the notice of the GDR.

After 1978 there were 133 combines created directly subordinate to the central authority, most of them a horizontal association of producers of identical or similar products. Monopolies were being deliberately created and anything that might have resulted in competition between enterprises or combines was eliminated. As a result they were in a position to dictate delivery terms. Innovations, as also the quality of products, were falling behind. In this situation the combines tended to develop into self-sufficient economic units, a trend promoted by the central authority by demanding that the combines produce their own equipment and devices for rationalisation. Thus they began to produce their required inputs themselves, like screws and nuts, instead of benefiting from mass production. From the viewpoint of the combines, this made sense so long as it was uncertain whether they would receive their inputs in any other way. For the economy as a whole, however, this attitude reduced the degree of division of labour and meant a considerable loss of efficiency.

In agriculture, too, the Party relied on economies of scale by creating more specialised mega-enterprises. In the Cooperative Crop Production Department, created as early as the end of the sixties, several Agricultural Production Cooperatives or people-owned estates jointly cultivated arable and grass land. These production units now reduced their cultivation programme to a few crops or cultures. From 1972/73 onwards the Cooperative Crop Production Departments were developed into ever larger agrarian complexes; these were specialised on individual foodstuffs. The participating Agricultural Production Cooperatives and people-owned estates jointly planned and organised their production, accountancy and the distribution both of their products and of their income. In 1975 about 1,200 such units cultivated 79 per cent of the farmland. Their average size was 4,130 hectares, which was fifteen times the size of the cooperatives at the end of collectivisation in the early sixties.[42] In the mid seventies a further step forward was taken when arable and stock farming were separated, and thus a tradition of German agriculture, where usually both were carried out together, was abandoned. The concentration of livestock corresponded to the concentration of acreage and decision power. At the end of the seventies just under one-third of fattening pigs were kept in sties with more than 3,000 boxes and Agricultural Production Cooperatives for animal production had on average more than 1,500 livestock units. The concentration reached its peak in 1977/78 with the 'Grüneberg Plan', so called after the responsible Politbüro member. This programme, orientated on American models, aimed at industrialising agriculture, eliminating the differences between town and country and 'advancing' the 'cooperative peasants' into a part of the working class.

The separation of animal and crop production led to sharp arguments about the volume, the quality and the dates of fodder deliveries, about manpower utilisation, supplies of natural manure and spread of liquid manure. In general the greater enterprises meant greater transport costs. The machines used were getting ever larger and heavier. As a result the soil got compacted, the top soil was destroyed and yields declined. This diminished the economies of scale, which had anyway been reduced by rising expenditure on epidemic control and hygiene in stockfarming, not to mention the growing environmental problems. Ultimately the large-scale fattening centres for cattle and pigs proved a failure. Any further concentration of agriculture was eventually halted in 1978 and after Grüneberg's death in 1981 a hesitant start was made at again reducing the size of units.[43] In the seventies agriculture again suffered several harvest failures whose extent was made worse by the organisational transformations. In order to safeguard supplies, additional grain imports from the West were necessary between 1971 and 1978, to a value of 3.8 billion Valutamarks, which had a corresponding impact on the balance of payments.[44]

And More Consumption?

At the beginning of the seventies it was still difficult to provide the necessary quantities of consumer goods in all price categories to meet Honecker's promises and to improve the living standard of the population. By the middle of the decade, however, it became possible to offer more goods that were satisfactory in choice, quality and price, as production of consumer goods had been stepped up, export of such products had been cut down and considerable imports had been received. Moreover, in 1971 consumer prices were frozen and eventually also prices within industry. While this helped to reduce the rise of consumer prices, it proved hardly possible to keep the prices of textiles and clothing stable, because increased production could only be ensured by the more expensive synthetic fibres. Enterprises tried, as before, to drive their cost and price calculation upwards by their 'well-tried' methods. Thus it was not possible to keep consumer prices constant everywhere. The share of price increases in the turnover growth found its level at about 25 per cent by the mid seventies. But this share rose again after 1977, also because of price increases in the world markets, so that by 1980 it nearly reached 60 per cent.[45]

Yet prices and tariffs for the population's basic needs had to be kept stable whatever happened. Hence as their costs rose as well, subsidies from the state budget had to be increased. These grew (excluding rent subsidies) from 7.4 billion Marks in 1970 to 21.5 billion Marks in 1982; their proportion of state expenditure increased from 13 per cent to 14 per cent. Thus in 1982 just under 16 per cent of the population's consumption-related expenses (other than rents) were subsidised; in 1967 it had been barely 7 per cent and in the year before Honecker's assumption of power if had been just over 10 per cent.[46] This policy was expected to result in increased performances by the workers. But as the relevant incentives were not directly linked to the social welfare regulations, the hoped-for results again failed to materialise. Indeed the improvement of the material standard of living and the apparent guarantee of social security – neither of them achieved or affected by one's own performance – had a long-term negative effect on performance motivation, the more so as neither the first nor the 'second wage packet' (health and social services, education and housing) made it seem possible to reach the level of West Germany, the constant reference point. At the same time the free or highly subsidised services and the subsidies for basic-needs goods and services were clearly rising faster than gross labour incomes. Broadly speaking, more was consumed in the seventies than produced.[47]

Net money incomes per head of the population in the seventies rose faster at 4 per cent annually on average than during the preceding decade (3 per cent) and between 1972 and 1974 increased by a leap.[48] As income increased and consumption-related benefits failed to give production and productivity the hoped-for stimulus, there was a shortage in the medium term of goods and services to satisfy a well-funded demand. It was still possible in the seventies to keep deficits small, so that retail turnover rose more rapidly than net money incomes and private households were being better supplied with industrial consumer goods.[49] However, the lag behind the Federal Republic continued to be considerable, especially with regard to motorcars and colour television sets, and certainly in product quality.

Table 5.1: Number of selected industrial consumer goods per 100 households in 1970, 1975 and 1980[50]

	1970	1975	1980
Motorcars	15.6	26.2	38.1
TV sets	73.6	87.9	105.0
Refrigerators	56.4	84.7	108.8
Washing machines	53.6	73.0	84.4

After 1977 the 'Exquisit' and 'Delikat' shops were further extended; they now also offered Western goods. This was designed to check the growing unrest caused by the 'Intershops', which sold Western and other high-quality articles for Western currencies. These had been created in 1962, initially to enable foreigners to make purchases for convertible currencies and to earn hard currency for the GDR. After 1974, when GDR citizens were permitted to own Western currencies, they too were allowed to shop there. In this way the 'Western money' accumulated in the pockets of GDR citizens was made useful for the state. 'Exquisit' and 'Delikat', on the other hand, increasingly became an inherent part of normal supplies. What seemed like growing affluence on the one hand was causing increasing shortages on the other. As early as 1977 enterprises and authorities were instructed to restrict their consumer goods and energy use to the absolutely necessary minimum. The central authority decreed further economy measures: street lighting was reduced, use of petrol and paper restricted; coffee, cocoa and tropical fruit must no longer be acquired with state money. These were harbingers of the coming crisis. Hidden price rises in 1977 led to hoarding purchases of textiles and foodstuffs. Because of rising world market prices it was decided in the summer of the same year that only two brands of coffee would be on offer, plus a mixture of coffee and a substitute. Public institutions were only allowed to offer the coffee mixture. This mixture, popularly nicknamed 'Erich's Krönung' (a reference to the well-known West German coffee brand 'Jacobs Krönung') caused further unrest. State authorities were flooded with complaints, so that crude coffee imports were again increased. However, the cheapest brand was taken out of the supply, a new more expensive one was introduced and thus the price of coffee increased on average. What the 'coffee crisis' revealed was a vicious circle of rising world market prices, supply disruptions and loyalty losses – a vicious circle from which the Party was unable to escape right up to its end.[51]

As demand continued to exceed the retail trade offer and as world market prices had once more greatly risen, Mittag, in the summer of 1979, instructed the State Planning Commission to work out proposals for price increases, half of which were to be shifted on to the population. In this way it was intended to pass on the growing import costs of raw materials and establish a balance of supply and demand on the domestic market. But Honecker rejected these proposals. Such a policy contradicted his understanding of socialism. The State Planning Commission's chief later had this to say about Honecker's reaction: 'The people need cheap bread, a dry apartment and work. If these three things are all right, nothing can happen to socialism.' He added: 'Any price modification leading to new burdens for the population was therefore unthinkable to Honecker. He always said that all the great counter-revolutionary developments in the other socialist countries, such as Poland, started with price rises.'[52] The Party chief believed that if price rises were to happen in the GDR, 'the Politbüro might as well resign and the government as well'.[53] And he threatened: 'At the next plenary session [of the Central Committee] anybody who runs down our consumer goods industry, this great development of the past few years, or the consumer goods turnover will get his face pushed in ...'[54] In this way all subsequent attempts to tackle the problem of consumer prices were fended off, while the problem got worse as a result of growing domestic costs and rising prices in the world market. As at the same time this attitude made it impossible to use price increases for lessening the imbalance between the purchasing power of the population and the goods on offer, the imbalance continued to increase. After this dispute Mittag never again opposed Honecker's policy. On the contrary, he not only seemed to follow it unconditionally, but he also made good use of the scope offered him by the economically inexperienced and uninterested Honecker.

The economic-policy course of the Honecker era produced ambivalent results in the economy of the seventies. Initially the country still profited from the yields of the late Ulbricht era and the growing costs were financed by increasing foreign debts. At just under 5 per cent the average annual growth rate of economic productivity between 1971 and 1982 was more or less at the level of the reform period. In the course of time, however, it dropped: from nearly 6 per cent in the first half of the seventies to just over 4 per cent in the subsequent years until 1982. This narrowed the distribution margin, which could only be enlarged at the expense of the balance of payments. Economic structure continued to develop as in the sixties: the share of industry in gross value added increased, reaching 62 per cent in 1982 and even 65 per cent in 1989. Agriculture declined in importance. At the beginning of the eighties it yielded 12 per cent, but in 1989 a mere 10 per cent. At the same time it was remarkable that transport and postal services, telecommunications and domestic trade were all losers in relative terms.[55] This reflected the unbroken priority of industry, whose structure became somewhat more modern during the seventies: the share of energetics and fuel as a proportion of industrial net production declined from 16 per cent to 12 per cent between 1970 and 1982, whereas the weight of the chemical industry rose from 23 per cent to 25 per cent, just as that of engineering and vehicle construction, whose share increased from 20 per cent to 22 per cent. Electrical engineering and electronics increased their share of industrial net production from 7 per cent to 10 per cent. The shares of the consumer-orientated industrial sectors of the light, textiles and foodstuffs industries, on the other hand, declined slightly.[56]

Debt Crisis

It was in consumption that Honecker wanted to show success: it was to go up, even though the total product gained did not grow as he hoped. As, however, in the interest of future growth, investments were not allowed to decline, more had to be imported than was exported. Already by 1972/73 the trade deficit vis-à-vis the Western world had greatly increased; total debts in the non-socialist economic area rose by 43 per cent from 1970 to 1971 and by a further 36 per cent by the end of 1972.[57] The State Planning Commission tried to put a brake on this at the beginning of 1973:

> The take-up of further credits is only acceptable from the standpoint of political elbow-room for our foreign policy, as well as with regard to economic strength, if equalised trade balances can be ensured for the next years and, beyond that, an export surplus for the financing of interests and services.[58]

Nevertheless, trade with the Western countries increasingly proceeded under the slogan: Whatever the cost, Western currency must be achieved. For that reason no efficiency gains were recorded below the line, but economic losses: what ultimately mattered was the availability of the imported goods.

When, as a result of the Yom Kippur war at the end of 1973, the world market prices for raw materials exploded for the first time, the GDR leaders initially regarded this as a phenomenon confined to the capitalist market; they believed that the prices would fall again in the foreseeable future. Because of the price-setting principles in Comecon, the market turbulences only reached the costs of GDR raw material imports with a delay; hence nothing was done at first in terms of economic policy. Admittedly, at the request of the Soviet Union, Comecon prices after 1975 were no longer, as until then, set for a five-year period – something the GDR had greatly profited from in the years before. In future they were to be based, each year anew, on the average of the world market prices for the past five years; i.e., the 1976 prices were based on the prices from 1971 to 1975. The increased world market prices were now more speedily noticed by the GDR also in its Comecon trade: until 1976 the GDR had been paying 50 per cent of the world market price for the crude oil imported from the Soviet Union; by 1978 it was 80 per cent.[59] The GDR imported crude oil, natural gas, copper, rolled steel and cellulose from the Soviet Union; the Soviets in return demanded 'hard' goods, such as chemical products and consumer goods that could have been marketed in the West too.

In theory the raw materials could have been just as well obtained from Western countries. But here the difficulty was the GDR's shortage of Western currency and the lacking competitiveness of its manufactures. Hence, if only on economic grounds, there was no alternative, quite apart from the political reasons that prohibited such an option. The Soviet Union used its partner's situation and demanded – as it had done before – that GDR production became even more focused on Soviet requirements. Thus the East German leadership found itself more and more in a dilemma: if it wanted to reduce its debt to the West it needed products that were marketable in the West; if it wanted to buy raw materials at relatively low prices it had to intensify its exports to the Soviet Union. Hence 'neither of the economic areas [West and East] was allowed to be neglected in export promotion'.[60] But to do both together was too much for the GDR economy.

Between 1971 and 1981, GDR imports from Western industrial countries exceeded the value of goods and services exported to those countries by nearly 40 billion Valutamarks. This cumulative deficit was more than double the GDR's 1981 exports to those countries.[61] But the GDR's resulting growing foreign debt in the seventies was not so much due to the population's improved supplies, but primarily to the diminishing international competitiveness of the GDR's investment goods sector and the country's dependence on raw materials.[62] After representatives of the State Planning Commission and the State Bank had warned against that course very early; the directors of two Party-owned research institutions, the Central Institute for Socialist Economy Management and the Academy for Social Sciences, pointed out to Honecker, in an analysis at the turn of 1974/75, that this policy was at the expense of the country's future economic possibilities because it was making debts abroad, investing too little and thus eating into its capital. They proposed that the subsidies from which the population benefited be reduced and that higher performances be more consistently demanded from the workers. These ideas, along with the other austerity measures they proposed, were by no means new. But the Party leaders ignored them and all other warnings, some of them put forward by the State Planning Commission chief, Schürer.[63] The Politbüro was less afraid of impending insolvency than 'that the economic situation might possibly compel us to make cuts in social benefits',[64] since these might result in incalculable reactions from the population.

The scope left to the GDR was narrowed down even further: the more expensive raw material deliveries from the Soviet Union demanded increased GDR deliveries in return or else an increase in the debt the GDR had with its hegemonic power. In March 1977 Schürer and Mittag alerted Honecker in a letter: 'For the first time we are in acute payment difficulties.' Honecker saw this as an attack on his person and policy and firmly rejected it. As such an attack came dangerously close to being seen as an infringement of Party decisions – a Communist sacrilege – the two authors gave way and promised to 'correct their formulations'.[65] To defuse the situation Honecker wanted to rapidly resort to the funds of the KoKo division.

The second price leap of crude oil in the world market in the period 1979–81 was again cushioned by Comecon price setting. The GDR was now able to process crude oil imported relatively cheaply from the Soviet Union and export it for foreign currency to the West; this prevented its debt to the West from rising any further. In this way it made maximal use of the subsidies implicitly granted by the Soviet Union; these arose from price differentials of the goods exchanged in relation to the world market. The oil business had initially been supported by the Soviet Union – presumably because they were expected to relieve some of its own burdens.[66] Later the Soviets viewed them with growing scepticism and in 1981 they eventually reduced their contractually agreed oil deliveries from 19 million tonnes to 17 million tonnes annually. This was no longer enough to cover both the GDR's domestic requirements and the exports needed to safeguard its balance of payments. In spite of vigorous efforts by the East German Party leadership Moscow did not yield, not even to the argument that this might destabilise the GDR. Indeed there were cryptic hints that the Soviet Union was itself on the brink of the abyss. In actual fact there had been a number of consecutive harvest failures, there was a shortage of essential industrial products, productivity was declining and costs were rising as a result of the new round of the armaments race. In the end the agreed quantity continued to be delivered, but the contentious 2 million tonnes now had to be paid for in convertible foreign currency, which shrank the GDR's holding of them even further.[67]

When Honecker came to power at the beginning of the seventies, the GDR's debts in the non-socialist economic area amounted to about 2 billion Valutamarks.[68] By 1980 they had risen to 23.6 billion Valutamarks, peaking in 1982 with 25.1 billion Valutamarks. Decisive for the GDR's foreign-currency liquidity and under political aspects, however, was its debt in convertible currency, which did not contain the special-terms credits from the Federal Republic and several developing countries. In this field the GDR's debts reached their peak in 1980/81 with about 20 billion

Valutamarks (almost 11 billion dollars). In 1980 this was four times and in 1981 – due to intensified export efforts – 'only' 2.9 times the GDR's exports in the same direction.[69] The State Planning Commission's chief had repeatedly warned against the consequences of such a development. At the beginning of 1979, along with the Minister of Finance and the presidents of the State Bank and the Foreign Trade Bank, he had pointed out that it was internationally assumed that borrowers did not use more than 25 per cent of their foreign currency incomes for redemption and interest. The GDR, however, they argued, already had a debt-servicing rate of 115 per cent; for the critical convertible foreign currency the figure was even 168 per cent. Their conclusion was: 'As foreign-currency expenditure on interest payments and credit redemption greatly exceed the income [in Western currencies], the cash deficits are growing larger every year. In order to balance them, further cash credits are being taken up, which further increases debts and interests. This spiral cannot be continued.'[70] The problem became even more acute when, at the end of the seventies and the beginning of the eighties, interest rates were rapidly rising in the international capital market. Even the Federal Republic's politically based transfer payments for road traffic, postal services, etc., which rose from about 800 million DM in 1975 to 1.8 billion DM in 1979, were no longer able to cover the burden of interest in the area of convertible currency after the end of the seventies.[71]

One group loyal to Moscow within the East German Party leadership did not at all like the trend of growing debts to the West and eventually denounced it in Moscow. As a consequence the East German Party leaders were now also being repeatedly warned by their Soviet comrades against allowing the GDR's dependence on the West to increase even further. Under Soviet pressure they decided in the summer of 1980 to halve their debt by 1985: the debt to the West, assumed at 25 billion Valutamarks for the end of 1980 was to be reduced to 13.9 billion Valutamarks by 1985. This amount was regarded by Mittag as 'politically and economically justifiable, given the international level'.[72] However, this could not be done in a hurry, either by increasing exports or reducing imports. The latter remained necessary, as in the rest of the Eastern Bloc states, in order to make up for the innovation deficits of the country's own system as well as the stagnating division of labour within Comecon. In addition to the Federal Republic it was now France, Austria and Japan that had become important trade partners of the GDR. During the seventies, grain and cattlefeed had been imported chiefly from the US because the Soviet Union, although it had promised to supply these, was unable to deliver. In 1981 agreed hard coal deliveries from Poland and the Soviet Union failed to materialise; these too had to be replaced by Western imports. When the Eastern hegemonic power finally cut its oil supplies and the West imposed a virtual credit boycott against the Eastern Bloc countries, the GDR, in view of the described developments and its debts, was very nearly insolvent in 1982. The main reasons were the lack of international competitiveness of East German products and the improved social benefits, which were not financed by its own growth of productivity. But there were also deeper causes: the system, having already, since the late fifties, proved itself largely incapable of transforming the economy from an extensive to an intensive growth path, was equally incapable, in the seventies, of reacting to the drastically changed global economic settings. An economic policy not adapted to that situation further intensified this inflexibility immanent in the system.

Notes

1. *Protokoll der Verhandlungen des VIII. Parteitages der SED, 15. bis 19. Juni 1971,* Vol. II, Berlin (East) 1971, p. 296.
2. Staritz, *Geschichte der DDR*, p. 278.
3. Peter Hübner and Jürgen Danyel, 'Soziale Argumente im politischen Machtkampf: Prag, Warschau, Berlin 1968–1971', *Zeitschrift für Geschichtswissenschaft* 50, 2002, pp. 804–32, quotation p. 807.
4. SPK, Staatssekretär: Persönliche Niederschrift über die Beratung der Grundlinie … im Politbüro [am 23.3.1971], 24.3.1971, BA Berlin DE1/56131.
5. SPK, Staatssekretär: Persönliche Niederschrift über die Beratung der Grundlinie … im Politbüro [am 23.3.1971], 24.3.1971, BA Berlin DE1/56131.
6. *Protokoll der Verhandlungen des VIII. Parteitages der SED*, Vol. I, p. 61.
7. SPK, Staatssekretär: Persönliche Niederschrift über die Beratung der Grundlinie … im Politbüro [am 23.3.1971], 24.3.1971, BA Berlin DE1/56131.
8. Niederschrift über die Diskussion in der Beratung des Ministerrates am 21.7.1971 zu den staatlichen Aufgaben des Fünfjahrplanes 1971–1975, BA Berlin DE1/56127.
9. Abt. Planung und Finanzen: Information zu politisch-ideologischen Problemen in der SPK, 3.12.1971, SAPMO-BA DY30 IV A2/2021/461.
10. SPK, Staatssekretär: Persönliche Notizen über die Beratung der Jahresaufteilung des Fünfjahrplanes 1971–1975 im Politbüro am 18.1.1972, BA Berlin DE1/56129.
11. SPK: Aufträge und Vorschläge aus der Beratung des Politbüros am 14.3.1972 …, 15.3.1972, BA Berlin DE1/56129.
12. Cf. the compilation of social-political measures in Johannes Frerich and Martin Frey, *Handbuch der Geschichte der Sozialpolitik in Deutschland*, Vol. 2: *Sozialpolitik in der Deutschen Demokratischen Republik*, Munich 1993, passim.
13. Steiner et al., *Statistische Übersichten*, Tables 8.1.3., 9.1.1.
14. Steiner et al., *Statistische Übersichten*, Table 3.1.1.1.
15. Ministerrat: Beschluß zu den Grundsätzen unserer Lohnpolitik vom 21.6.1972, BA Berlin DC20-I/3-964.

16. Staatssekretär für Arbeit und Löhne, Rademacher to Schürer, 19.4.1974: Beschlußentwurf. Volkswirtschaftliches Tarifprojekt, 18.4.1974, BA Berlin DE1/VA-56159.
17. Schürer to Krolikowski: Vorschlag zur Arbeit am volkswirtschaftlichen Tarifprojekt, 27.1.1975, BA Berlin DE1/56135.
18. SPK: Vorschläge zur weiteren Durchführung der Beschlüsse des VIII. Parteitages der SED über die Planung und Bilanzierung ... [14.4.1972], BA DC20-I/3-953.
19. SPK, Vorsitzender: Information über die bisherige Verwirklichung der ... festgelegten Maßnahmen zur Verbesserung der Planung, Leitung und Bilanzierung, 17.2.1971, BA Berlin DE1/51851; Steiner, *DDR-Wirtschaftsreform*, pp. 546 f. Cf. also Ian Jeffries and Manfred Melzer, 'The New Economic System of Planning and Management 1963–70 and Recentralisation in the 1970s', in idem (eds), *The East German Economy*, London 1987, pp. 35 ff.
20. Material über die Plandurchführung 1971. [Januar 1972], SAPMO-BA DY30/2733.
21. Abt. Sozialistische Wirtschaftsführung/Zentralinstitut für Sozialistische Wirtschaftsführung: Information zur vollen Wahrnehmung der Verantwortung ..., 1.2.1979, SAPMO-BA DY30 IV 2/2101/61.
22. *Statistisches Jahrbuch 1968*, p. 115; 1971, p. 103.
23. Ebbinghaus, *Ausnutzung und Verdrängung*, p. 193.
24. Schlußwort Honeckers auf der 4. ZK-Tagung im Dezember 1971, quoted from Monika Kaiser, *1972 – Knockout für den Mittelstand. Zum Wirken von SED, CDU, LDPD und NDPD für die Verstaatlichung der Klein- und Mittelbetriebe*, Berlin 1990, p. 40.
25. Calculated according to SZS: Sammelband ausgewählter Kennziffern über die Entwicklung der Volkswirtschaft 1960–1971, BA Berlin DE2/30191/0014157.
26. *Statistisches Jahrbuch 1972*, p. 118.
27. Productivity as gross value added per capita calculated according to *Einheitliche Datenbasis*.
28. The share of gross investments of gross value added calculated according to *Einheitliche Datenbasis*; *Statistisches Jahrbuch 1990*, p. 113 f.
29. Related to the spheres of the industrial ministries: SZS: Statistischer Bericht über den Stand der Verwirklichung der Direktive des VIII. Parteitages und des Gesetzes über den Fünfjahrplan im Jahre 1972, 14.3.1973, BA Berlin DC20-I/3-1023.
30. Partially calculated according to *Einheitliche Datenbasis*; *Statistisches Jahrbuch 1990*, p. 121.
31. Hans-Hermann Hertle, 'Die Diskussion der ökonomischen Krisen in der Führungsspitze der SED', in Theo Pirker, M. Rainer Lepsius, Rainer Weinert and Hans-Hermann Hertle, *Der Plan als Befehl und Fiktion. Wirtschaftsführung in der DDR. Gespräche und Analysen*, Opladen 1995, pp. 309–45, here 322 ff.
32. Partially calculated according to Karlsch, 'Wirtschaftliche Belastungen'; *Einheitliche Datenbasis*; Steiner et al., *Statistische Übersichten*, Table 0.2.0.1.

33. Abt. Forschung und technische Entwicklung: Auswertung der internationalen Übersichten über die Entwicklung des Außenhandels 1972, 15.5.1973, SAPMO-BA DY30/2881.

34. Ahrens, *Gegenseitige Wirtschaftshilfe?*, p. 267.

35. Bericht über Schlußfolgerungen aus der 2. Tagung des ZK zur Beschleunigung des wissenschaftlich-technischen Fortschritts auf dem Gebiet elektronischer, insbesondere mikroelektronischer Bauelemente ..., 28.2.1977, SAPMO-BA DY30 IV 2/2101/41.

36. Unsigned letter, presumably from Schalck-Golodkowski to Mittag concerning the Bericht über Schlußfolgerungen ..., 28.2.1977, SAPMO-BA DY30 IV 2/2101/41.

37. Calculated according to Jörg Roesler. 'Zu groß für die kleine DDR? Der Auf- und Ausbau neuer Industriezweige in der Planwirtschaft am Beispiel Flugzeugbau und Mikroelektronik', in Fischer et al., *Wirtschaft im Umbruch*, 307–34, here 325; as well as *Enheitliche Datenbasis*.

38. According to internal analyses of the Ministry for Finances and the State Bank from H. Jörg Thieme. 'Notenbank und Währung in der DDR', in Deutsche Bundesbank, *Fünfzig Jahre Deutsche Mark*, pp. 609–53, here 648. For a compilation of alternative estimates see: Albrecht Ritschl. 'Aufstieg und Niedergang der Wirtschaft der DDR: Ein Zahlenbild 1945–1989', *Jahrbuch für Wirtschaftsgeschichte* 1995, 2, pp.11–46, here 36.

39. Stenographische Niederschrift der 2. Parteitagung des Forschungsrates am 12.11.1962, SAPMO-BA DY30 IV 2/607/33.

40. Dieter Lösch and Peter Plötz, 'HWWA-Gutachten. Die Bedeutung des Bereichs Kommerzielle Koordinierung für die Volkswirtschaft der DDR', in Deutscher Bundestag (ed.), *Der Bereich Kommerzielle Koordinierung und Alexander Schalck-Golodkowski. Bericht des 1. Untersuchungsausschusses des 12. Deutschen Bundestages. Anhangband 1994*, pp. 3–158, here 48; Hertle, 'Diskussion der ökonomischen Krisen', p. 316.

41. Lösch and Plötz, 'Bedeutung des Bereichs Kommerzielle Koordinierung', p. 44.

42. Calculated according to Statistisches Bundesamt, *Ausgewählte Zahlen zur Agrarwirtschaft 1949 bis 1989* (Sonderreihe mit Beiträgen für das Gebiet der ehemaligen DDR, No. 8), Wiesbaden 1993, pp. 14 f.

43. Bauerkämper, *Ländliche Gesellschaft*, pp. 199–203, 403.

44. Betr.: b. Stand der Zahlungsbilanz ...,1.2.1979, BA Berlin DE1/56323, according to Jonathan R. Zatlin, *The Currency of Socialism. Money and Political Culture in East Germany*, Cambridge 2007, p. 73.

45. André Steiner. 'Preisgestaltung', in Christoph Boyer et al. (eds), *Geschichte der Sozialpolitik in Deutschland seit 1945*, Vol. 10: *Deutsche Demokratische Republik 1971–1989. Bewegung in der Sozialpolitik, Erstarrung und Niedergang*, Baden-Baden 2008, pp. 304–23, here 314.

46. Partly calculated according to: Steiner et al., *Statistische Übersichten*, Tables 0.2.1.3., 0.4.2.0.

47. Steiner et al., *Statistische Übersichten*, Tables 0.2.1. and 1.2.1.

48. Calculated according to Steiner et al., *Statistische Übersichten*, Table 0.4.1.0.

49. Calculated according to *Statistisches Jahrbuch 1990*, pp. 52, 55. Cf. also Steiner et al., *Statistische Übersichten*, Table 0.4.1.0.
50. *Statistisches Jahrbuch 1990*, p. 325.
51. Cf. Stefan Wolle, *Die heile Welt der Diktatur*, Bonn 1998, pp. 199 ff.; Volker Wünderich, 'Die "Kaffeekrise" von 1977. Genußmittel und Verbraucherprotest in der DDR', *Historische Anthropologie* 11, 2003, pp. 240–61.
52. Schürer in 'Die gescheiterte Preisreform 1979 in der DDR. Protokoll einer Diskussion', in Rainer Weinert (ed.), *'Preise sind gefährlicher als Ideen'. Das Scheitern der Preisreform 1979 in der DDR. Protokoll einer Tagung.* (POLHIST Arbeitshefte der Forschungsstelle Diktatur und Demokratie am Fachbereich Politische Wissenschaften der Freien Universität Berlin. No. 10) Berlin 1999, p. 26.
53. Notizen zur Beratung des Politbüros des ZK der SED zum Planentwurf 1980 am 27.11.1979, BA Berlin DE1/56296, quoted according to Hertle, 'Diskussion der ökonomischen Krisen', p. 318.
54. Walter Halbritter, 'Vermerk über ein Gespräch beim Generalsekretär des ZK der SED, Gen. Erich Honecker, am 29.10.1979 (anwesend Mittag, Jarowinsky, Halbritter)' in Weinert, *'Preise sind gefährlicher als Ideen'*. For an exact account see also Steiner, 'Preisgestaltung', pp. 317f.
55. Calculated according to *Einheitliche Datenbasis*.
56. Calculated according to SZS: Sammelband ausgewählter Kennziffern über die Entwicklung der Volkswirtschaft 1988, BA Berlin DE2/30103/0012918.
57. [Material from Mittag to Honecker:] V. Zur Verschuldung der DDR im Handel mit den kapitalistischen Ländern, SAPMO-BA DY30/2725.
58. SPK, Staatssekretär: Probleme der Entwicklung der Außenwirtschaftsbeziehungen in den Jahren 1974 und 1975, 19.1.1973, BA Berlin DE1/52118/1.
59. Harm G. Schröter, 'Ölkrisen und Reaktionen in der chemischen Industrie beider deutschen Staaten. Ein Beitrag zur Erklärung wirtschaftlicher Leistungsdifferenzen', in Johannes Bähr and Dietmar Petzina (eds), *Innovationsverhalten und Entscheidungsstrukturen. Vergleichende Studien zur wirtschaftlichen Entwicklung im geteilten Deutschland*, Berlin 1996, pp. 109–38, here 114.
60. Ahrens, *Gegenseitige Wirtschaftshilfe?*, p. 281.
61. Calculated according to *Statistisches Jahrbuch 1990*, pp. 32 f.
62. Ahrens, *Gegenseitige Wirtschaftshilfe?*, pp. 262–68.
63. Hertle, 'Diskussion der ökonomischen Krisen', pp. 312 f.
64. Christoph Boyer and Peter Skyba, 'Sozial- und Konsumpolitik als Stabilisierungsstrategie. Zur Genese des "Einheit von Wirtschafts- und Sozialpolitik" in der DDR', *Deutschlandarchiv* 32, 1999, 577–90, p. 588.
65. Mittag and Schürer to Honecker, 14.3.1977; Schürer: Persönliche Aufzeichnungen, 27.4.1977; both BA Berlin DE1/56323, quoted according to Hertle, 'Diskussion ökonomischer Krisen', p. 314.
66. See Gerhard Schürer: Information über die Beratung mit Genossen Tichonow am 25.9.1973, 26.9.1973, BA Berlin DE1/56094.

67. On the procedure and its dramatic circumstances cf. Herle, 'Diskussion der ökonomischen Krisen', pp. 320 ff.; Ahrens, *Gegenseitige Wirtschaftshilfe?*, p. 333.

68. According to Gerhard Schürer, Gerhard Beil, Alexander Schalck, Ernst Höffner, and Arno Donda, 'Vorlage für das Politbüro des Zentralkomitees der SED. Analyse der ökonomischen Lage der DDR mit Schlußfolgerungen vom 30.10.1989', *Deutschland-Archiv* 25, 1992, pp. 1112–20, here 1114.

69. Deutsche Bundesbank, *Die Zahlungsbilanz der ehemaligen DDR 1975 bis 1989*, Frankfurt 1999, p. 60; Arnim Volze. 'Zur Devisenverschuldung der DDR – Entstehung, Bewältigung und Folgen', in Eberhard Kuhrt (ed.), *Die Endzeit der DDR-Wirtschaft – Analysen zur Wirtschafts-, Sozial- und Umweltpolitik*, Opladen 1999, pp. 151–83, here 178 ff.

70. Schürer, Böhm, Kaminsky, Polze: Stand der Zahlungsbilanz der DDR gegenüber dem nichtsozialistischen Wirtschaftsgebiet 1978 und 1979 sowie erforderliche Maßnahmen, 1.2.1979, BA Berlin DE1/56323, quoted according to Hertle, 'Diskussion der ökonomischen Krisen', p. 318.

71. Volze, 'Zur Devisenverschuldung der DDR', p. 183.

72. Mittag to Honecker, 28.10.1980: Vorschlag zur Durchführung des Außenhandelsplanes ..., SAPMO-BA DY30/2730.

Chapter 6

Continued Economic Decline
1982–1989

In the end it was the Federal Republic that helped the GDR get out of its debt crisis of the early eighties, with the new government, led by the Christian Democratic Union (CDU), continuing the German and Eastern policies of its social-liberal predecessors. In the first half of the eighties, however, the GDR did manage to reduce its obligations to the West, though this happened at the expense of its economic substance as Honecker's consumer-oriented and social programme was adhered to despite the changed conditions in the world economy. The Soviet Union – impeded by multiple changes at the top as its aged rulers died one after another – was unable to give additional support to the GDR; it was too busy struggling with the consequences of the long years of stagnation under Brezhnev. Nevertheless, Moscow repeatedly opposed any further rapprochement between the two German states. Thus Honecker's long hoped-for visit to Bonn was not realised until 1987. In terms of foreign policy the GDR was then at the zenith of its reputation, though economically it was being progressively eroded. The living standard of the population worsened with ever greater shortages in supplies. The new and growing demands of the rising generation could no longer be satisfied. The binding power of the barter deal of political tranquillity against promises of affluence was diminished: the number of GDR citizens applying for permits to leave the country was increasing, and a multiplicity of political oppositional and environmental groups, founded mostly under the umbrella of the Church, sprang up.

When, in the mid eighties, a younger politician, Gorbachev, assumed power in Moscow and began to reshape the Soviet Union, the majority of the East German Party leaders showed a lack of understanding for this and thereby got into ever greater conflict with the population, which had sympathies for the new Soviet policy. An accumulation of mistaken political decisions in the course of 1989 promoted the growth of mass emigration, escape and protest, leading ultimately to the events of the autumn of 1989 and to the fall of the Berlin Wall.

Getting out of Debt?

With Poland declaring itself insolvent in 1981 and with Romania suspending debt servicing, confidence in the Eastern Bloc countries collapsed in the Western credit markets. With the Western credit boycott the GDR also stood on the brink of insolvency. In the first half of 1982 alone Western creditors withdrew 40 per cent of their short-time deposits in the GDR.[1] The Federal Republic's government, however, fearing incalculable consequences of a political crisis in the GDR along the Polish model, offered a way out. In this way it honoured perhaps Honecker's readiness to continue the dialogue with the West against Moscow's wishes – in spite of the renewed hardening of the East–West conflict, due to the Soviet invasion of Afghanistan and the debate about the NATO Double-Track Decision of 1979. In 1983 and 1984 the Federal government guaranteed two unbound credits of West German Land and private banks to an amount of 1 billion and 950 million DM respectively. These two credits gave the GDR the basis for the necessary debt conversions, as they were again deposited as accounts with Western banks, thus suggesting the GDR's solvency. In addition the overdraft credit granted the GDR in intra-German trade by the Federal Republic, the 'Swing', and other annual payments made to the GDR by the West, gave it a certain amount of financial elbow room. Moscow admittedly criticised the East German leaders for their course – financial dependence on the Federal Republic and continuation of the dialogue with the West at the time of a renewed Cold War – but it had no economic alternative to offer. With the two billion credits once more 'rescuing' the GDR, Honecker now saw less reason than ever to revise his policy.[2] In this respect the credits had a stabilising effect in the short term, but a destabilising effect in the medium term.

Also, because the Soviet Union had reduced its supplies of crude oil, the GDR's coal-chemical industry was kept going and partially expanded. The programme, started in 1978, of replacing heating oil and imported gas with domestic brown coal was continued on an undiminished scale. In this way the raw material basis of energy production and of the chemical industry was to be restructured; in the sixties it had been partly switched over to crude oil. Faced with increased Comecon contractual prices, these two industrial branches once again had to make more extensive use of native brown coal. Available crude oil was no longer to be used for energy production, but was to be 'fractionated more deeply' in order to sell the products thereby gained in the West. In this way it was intended to reduce crude oil imports while at the same time earning convertible foreign currency. It proved possible by 1981, with investments of 15 billion Marks, to save 6 million tonnes of oil products annually and make it available for export to the West. Simultaneously the coal-chemicals industry was intensified, even though it was more expensive and costly in terms of energy. Thanks to further investments it was eventually possible to cut the use of heating oil to nearly one-half. In order to increase the Western currency yield of the export of oil products, modern processing plants were imported from the West, which again required credits. But as these exported products could only be sold in the Western markets at dumping prices, these deals also ate into the GDR's economic substance.[3] To make up for the saved crude oil and its processing products the mining of crude brown coal, which had stagnated since the sixties, was to be stepped up again at any cost. At the same time, however, mining conditions were steadily deteriorating. The cost of mining one tonne of crude brown coal increased from 7.70 Marks to 13.20 Marks between 1980 and 1988.[4] The costs of this switch of energy sources were eventually higher than the saving effect for the oil products, although they gained convertible foreign currency. However, this task used investments and capacities that might otherwise have been used for modernising the economy. As it was simply the replacement of one energy source by another, the GDR economy did not, for this effort, gain in real economic strength. Moreover, the switch had disastrous effects on the environment: power stations were not modernised to the required extent and investments in air purification were limited. While brown coal mining rose by 20 per cent from 1980 to 1987, sulphur dioxide emission went up by 30 per cent.[5] A high price had therefore to be paid for earning an export surplus.

Initially the GDR managed to 'keep its head above water' with its debt conversions. By cutting down on imports from the West, by rearranging the country's structure of imports and by pushing exports at any cost – 'Liquidity comes before profitability' – the GDR eventually even managed to stabilise its balance of payments vis-à-vis the West. While trade balance surpluses were achieved in this way, the domestic market was being deprived of investment goods, of consumer goods and of foodstuffs. Attempts were moreover made to back up the reduction of debts by increased cooperation with West German partners. These attempts included licence productions (the manufacture of West German brands in GDR enterprises), completions (the fitting of Western components into East German products), as well as compensation deals, when the construction of complete factories and plants in the GDR by Western contractors would be paid for with the goods produced in those factories. However, the volume of these forms of cooperation was too slight to reduce the GDR's indebtedness to any marked degree. The Party leaders also tried to make greater use of family visits from Western Germany as a source of foreign currency. The minimum currency exchange for

Federal citizens visiting the GDR was increased with the justification that they were benefiting from their subsidised purchases. Also, the number of Intershops and the goods they offered were increased. Their turnover rose by 66 per cent between 1977 and 1989, representing considerable Western currency surpluses: their gross revenue in 1988 came to nearly 10 per cent of the GDR's total Western exports.[6] This encouraged the politically and morally dangerous trend triggered already by the circulation of the D-Mark as a second currency, but all these measures made an effective contribution, in the short term, to averting the GDR's insolvency. After the drastic increase of the GDR's debt up until 1981/82 it proved possible to reduce the debt to the non-socialist countries by 1985 to 15.5 billion Valutamarks (5.2 billion dollars), the amount in convertible foreign currency being just under 12 billion Valutamarks (just under 4 billion dollars). In terms of dollars, therefore, the debt – as had been demanded in 1980 – had been more than halved and now amounted to 'only' about 80 per cent of exports in the same direction.[7]

At the same time there was, during those years, a very considerable increase in trade 'outside the plan', which included in particular the business of the KoKo division ('Commercial Coordination'). Whereas in 1976 these still amounted to less than 18 per cent of the total foreign trade turnover in the non-socialist economic area, they reached their peak of 44 per cent in 1984.[8] Anything that could be quickly turned into 'hard' currency was exported, sometimes secretly: from antiques to paving stones and weapons, all the way to political detainees. Quite apart from the extortionate methods applied and the moral questionability of the procedure, the profits of these exports did not noticeably relieve the economy. Moreover, the meat exports, greatly stepped up at the beginning of the eighties, eventually had drastic consequences for the population's supplies and for the future holdings of livestock. Even so, the trade balance of KoKo continued to be in the red even during the first half of the eighties because its imports were also increasing. These consisted of modern technological plants which, for reasons of secrecy or better-looking liquidity, were not to appear in the planned trade. Even so the amount that Mittag and Honecker 'injected' into the balance of payments each year from the Western currency earned by KoKo rose from about 1 billion DM in the seventies to nearly 2 billion DM in the eighties. Half of this amount came from the Intershops and similar sources, as well as from visitors from the Western countries, especially the Federal Republic. The rest was earned by KoKo in foreign trade and with financial investments and transactions in securities. All in all, KoKo, between 1972 and 1989, earned some 25 billion Valutamarks,[9] which corresponded to the peak level of the net debt to the non-socialist economic area in 1982. The importance of this special division should not therefore be underrated, but equally not overrated: it, too, was unable to solve the fundamental problems of the GDR's foreign trade.

Although it had been possible to reduce the GDR's debt to the West by the mid eighties, conditions for the GDR changed now once more: because of the delayed adjustment of Comecon contractual prices to those of the world market, the GDR, from 1985, had to pay a high oil price to the Soviet Union; this was thirteen times the 1970 level.[10] But just at the end of 1985 the crude oil price in the world market collapsed. The advantages of the first half of the eighties – low import prices for crude oil and higher export prices for oil products – were reversed into their direct and foreseeable opposite: relatively high prices for imported crude oil and relatively low prices for oil products. Thus the mineral oil exports to the West no longer yielded as much additional foreign currency income as before. Whereas in 1985 they had still earned over 2.5 billion Valutamarks, the figures for 1986 were only 1 billion and for 1987 only 900 million Valutamarks.[11] It was not possible to replace the declining yields from the sale of oil products by offering other products. The GDR's engineering industry, just as electrical engineering and electronics – with the exception of sectors covered by the microelectronics programme – had shown a decline in innovation and had been insufficiently endowed with investments. This resulted in growing wear and tear on the plants and eventually – moreover in the GDR's principal export ranges – in diminishing competitiveness of its products on the world market; mostly they could only be sold in the Eastern Bloc. As a result, the GDR depended in particular on demand from the Soviet Union, which increasingly prescribed what the GDR had to deliver. In a whole string of combines, especially in engineering, Soviet requirements had a considerable impact on what was being produced. The lag in productivity got worse and relative manufacturing costs rose, which was reflected in diminishing foreign currency earnings. In 1980, for every Mark spent within the country the GDR only earned 0.45 Valutamarks with her products exported to the West, and in 1988 a mere 0.25 Valutamarks.[12] In the final years of the GDR the share of machinery in Western trade rose once more, but this was at the expense of profitability and – especially in view of the GDR's worn-out machinery and plants – was therefore to be regarded 'in export as an extreme emergency solution and in import as a cover of the most urgent catch-up needs'.[13] Thus all plans for a comprehensive reduction of debts were based on unrealistic foundations.

Dispensing with Reforms in the Controlling of the Economy

In order to meet the changes in the world economy and to finally force the GDR's economy into intensive growth, the control mechanism was – as it was put – to be 'perfected' at the beginning of the eighties. The need to intensify economic activity, i.e., to ensure better use of all available production factors, was greater than ever; the 'main task' with its consumer-policy and social-policy emphasis was to be implemented further, future growth potential guaranteed and foreign debts reduced. Continuation of the social-policy programme had not been without controversy among the Party leaders at the beginning of the eighties in view of the worsening framework conditions. But as it was believed that abandonment of this policy might produce similar reactions as in Poland, it was decided to carry on with it. This was another reason for making better use, at long last, of economic potentials, as intensification had until then been carried out only rudimentarily. To this end central planning was to be more precise and cost-benefit thinking was to be encouraged among executives of enterprises and combines. About ninety plan indicators were to be used by the central authority to control the economic units, with four indicators – net production, net profit, products and services for the public as well as the export – being of special importance. This was a turning-away, once again, from using 'commodity production' as the central criterion of success because, as a gross index, it tended to encourage wasteful use of resources and thus militated against the goal of intensification. In order to strengthen the central control of resources the number of goods-distribution balances was increased and, above all, their formulation concentrated in the hands of the central authorities. These now compiled 2,136 balances for materials and semi-finished goods and with them controlled about 76 per cent of industrial inputs. The combines prepared a further 2,400 such balances themselves.

In the second half of the eighties the indirect, finance-oriented steering instruments were to be further developed, and at the same time additional control mechanisms were to be introduced, as well as the number of plan indicators further increased. From 1988 in sixteen combines, for instance, experiments were started with the principle that the combines had to earn their own finances (*Eigenerwirtschaftung der Mittel*), previously already practised during the reform in the sixties. Although responsibility for about 1,000 balances, which had been centrally prepared until then, was transferred to the combines, the central authority retained the final say. Thus enterprises and combines continued to be squeezed into a centrally fixed corset. Moreover, through dues payable to the state, the

major part of their profits, sometimes also their depreciation, were withdrawn from them, so that they had to take up credits for the financing of
their investments, thus getting formally into debt. This was a way of con-
cealing the domestic state indebtedness. It undermined furthermore the
incentives for enterprises and combines. Moreover, the multiplicity of
amendments and new measures in the control mechanism, designed
mainly to generate innovations, made the rules of procedure ever more
complicated.[14] Altogether certain elements already discussed or applied
during the economic reform in the sixties were to experience a renais-
sance. As, however, the overall character of the mechanism was not
changed, they remained without any major effect on the rationality of the
economy or on the economic results. Thus in the eighties the control
mechanism was still centralistic and inflexible. As before, the limitations
of the system became obvious in the generation of innovations and in
promoting intensive growth. In the end 'the chasm between plans and
economic reality became even deeper', which manifested itself in corrections to the plan downwards and in (self-) deception.[15]

When the new Soviet Communist Party leader Gorbachev, who was
younger than the GDR leaders, began, in the mid eighties, to use
Perestroika and Glasnost to lead the Soviet Union out of its economic stagnation, the East German Party leaders did not feel that this concerned
them. After all, the economy and the living standard in the GDR were
markedly higher than in the Soviet Union, as internationally agreed. In
point of fact, the GDR's problems did differ from the Soviet ones. But this
assumed 'superiority' ruled out, among the leaders around Honecker, any
thought of an economic reform, even in the face of the obvious economic
difficulties. Towards the end of 1987 the Party chief declared in the
Politbüro: 'We don't need any new theory for the development of the
planned economy in the GDR. What has proved successful should be continued, what impedes us should be got rid of. It is clear that we have the
population behind us. But if we fail to understand the present signals,
then we shan't retain their confidence.'[16] Quite obviously they did not
understand the signals. Reforms were out of the question because the
leaders were afraid of political consequences. In a consultation with
Honecker the Politbüro member responsible for trade and supplies made
this uncontradicted statement: 'No one [in the other Eastern Bloc coun-
tries] has achieved better solutions with so-called economic reforms. They
all have debts, but the foundation of trust and optimism has been
destroyed. We've got to keep the GDR stable.'[17] In point of fact, the economic elbow room necessary for a reform could probably only have been
provided with the support of the Federal Republic as, in the second half
of the eighties, the Soviet Union increasingly freed itself from its obligations vis-à-vis its allies. Besides, after the experience of the sixties, an

upswing could only have been achieved by a more consistent flexibilisation of the system's control mechanism and by a major retreat of the state and the central authority. But that was more than the Party leaders, anxious to hold on to power, could permit: that would have abolished the whole system. Seen thus there was certain logic in the growing isolation of the East German Party leadership in the Eastern Bloc as a stronghold of orthodoxy in the eighties.

In view of the Soviet concepts of Glasnost and Perestroika, the GDR citizens were hoping for a rejuvenation of the Party's Politbüro, with reforms touched on and suggested by itself; however, the status quo of the established system remained unchanged, though now called 'Socialism in GDR colours'. This slogan stood for 'Carry on as before'. Hence the activity of enterprises and combines, and even the central authorities, in the eighties, was primarily focused on coping with the changing economic crises, big and small, caused by domestic economy and foreign trade. The greater the difficulties, the more the central authority intensified its control. Mittag now demanded reports every ten days, sometimes even daily. This encouraged the managerial staff in enterprises and at the middle level even more than before to manipulate their figures. Ever since the seventies the managerial staff had increasingly regarded this as 'a phase of muddling through and extensive improvisation, but also of resignation'.[18] The morale of management personnel in the economy, just as that of Party officials at the bottom and middle level, broke down – a fact certainly noted by the Ministry for State Security. The 1982 payments balance crisis was seen by many people in responsible posts as a break demonstrating to them that the policy pursued by the Party leaders was bound to wreck the economy.[19] But a mixture of internalised Party discipline, belief in the values and ideology of socialism, a sense of responsibility and material interests made most of them stay in their posts.

Growing Loss of Assets

In macroeconomic terms the decline of the GDR's economy was revealed in the declining growth rates of economic productivity: since 1984 this had been continually declining. Whereas the gross value added per head of population was still increasing by more than 5 per cent in 1984, the figure for 1989 was barely 3 per cent.[20] Productivity in the GDR at its end was about two-thirds below that of the Federal Republic.[21] The widening of the gap since the beginning of the fifties, when it amounted to only one-third, demonstrates the growth losses that were due to the economic system. With growth rates declining, three objectives were increasingly competing: expenditure for the maintenance or improvement of the living standard;

increasing debt service obligations (redemption and interest) in the Western countries at the same time as attempts to reduce these debts; and increased investments. In its efforts to cope with all these, the state was increasingly falling into debt, not just abroad but also domestically. In 1970 the state budget's debt with the credit system was still about 12 billion Marks; by 1980 it rose cumulatively to 43 billion Marks and in 1988 it amounted to 123 billion Marks. At the end of 1989 it eventually reached 130 billion Marks. In 1988 this was more than one-half of the state's budgetary expenditure.[22] To perform this 'soundless' financing of state expenditure the population's savings deposits were mainly drawn upon and additional money was created – as already mentioned – by way of the finances of enterprises. When even this source of money was no longer sufficient, the first of the three targets to be reduced was investments; the other two targets were untouchable for political reasons. The narrower the financial scope became, the more even the military and state security spheres had to be content with ever smaller shares of the budgetary expenditure: in 1982/83 it was 11 per cent, in 1989 it was only 8 per cent.[23]

While it was still possible, in the seventies, with an only slightly diminishing investment quota, to cover the increasing share of consumption in the total product by an increasing foreign indebtedness, in the eighties the share of private consumption in the domestic use of the gross domestic product, which had risen up to 1984 and thereafter stagnated (1980: 59 per cent; 1984: 62 per cent; 1989: 62 per cent), had to be paid for with a more strongly retrograde investment quota. Between 1982 and 1986 the investment volume was, in absolute terms, below the 1981 level. The proportion of gross investment in the gross value added declined from 30 per cent in 1980/81 to 23 per cent in 1985/86. Even more dramatic was the decline of the proportion of net investments in the 'producing' sphere – crucial for future growth – dropping over the same period from 12 per cent to under 7 per cent. Although the investment quota rose slightly after 1986, this did not essentially change the declining trend of the eighties.[24]

With declining investment quotas, particular importance attached to how the extension funds were applied. Right up to the end of the GDR the Party leaders concentrated them strongly on industry, which they continued to believe was the core of the economy. Transport and communications in particular had been neglected for a long period, which resulted in a huge shortage of private telephone connections and to appalling conditions on the railways and the road network. By the end of the eighties 17 per cent of the rail network could only be travelled over at a reduced speed, or was closed altogether. On certain track sections express trains could only travel at 10 km/h. Of the rail track dismantled after the end of the war the second or third track was still missing in 1989 on 500 km of the network. Nearly half the autobahn surfaces exhibited considerable damage, which impaired traffic, and 18 per cent of the road network was classified as 'barely passable'.[25] This lengthened transportation times, resulting in goods being spoilt, in production stoppages and in growing delays in personal transport. Communal utilities and the service sector were also insufficiently endowed with investment funds. On the other hand, investments for the residential building programme were further increased after 1982. In 1985 14 per cent of total investments in the economy as a whole went to this sector, though this share declined in the subsequent years to 11 per cent.[26] Even so, expenditure in this sphere was higher than in the preceding decades and, considering the extent and conditions of the housing stock, it was certainly necessary. At the same time, however, old building assets were being neglected, which limited the net effect. Although the average living space per inhabitant rose from 20 to 27 sq.m. between 1971 and 1989, and although the equipment of apartments improved, the ambitious targets of the residential building programme – the centre of Honecker's social policy – were not reached. Of the apartments originally promised only 60 per cent were newly built or modernised between 1975 and 1989.[27]

Within industry in the eighties it was the modern branches of engineering and vehicle manufacture, and after 1986 also electrical engineering and electronics, which again received more investments. This was due to the microelectronics programme by means of which the Party leaders around Honecker, in the final third of the seventies, had again begun to focus their support on forward-looking branches. This programme was an absolute necessity for the GDR: efficient modern engineering was ever more insistently calling for microelectronic parts. As the COCOM (Coordinating Committee for East–West Trade Policy) list prevented the sale of modern Western technologies to the Eastern Bloc; as the GDR continued to suffer from a chronic shortage of Western currency; as cooperation with the Comecon countries – an obvious choice – had not proved very successful; and as cooperation with the military-industrial complex of the Soviet Union was limited to what the Soviets demanded; the GDR had no other choice than to turn to the manufacture of microelectronic parts itself.

Between 1986 and 1989 alone this devoured some 14 billion Marks of investments, of which three combines were the principal beneficiaries: Carl Zeiss Jena, Mikroelektronik Erfurt and Robotron Dresden. In addition, a further 14 billion Marks was spent on research and development, as well as about 4 billion Valutamarks on imports from the West.[28] It was one of the tasks of the Sector for Science and Technology of the Hauptverwaltung Aufklärung (Main Directorate for Reconnaissance, the foreign intelligence service) of the Ministry for State Security, as well as of KoKo, to evade the Western embargo regulations and to get hold, illegally, of the microelectronic parts to be 'developed', as well as of the necessary know-how and production plant as prototypes in order then to copy them. The purchase of licences in Japan, for instance, was prevented by the US by reference to the technology embargo. Quite apart from the fact that, in the mid eighties, one had reached the limits of 're-inventing' microchips, the fundamental problems of technology transfer could not be solved in this manner. Even though the relevant Directorate of the Ministry for State Security demonstrated what sums it was saving the economy by illegally obtaining Western technology, it remains questionable, given the conditions of the GDR, to what extent efficient use could actually be made of this technology. If only because of its enormous costs, which did not remain hidden from the public, the microelectronics programme had to be propagandistically dressed up as a model of forward-looking economic and structural policy. At the same time the costs for the production of a single 256 K memory circuit amounted to 534 Marks; in the world market the same part was available for four to five Valutamarks. This means that every circuit had to be subsidised by 517 Marks from the state budget. Meanwhile the GDR was lagging about eight years behind the international state of development and producing only 10 per cent of the number of pieces produced by Western manufacturers.[29] These efforts could not be measured by economic criteria. They presupposed the continued existence of the Eastern Bloc, where the GDR could market it's – by Eastern Bloc standards – peak products. But when the other Comecon countries began increasingly to sell their raw materials and energy sources in the world market and there, in return, to acquire the most modern technology, the microelectronics programme lost its strategic basis. The credits taken up for financing the imported manufacturing plants could not be repaid in this way and thus became a further burden on the GDR's future balance of payments.

Another investment priority in the eighties was the motorcar industry. An ambitious innovation programme for this branch had collapsed in the seventies and 'two absolutely outdated models' continued to be 'manufactured by largely outworn equipment'. The Party leadership therefore decided in 1983 to embark on a new – though limited – development programme for motorcar production.[30] In order to keep costs low, models would not be changed: the GDR's only own makes, Trabant and Wartburg, were merely to be equipped with a modern four-stroke engine. The fact was that the GDR models with their two-stroke engines were being increasingly rejected in the other Eastern Bloc countries because of their unfavourable fuel consumption and their high car emissions, harmful to the environment. In view of the reduced crude oil deliveries from the Soviet Union the fuel consumption of cars had to be lowered also. Added to this was the domestic public's dissatisfaction with the cars on offer. The West German Volkswagen AG supplied the complete manufacturing plant for a four-stroke engine and, in return, was to receive a proportion of the engines manufactured there. This compensation deal promised the GDR motor industry a chance to catch up with the international standard, at least in terms of engines. To what extent this would actually satisfy the consumer needs of the East German public was questionable. As with many other investment projects, the costs of this programme exploded during realisation: in the second half of the eighties it devoured 11 billion Marks, nearly double the 1985 investments in the entire engineering and vehicle industry. Honecker felt cheated: instead of a new engine one would now build an almost completely new car. In the Politbüro he said: 'Surely we have the Wartburg and our Trabi; we can continue to manufacture them.'[31] The first Wartburg with a four-stroke engine came off the assembly line in October 1988. For all its shortcomings in terms of quality this model was a success – until the fall of the Wall. After that it had no chance against the models offered by the West.

Such programmes did not, of course, do away with the obstacles to innovation caused by the system. On the contrary: in the branches that were not promoted they actually made matters worse. In particular, the monopoly position of the combines, the relatively slight qualitative demands in Comecon trade, as well as a control mechanism that continued to reward quantitative growth, prevented a successful renewal of production. The same effect was created by the foreclosure from the international division of labour and the resulting rather broad range of products manufactured. This splintered research and development and hence yielded few results. For this reason also industry's equipment with modern plants and machinery was – contrary to the Party's propaganda assurances – poor compared to international standards. In the mid eighties 300 numerically or computer-numerically controlled (NC or CNC) machines were in use per 100,000 employees in the GDR's metal-processing industry; the figure for the Federal Republic was 2,600. Industrial robots came somewhat closer to the Western competitor: per 100,000 industrial employees the GDR had 133, the Federal Republic 145, while Japan had 602. Their efficiency was largely determined by their combined use with NC or CNC machines; because of their lesser numbers, their efficiency was also lower in the GDR than in the Federal Republic.[32]

As a result of the concentration of funds on the prioritised sectors the proportion of uncompleted investment projects and hence that of partially or totally production-ineffective funds continued to rise. By international comparison the technological level of many products was still inadequate. Industrial investments, in particular, were predominantly extensive, which meant that for the start-up of the newly created capacities still more manpower was needed than was freed by them; in other words the investments generated a need for more manpower.[33] However, there were no manpower reserves left: with the internationally very high employment quota of 91 per cent in 1985 the limit was reached.[34] More and more often the Army was drawn upon – a quick and, above all, available manpower reserve. In addition, the enterprises were demanding more foreign 'contract workers', because these were 'incomparably cheaper than any freeing of manpower through investments'. In consequence their number multiplied from 24,000 in 1981 to 94,000 in 1989.[35] But, at best, this did no more than ease the manpower problem to some extent.

In order to finance the priority programmes, funds amounting to a whole year's investments were redirected in the eighties alone; these should instead have served the maintenance of existing plants and machinery.[36] The result was the creation of a few ultramodern enterprises, while elsewhere buildings and plants in the same industrial sector were going to ruin. Their wear rate rose in the 'producing' sector from 43 per cent to 47 per cent between 1980 and 1989; for machinery and equipment the increase was even from 51 per cent to 55 per cent. The situation in the crafts, in building, in transport and communication was even a great deal worse.[37] Soon the deplorable condition of production plants was causing more and more breakdowns and accidents, some fatal, and increasingly affecting the health of the workers. Besides, it drove up the costs of repair and maintenance and, in consequence, the production costs, as well as tying down a lot of manpower in the repair and maintenance sector. Because the ancillary industries were also receiving too few investments, their capacities increased – as they had done towards the end of the Ulbricht era – more slowly than those of the final producers. In order to limit the resulting disruptions, the required inputs were more and more often imported, or else the enterprises made use of the grey, and increasingly also the black, market. For that, alongside saleable products (of their own) they also, in the second half of the eighties, employed Western currency. This was illegal, but it was tolerated and sometimes even encouraged, because that way the plan could be fulfilled. Admittedly this raised the costs even further. Altogether the volume of investment was rather restricted, because of the overemphasised social welfare policy: what was available was expended without achieving any real improvements in structure or efficiency. The long-term lowering of the investment level and the inadequate incentives due to egalitarian wage structures greatly impaired the efficiency of the GDR's economy.

The same applied to agriculture. At the end of 1981 the Party abandoned its overemphasised industrialisation policy in the country and brought crop and livestock farming back together. The acreages farmed by individual enterprises were to be reduced, step by step, largely because the yields of crop production by mega-enterprises had declined due to water and wind erosion, as well as through increasing soil compaction. In actual fact, the acreage reduction progressed only by small steps. The average size of Agricultural Production Cooperatives and People-Owned Estates only diminished, between 1980 and 1989, from 4,754 and 5,454 hectares respectively to 4,528 and 5,030 hectares.[38] At the same time more fertiliser and pesticides were applied; these seriously affected the soil and ground water. Even the minimal decline at the end of the eighties was due not so much to ecological motivations as to economic constraints. To obtain the urgently needed Western currency, fertilisers and crop-protection chemicals, as well as agricultural machinery were exported. In consequence there was a dramatic fall in investments in agriculture: starting from a level that, in 1981, was, measured by the available fixed assets, anyway 18 per cent less than in industry, investments in agriculture declined by nearly 30 per cent between 1981 and 1985. Wear and tear of machinery in agricultural enterprises was thus greater in 1989 than in the 'producing' spheres as a whole.[39] The efficiency problem that already existed in many agrarian enterprises – in 1980 15 per cent of crop farms and 30 per cent of livestock farms made no profit – was bound to get worse.[40] In order to ensure an income for these enterprises and to strengthen agriculture, an agrarian price reform was carried out in 1984; as a result it was possible to reduce subsidies for agriculture from 11.4 billion Marks in 1983 to 6.2 billion Marks in 1985 – in other words, they were almost halved.[41] As, however, consumer prices for foodstuffs remained constant, the sum for the support of foodstuff prices rose from 12.1 billion Marks to 27.6 billion Marks over the same period. The agrarian price reform therefore resulted in surplus costs of 10 billion Marks – an amount that was to increase further in the following years. Thus the proportion of foodstuff subsidies of the total budgetary expenditure rose from 7 per cent to 13 per cent. In 1983 the population's food consumption had been subsidised at 26 per cent, after the agrarian price reform in 1985 at just under 44 per cent and in 1989 at 46 per cent.[42] This meant that, in order to realise cost-covering prices, private consumers would have had to pay almost double the amount for their food. This increase in subsidies considerably narrowed the margin of distribution. Quite obviously the Party leaders would soon have had to slaughter their 'sacred cow', stable prices.

Yet the production effect of this price reform was slight: although, thanks to good weather, agricultural production was increased in 1984, it stagnated after that date. The development of the agricultural sector was also affected by the balance of payments. In order to limit imports of foodstuffs, the Party leaders again upgraded the private small farms towards the end of the seventies. For the same purpose the acreage under bread grain was increased by 18 per cent in 1983 at the expense of fodder grain. As a result, considerable quantities of fodder grain had to be imported in the second half of the eighties. Inadequate provision of feeding stuff and increased exports of meat products – including young animals – resulted in sharp drops in livestock production in 1982/83 and 1988; these had a serious effect on the supply of meat and meat products for the population.

More Money, Fewer Goods

Since the beginning of the eighties there were two limitations to the growth of goods on offer for the consumer: first, imports were to be reduced in order to lower the GDR's debts to the West; secondly, the investment policy had a negative effect on the consumer goods industry. In consequence, the goods on offer were, in their structure, less and less up to demand. While the net money income of the population was rising by just under 4 per cent in the eighties, retail turnover rose by only 3 per cent. Hence the surplus purchasing power increased and, according to data of the GDR State Bank, in the years 1986 to 1989, reached 12 to 14 billion Marks. This was a little over 4 per cent of the gross domestic product during those years and a little more than 8 per cent of realised private consumption. The surplus purchasing power was reflected also in the savings quota, which had averaged about 6 per cent in the sixties and declined to about 5 per cent on average in the consumption-intensive seventies. In the eighties it rose from its low point of under 3 per cent (1980) to 7 per cent (1987/88), an indication of just how much the supply of goods and services for the population had deteriorated in the course of the eighties. Admittedly, the surplus purchasing power was not felt equally everywhere. In particular, the 30 per cent of the population who really depended on subsidised products, rents and services were scarcely aware of it. The situation was different for the roughly 15 to 20 per cent who were able to afford practically everything; they had costly consumer items twice or even three times.[43] Instead of experiencing any surplus purchasing power, many pensioners experienced poverty, as they had only slightly benefited from the additional welfare measures. However, the Party leaders shied away from changing this policy to one that would assign to the needy directly higher pensions, welfare benefits or higher child benefits instead of subsidies. The leaders feared that disturbances might follow the abandonment of the principle of stable prices.

Because of the rising costs, keeping the prices of basic necessities and rents stable required a further increase in subsidies financed by the state budget. Not counting the indirect subsidising of rents, these rose from 21.5 billion in 1982 to an exorbitant 50.6 billion Marks in 1989, i.e., they more than doubled. Thus their share of budgetary expenditure grew from just under 14 per cent to 21 per cent. In consequence the subsidised part of the consumption expenditure of the population (not counting rents) rose to over 26 per cent. If one includes the indirectly subsidised rents, the quota of the population's subsidised consumption was probably about one-third. As in the seventies, the free or highly subsidised benefits of the 'second wage packet' increased more quickly than work earnings. This meant that an ever smaller part of the population's gross income came from their occupational activity: in the Ulbricht era this had been 80 per cent or more, but from the seventies onwards this figure dropped abruptly to about 75 per cent or less. Inversely the part of income from 'social' funds, which were only loosely related to work performance, increased from about 17 per cent to 21 per cent.[44] Generally speaking, living standards depended less and less on a person's own performance, while more and more of the productivity growth was being spent on private incomes.

As the population's incomes went up, so, naturally enough, did their demands for consumer goods, but in the eighties these were less and less satisfied. Although basic food needs were met in principle, the choice was increasingly narrowed down in the eighties. Temporary difficulties in meat supplies were already nothing unusual, to be later joined by milk and butter. Fruit, vegetables, and tropical fruit in particular, had not been available in adequate quantities for some time. All this caused considerable resentment among the population. At the same time, highly subsidised prices for goods for basic needs were favouring an already health-impairing high per-capita consumption of meat, fats and sugar, leading moreover to a waste of bread and other foodstuffs. In addition, the subsidies resulted in a growing use of energy, with fatal consequences for the environment. At the same time the subsidies for basic needs were accompanied by high product-related charges for higher-value foodstuffs and technical consumer goods, which were becoming a lot more expensive. The circumstance that manufacturers were able to get the prices of their products raised after only trifling improvements of their user value drove up prices even further. The growth of the retail turnover was thus more and more based on price increases, while the quantitative turnover rose only slightly or even stagnated. The inflation rate for the whole of the Honecker era is thought to have averaged about 1.5 per cent annually, although price increases in the different categories of goods varied greatly. Besides, towards the end of the seventies and the beginning of the eighties consumer prices were rising significantly faster than before or afterwards.[45]

Despite repeated programmes for increasing the output of consumer goods, many of these were not available either in the volume demanded or of the required quality. The situation worsened even further in the eighties. More and more goods, such as textiles, were being exported in the interest of solvency, even though the foreign currency earned by them was slight. Following a particular negative experience of his grandson, Honecker himself grumbled in the Politbüro: 'I am not advocating our people running about naked because of our exports!'[46] Although the proportion of households equipped with technical consumer items improved in the eighties, it nevertheless lagged qualitatively and quantitatively behind what was available in the West, and this was known from Western television, the Intershops and from trips to the Federal Republic. Some modern consumer goods, moreover, were not available at all.

Particularly explosive was the availability of motorcars. According to the official GDR statistics, in 1989 only just over one-half of all households possessed a motorcar. Most of these were of domestic manufacture: 54 per cent were 'Trabant' models and a further 17 per cent were 'Wartburg' models. Only 0.1 per cent of motorcars in the GDR came from the West or from Yugoslavia, the rest came from other Eastern Bloc countries. Of the privately owned cars, 61 per cent were over ten years old, which drove up the demand for (equally unavailable) spare parts and repairs. The waiting time for a new motorcar was, varying according to model, between 12.5 and 17 years. This situation had absurd consequences: on the one hand a flourishing black market in used cars, which could cost more than twice or three times their new price, or even more for Western models. On the other hand, because of the registration system no one was quite sure how great the demand actually was. To be on the safe side, almost everybody had himself put on a list for a car and these places on the list were then traded for between 2,000 and 40,000 Marks.[47] In this way one could advance oneself in the waiting queue. Thus the socialist shortage economy developed its own way of options trading. In the East German economic policy the motorcar never occupied a particular position. Nor was its significance recognised as a growth engine of the economy, as observed in the Western industrialised countries during the boom years. As late as December 1988 Honecker reminded the Politbüro that the public had been promised the solution of the housing problem, 'but it was never promised that every family must have a car by 1990'.[48] Evidently the Party leaders, most of whom became socialised before 1945, failed to understand that because of the increased incomes previously 'unthinkable' consumer wishes had meanwhile become 'normal' for GDR citizens – the more so against the background of the affluent society in the Federal Republic. However, car ownership was only one – albeit a special and symbolic – illustration of the supply situation.

As early as 1987 the Ministry for State Security informed the Party leaders that 'a considerable increase of critical discussion can be observed'. These 'negative and disparaging remarks about the goods on offer' were 'increasingly … accompanied by openly voiced doubts of the objectivity and credibility of the economic surveys and results periodically published by the GDR's mass media'. Besides, there were 'increasingly frequent and increasingly aggressive' complaints about the better supply situation in Berlin, as well as about 'corruption and bribery in the commercial and services sector'.[49] Even in the 'Exquisit' and 'Delikat' shops, which were increasingly being extended at the expense of standard supplies, the goods on offer were quantitatively and, more and more also qualitatively, below demand. Meanwhile the GDR citizens obtained the lacking commodities, especially high-value consumption items, from the Federal Republic. It is thought that these private 'imports' reached a volume of 20 to 25 billion Marks in terms of GDR prices until 1989. At the end of the seventies the privately imported quantities of certain goods, such as cocoa, clothing and footwear, amounted to about one-third of these goods available in the GDR retail trade. At the end of the eighties the private imports probably exceeded the supply available in the GDR trade.[50] This further increased the surplus purchasing power and demands on the GDR supplies were raised. As a growing number of commodities were not available in sufficient quantities, the frustrated consumers purchased any available goods or they bought them not when they needed them but when they were available. More and more often employees would leave their workplace during working hours in order to queue for goods in short supply. In 1989 unauthorised absences per worker amounted to six hours a week on average.[51] The shortages undermined the incentives for the workers, anyway poor, and the Party's slogan of the eighties '*Ich leiste was, ich leiste mir was!*' ('At work I am good, so I treat myself to some goodies') must have sounded to many like mockery. For the Party leaders, guaranteed provisions were the most important prerequisite for maintaining the status quo. For that reason special imports were arranged before political 'great events', such as Party Congresses, elections or jubilees; these improved the supplies in the trade.

In the second half of the eighties it was mainly the supply shortages that annoyed the population and caused widespread resignation. The economic situation, people thought, would not improve anyway. They were confirmed in this belief by the impressions and experiences of the growing number of citizens who were granted the opportunity of visiting the Federal Republic. Some of these did not return and the number of exit applications steadily rose throughout the eighties. As before 1961, there was a multitude of reasons for this, in addition to the inadequate supply of consumer goods: the economic situation, universally regarded as desperate; the comparably low living standard; the growing political ossification and immobility. Whereas in the past the number of authorised emigrations had been small, between 1980 and 1988 the GDR lost more than 21,000 citizens on average per year to the Federal Republic. Of particular economic concern was the fact that 42 per cent of them belonged to the especially keen and well-trained age groups between 18 and 40.[52] These were the up-and-coming generations for whom the successes of postwar reconstruction and guaranteed basic requirements had long become a matter of course, who were interested in individual develop- ment opportunities and a scope for movement, and who oriented them- selves by Western consumer standards.

This renewed flight from the GDR – for some of them also into a drop- out existence – was only one symptom of the lessening cohesiveness of the system. In the economy this showed itself also in the expanding black mar- ket for all goods in short supply; this gave rise to a new social differentia- tion. To obtain scarce consumer goods, corruption and nepotism played an increasing part. The black market, 'compulsory savings' and price increas- es for commodities of elevated demand eventually brought about a situa- tion in which the GDR currency could only limitedly perform all the func- tions of money: the 'second currency', the D-Mark, increased in impor- tance; whoever paid in D-Marks need not wrestle with shortages or exces- sive prices. The two-class society resulting from the availability of Western money was not only accepted by the state but actually promoted with its Intershops. The decline of the DDR-Mark was reflected, from the mid sev- enties, by the almost steadily rising black-market rate of the (Western) D- Mark. According to estimates, the share of D-Marks in circulation in the GDR (calculated by the black-market rate) as a proportion of the total GDR money volume rose from over 1 per cent in 1974 to over 13 per cent in 1988. The stocks of D-Marks held cash in the GDR (often serving as a store of value and therefore not fully effective in circulation) in 1988 reached a share of 62 per cent of all cash in circulation.[53] Whether or not this estimate is accurate in detail, it demonstrates the loss of confidence in the GDR cur- rency and is evidence that the system had failed economically, ideological- ly and eventually also morally.

Final Crisis

Because of the retained inflexible system structure on the one hand, and earlier decisions on the other, the Party's scope for action in the sphere of economic policy had become increasingly narrow. In view of the domes- tic and foreign debts the chief of the State Planning Commission realised at the start of 1988 that the economic problems could not be solved by the traditional means. The Eastern Bloc countries were no longer meeting their contractual obligations in full and the Soviet Union had announced that after 1990 it would further reduce its supplies of crude oil. It was also clear that the foreign currency expenditure on microelectronics could not be refinanced. On the contrary, this sector demanded new funds of astronomical dimensions from the State Planning Commission in the new plans. At the end of April 1988, therefore, Schürer decided on an unusual step. Bypassing Mittag and the Politbüro, he sent a paper to Honecker that cautiously proposed a limited change in economic policy because the necessary investments, the supplies for the population and the demands resulting from the balance of payments could not be balanced in the draft plan for 1989. In detail he suggested halting the further development of microelectronics, making the funds thus freed available for processing engineering as an engine for exports, to strengthen the production of semi-finished articles at the expense of final producers, to promote a economic energy consumption, to lower state consumption including its welfare-motivated part and to cut back subsidies for rents, energy, children's articles and all other products not serving basic needs. Honecker, however, saw Schürer's ideas as a 'frontal attack against the policy of a speedy development of microelectronics, as well as against the "unity of economic and social policy"' and against his person. When the Party chief handed Schürer's document to Mittag, he rejected it on the grounds that it ran counter to Party resolutions. By using this political judgement he avoided economic arguments. Mittag merely emphasised that the development of microelectronics was 'a strategic task of the first order' and that only with it could the GDR gain scope for action and hold its place in the world markets.[54] Both positions were justified and merely represented different moments in a vicious circle: to reduce debts, the competitiveness of GDR products must be improved, which in turn required modern technology. But because of the system-immanent limitations this could not be developed within the country but had to be imported, which further increased the GDR's debts. However, the strategy of employing on-credit modern technology in order to reduce debts at a later stage had long suffered shipwreck in view of the slight endogenous performance and innovation incentives and the changed foreign trade conditions. Hence an austerity policy was urgently needed.

Instead of receiving support, Schürer was instructed by the Politbüro to 'continue the line of the main task in the unity of economic and social policy by stopping further debts and gradually reducing them'.[55] This squaring of the circle was bound to fail. The relative, and at times even absolute, decline of investments in the eighties and their simultaneous concentration on a few priorities had resulted in investment gaps in all other sectors, which was why their representatives were now demanding compensation. Therefore it was less and less possible to balance the plans. In the end the Politbüro regarded the population's consumption demands as the root cause of the problem. It was said: 'Our people want from us social security, safety, assured workplaces and education – plus the department stores of the Federal Republic.'[56]

The debt situation continued to escalate and a sense of crisis spread even among the Party leaders. Eventually, after the autumn of 1988, there were discussions in the leadership circle and finally, in the narrowest circle, by the economic officials in Mittag's office, on whether the living standard should be lowered and to what extent subsidies could be cut back. The result was half-hearted decisions. Egon Krenz, who was to inherit Honecker's post a few months later, remarked in May 1989 that it was just the continuation of the 'unity of economic and social policy … that is socialism in the GDR'.[57] And that of course was not to be questioned. But various events, such as the ban of the Soviet periodical *Sputnik* at the end of 1988, the obvious fraud of the communal elections in May 1989 and the opening of the Hungarian–Austrian frontier for GDR citizens led to a growing erosion and delegitimation of the Party's power. At the same time thousands were fleeing to the West via Hungary or through the Federal Republic's embassies in Prague and Warsaw. From the end of September 1989 there were the 'Monday demonstrations' in Leipzig, where the call for reforms was becoming ever louder. The 'double movement of mass emigration and mass protest' now drove even some Politbüro members to action and in mid-October 1989 they replaced Honecker and Mittag.[58]

The new leaders under Krenz received an analytical report on the true economic situation in the autumn of 1989. It was concluded that the GDR's solvency could only be saved if the consumption of the population was lowered by 25 per cent to 30 per cent. To avoid this, the authors of this report proposed negotiating with the Federal Republic about the necessary credits, amounting to billions, offering as a trade-off that 'these and further measures of economic and scientific–technological cooperation between the GDR and the Federal Republic would, before the end of the century, create conditions in which the frontier between the two German states, in the form in which it exists today, would become superfluous'.[59] But with the fall of the Wall on 9 November 1989 this could no longer be a bargaining chip. What had been until then a closed economy had overnight become an open one. Hence the economic reform suggested in the analytical report at the end of October had been deprived of its basis too.

After the collapse of the GDR the most varied data circulated about the scale of its debt to the West. Mittag had seen to it that even the topmost economic officials were only incompletely informed. On the one hand he was anxious to present the GDR's soundness in the best possible light in order to safeguard their creditworthiness. On the other hand 'the debts to the West were to appear greater in the State Planning Commission's balance of payments … than they actually were in order to prevent the greediness of the Politbüro, of industry and perhaps also the State Planning Commission and to create secret reserves for threatening new liquidity bottlenecks'.[60] As a result both the Party's Politbüro and the economic authorities were inaccurately informed on the debt to the West. In the analysis of the economic situation submitted to Krenz in the autumn of 1989 a debt of 49 billion Valutamarks (26.5 billion dollars) was recorded.[61] The concealed outstanding debts and foreign currency reserves, including obligations not until then taken account of, meant that the GDR's balance of payments vis-à-vis the West at the time of the fall of the Wall actually showed a deficit of 'only' just under 20 billion Valutamarks (10.8 billion dollars). Among them the politically relevant debt in convertible foreign currency amounted to 15.2 billion Valutamarks or 8.2 billion dollars. This represented 175 per cent of exports to Western industrial countries in 1989 (not counting intra-German trade) or about one-fifth of the gross domestic product earned in the same year.[62] This order of magnitude, purely in terms of quantity, should have been manageable. To that extent the GDR was not (yet) 'broke' in the strict sense of the word. What was much more serious was the fact that, for several years past, there had been considerable difficulties in maintaining exports to Western countries, as the international competitiveness of GDR products had been steadily deteriorating. It would therefore have become increasingly difficult for the GDR to earn the Western currency needed to service its debts.

The crucial factors that led to this situation were to be found in the Party leaders' economic policy and its domestic economic consequences. Moreover, during the final two decades of its existence the foreign-trade framework conditions had radically changed for the GDR. One of the fundamental problems remained the lack of progress with the division of labour within Comecon or with the economic integration of its member countries. Besides, since the late sixties the GDR had been extremely cautious and conservative vis-à-vis all reforms proposed within the Eastern Bloc economic alliance. It maintained a sceptical attitude towards all attempts to develop Comecon into a common market with a certain opening towards the world markets. The Party leaders – at least instinctively – recognised the potentially system-exploding dimension of such proposals and thus, from their own point of view, were acting quite consistently. Their prime interest was to keep trade practices among the Comecon countries unchanged in order to gain for themselves the subsidies implicitly granted to them by the Soviet Union in trade exchange. There is some doubt whether, in the second half of the eighties, they had lost this anyway as a result of the fundamental changes in exchange and price relations. All the changes in domestic and foreign economic conditions, some of them brought upon themselves by the Party leaders, narrowed down their scope of decision-making.

The socialist economic system's immanent incapacity to produce structural and technological or innovatory change was the decisive cause of the GDR's economic weakness in its final decade. The system was unable to react and adapt to the new framework conditions – worldwide changed prices of important resources and the international spread of a post-Fordist production regime on the basis of flexible technologies. The system's limits were, principally, a consequence of the inflexibility and the inadequate incentives of the control mechanism, as well as of the basic economic-policy decisions that were made at the expense of its economic capital. While external economic problems exacerbated the problems, they were not their root cause. Because of its own economic difficulties the Soviet Union was no longer in a position to compensate for the GDR's economic weakness. Moreover, the system's development potential and that of the GDR's economy seem to have been exhausted in the eighties. For years the GDR had lived above its means, as reflected in its domestic and foreign indebtedness and in the decay of its capital stock. Indeed, the economic break-up should have been foreseeable if there were no thorough-going changes to the system's economic conditions. Inability to meet the public's growing quantitative and qualitative consumer demands accelerated the decline and contributed to the political upheaval of the autumn of 1989 that eventually, in November 1989, led to the fall of the Berlin Wall and hence brought to an end the existence of the GDR as a (relatively) enclosed economy.

Notes

1. Dokumente über Beschlüsse zur Zahlungsfähigkeit der DDR …, 5.5.1989, BA Berlin DE1/56323, according to Zatlin, *The Currency of Socialism*, p. 139.
2. Cf. Zatlin, *The Currency of Socialism*, pp. 143 f.
3. Schröter, 'Ölkrisen und Reaktionen in der chemischen Industrie', pp. 115–24.
4. Günter Kusch, Rolf Montag, Günter Specht and Konrad Wetzker, *Schlußbilanz – DDR. Fazit einer verfehlten Wirtschafts- und Sozialpolitik*, Berlin 1991, pp. 128 ff.
5. Calculated according to *Statistisches Jahrbuch 1990*, pp. 146, 174.
6. Lösch and Plötz, 'Bedeutung des Bereichs Kommerzielle Koordinierung', p. 70.
7. Deutsche Bundesbank, *Zahlungsbilanz der ehemaligen DDR*, p. 60; Volze, 'Zur Devisenverschuldung der DDR', pp. 180 f.
8. Calculated according to Ministerium für Außenhandel, NSW-Gesamthandel zu internen Umrechnungsverhältnissen, [1989]. These data were made available to the author by courtesy of Hans-Hermann Hertle.
9. Lösch and Plötz, 'Bedeutung des Bereichs Kommerzielle Koordinierung', pp. 88 f.

10. Übersicht über das Wirken ökonomischer Faktoren ..., BA Berlin DE1/56317, quoted according to Christoph Boyer, 'Politische Rahmenbedingungen 1981–1989', in Christoph Boyer et al. (eds), *Geschichte der Sozialpolitik in Deutschland seit 1945*, Vol. 10: *Deutsche Demokratische Republik 1971–1989. Bewegung in der Sozialpolitik, Erstarrung und Niedergang*, Baden-Baden 2008, pp. 35–66, here 48.
11. Charles S. Maier, *Dissolution. The Crisis of Communism and the End of East Germany*, Princeton 1997, pp. 66f.
12. Thieme, 'Notenbank und Währung in der DDR', p. 648; Ritschl, 'Aufstieg und Niedergang', p. 36.
13. Ahrens, *Gegenseitige Wirtschaftshilfe?*, p. 326.
14. On this and the preceding cf. Manfred Melzer, 'The Perfecting of the Planning and Steering Mechanism', in Jeffries and Melzer, *East German Economy*, pp. 99–118; Phillip J. Bryson and Manfred Melzer, *The End of the East German Economy. From Honecker to Reunification*, London 1991, pp. 31–47; Kusch et al., *Schlußbilanz – DDR*, pp. 100–20.
15. Boyer, 'Politische Rahmenbedingungen', p. 44 f.
16. Niederschrift über die Beratung des Politbüros zum Entwurf des Volkswirtschaftsplanes und des Staatshaushaltsplanes 1988 am 17.11.1987, SAPMO-BA DY30/3755.
17. [Wenzel:] Arbeitsniederschrift über eine Beratung beim Generalsekretär ..., 6.9.1988, SAPMO-BA DY30/3755.
18. Peter Hübner, 'Industrielle Manager in der SBZ/DDR. Sozial- und mentalitätsgeschichtliche Aspekte', *Geschichte und Gesellschaft* 24, 1998, 55–80, p. 74.
19. Maria Haendcke-Hoppe-Arnd, 'Die Hauptabteilung XVIII: Volkswirtschaft', in Siegfried Suckut, Clemens Vollnhals, Walter Süß and Roger Engelmann (eds), *Anatomie der Staatssicherheit. Geschichte, Struktur und Methoden* (MfS-Handbuch, Vol. III/10), Berlin 1997, p. 78 f.
20. Calculated according to *Einheitliche Datenbasis*.
21. Cf. Ritschl, 'Aufstieg und Niedergang', p. 16.
22. Data for 1970, 1980 and 1988 according to Schürer et al., *Analyse der ökonomischen Lage der DDR*, p. 1115. Figure for the end of 1989 according to Kusch et al., *Schlußbilanz – DDR*, p. 20. Calculation according to Steiner et al., *Statistische Übersichten*, Table 0.2.0.1.
23. Partly calculated according to Karlsch, 'Wirtschaftliche Belastungen'; *Einheitliche Datenbasis*; Steiner et al., *Statistische Übersichten*, Table 0.2.0.1.
24. Calculated according to *Statistisches Jahrbuch 1990*, pp. 110, 113; *Einheitliche Datenbasis*. As the prices of machines and equipment had in fact increased by more than allowed for in the GDR statistics, the real investment strength was even lower. At an estimate the price-adjusted physical volume of investments in the 'producing' sphere in 1987 was no greater than in 1975. (See Kusch et al., *Schlußbilanz – DDR*, p. 24.)
25. Burghard Ciesla and Helmuth Trischler, 'Die andere "Verkehrsnot". Verkehrspolitik und Leistungsentwicklung des ostdeutschen Verkehrssystems', in Lothar Baar and Dietmar Petzina (eds), *Deutsch–Deutsche Wirtschaft 1945 bis*

1990. Strukturveränderungen, Innovationen und regionaler Wandel. Ein Vergleich, St. Katharinen 1999, pp. 153–92, here 162 ff.; Kusch et al., *Schlußbilanz*, p. 61.

26. Calculated according to *Statistisches Jahrbuch 1990*, pp. 113 f.
27. Hansjörg F. Buck, 'Wohnungsversorgung, Stadtgestaltung und Stadtverfall', in Eberhard Kuhrt (ed.), *Die wirtschaftliche und ökologische Situation der DDR in den 80er Jahren*, Opladen 1996, pp. 67–102.
28. Hertle, 'Diskussion der ökonomischen Krisen', pp. 335 f.; Kusch et al., *Schlußbilanz – DDR*, p. 37.
29. Hertle, 'Diskussion der ökonomischen Krisen', p. 336; Diskussionsbeitrag von Werner Jarowinsky auf der 10. Tagung des ZK der SED vom 8. bis 10. November 1989, in Hertle and Stephan, *Ende der SED*, pp. 389–94, here 392. On the microelectronics programme cf. also Maier, *Dissolution*, pp. 73–75.
30. Reinhold Bauer, *PKW-Bau in der DDR. Zur Innovationsschwäche von Zentralverwaltungswirtschaften*, Frankfurt 1999, pp. 16, 287 ff.
31. Niederschrift über die Beratung des Politbüros zum Entwurf des Volkswirtschaftsplanes und des Staatshaushaltsplanes 1988 am 17.11.1987, SAPMO-BA DY30/3755.
32. Kusch et al., *Schlußbilanz – DDR*, p. 59.
33. Cf. Statistisches Amt der DDR, *Statistisches Jahrbuch für die Industrie 1989*, BA Berlin DE2/21006/0014040; id., *Statistisches Jahrbuch über ausgewählte Kennziffern der Investitionen 1990*, BA Berlin DE2/21006/0014032.
34. Steiner et al., *Statistische Übersichten*, Table 3.1.1.1.
35. Sandra Gruner-Domic, 'Zur Geschichte der Arbeitskräfteemigration in die DDR. Die bilateralen Verträge zur Beschäftigung ausländischer Arbeiter (1961–1989)', *IWK* 32, 1996, pp. 204–30, quotation and figures p. 277.
36. Kusch et al., *Schlußbilanz – DDR*, p. 38.
37. *Statistisches Jahrbuch 1990*, pp. 120 f.; Kusch et al., *Schlußbilanz – DDR*, p. 56.
38. Calculated according to *Statistisches Jahrbuch 1990*, p. 212.
39. Cf. *Statistisches Jahrbuch 1990*, p. 121; *Einheitliche Datenbasis*.
40. Adolf Weber: 'Ursachen und Folgen abnehmender Effizienz in der DDR-Landwirtschaft', in Eberhard Kuhrt (ed.), *Die Endzeit der DDR-Wirtschaft – Analysen zur Wirtschafts-, Sozial- und Umweltpolitik*, Opladen 1999, pp. 225–69, here 251.
41. *Statistisches Jahrbuch 1986*, p. 261.
42. Cf. Steiner et al., *Statistische Übersichten*, Table 0.2.1.3.; *Statistisches Jahrbuch 1990*, p. 270.
43. Data calculated in part according to Staatsbank der DDR, *Jahresbericht 1989*, Berlin (East) 1990, p. 4, quoted according to Bodo von Rüden, *Die Rolle der D-Mark in der DDR. Von der Nebenwährung zur Währungsunion*, Baden-Baden 1991, p. 35; *Statistisches Jahrbuch 1990*, p. 55; Steiner et al., *Statistische Übersichten*, Table 0.4.2.0.; Statistisches Bundesamt (ed.), *Entstehung und Verwendung des Bruttoinlandsprodukts 1970 bis 1989* (Sonderreihe mit Beiträgen für das Gebiet der ehemaligen DDR, No. 33), Wiesbaden 2000, p. 137; Günter Manz: 'Subventionspolitik als Teil der Sozialpolitik', *Wirtschaftswissenschaft 38*, 1990, pp. 494–503, here 497; Zatlin, *The Currency of Socialism*, p. 170.

44. All data calculated in part according to Steiner et al., *Statistische Übersichten*, Tables 0.2.1.0., 0.2.1.3., 0.4.1.0., 0.4.2.0. and 1.2.1.
45. Steiner, 'Preisgestaltung', p. 315.
46. Klopfer: Persönliche Niederschrift über die Beratung im Politbüro, 19.1.1988, SAPMO-BA DY30/3755.
47. Gernot Schneider: 'Lebensstandard und Versorgungslage', in: Kuhrt, *Die wirtschaftliche und ökologische Situation der DDR*, pp. 111–30, here 125 ff.; Zatlin, *The Currency of Socialism*, pp. 203–33.
48. Klopfer: Persönliche Notizen über die Beratung der Wirtschaftskommission des Politbüros vom 17.12.1988, BA Berlin DE1/56285, quoted according to Zatlin, *The Currency of Socialism*, p. 217.
49. MfS: Information über Reaktionen der Bevölkerung zu Problemen des Handels und der Versorgung, 14.8.1987, BstU ZAIG 3605, quoted according to Schneider, *Lebensstandard und Versorgungslage*, p. 113.
50. Manz, 'Subventionspolitik', p. 497. For the end of the seventies see Judt, *DDR-Geschichte*, p. 157; *Statistisches Jahrbuch 1980*, pp. 228, 277. For the end of the eighties see Annette Kaminsky, *Wohlstand, Schönheit, Glück. Kleine Konsumgeschichte der DDR*, Munich 2001, p. 158.
51. Klopfer: Persönliche Notizen über eine Beratung im Politbüro am 14.2.1989, BA Berlin DE1/55384, according to Zatlin, *The Currency of Socialism*, p. 161.
52. Calculated according to Steiner et al., *Statistische Übersichten*, tables 0.1.1.7. and 0.1.1.8.
53. On the whole section cf. von Rüden, *Rolle der Mark*, pp. 39, 45, 80 f., 98-101.
54. Hertle, 'Diskussion der ökonomischen Krisen', pp. 336–40.
55. Niederschrift des Redebeitrags von Willi Stoph im Politbüro am 10.5.1988, BA Berlin DE1/56320, quoted according to Hertle, 'Diskussion der ökonomischen Krisen', p. 341. See there also on the following.
56. [Wenzel:] Arbeitsniederschrift über eine Beratung beim Generalsekretär ..., 6.9.1988, SAPMO-BA DY30/3755.
57. Klopfer: Persönliche Notizen über die Beratung beim Generalsekretär ..., 16.5.1989,BA Berlin DE1/56317, quoted according to Hertle, 'Diskussion der ökonomischen Krisen', p. 344.
58. Hertle, 'Diskussion der ökonomischen Krisen', p. 344.
59. Schürer et al., *Analyse der ökonomischen Lage der DDR*, pp. 1116, 1120. Cf. also Hertle, 'Diskussion der ökonomischen Krisen', p. 344.
60. Arnim Volze: 'Ein großer Bluff? Die Westverschuldung der DDR', *Deutschland-Archiv 29*, 1996, pp. 701–13, here 702 f.
61. Schürer et al., *Analyse der ökonomischen Lage der DDR*, p. 1114.
62. Bundesbank, *Zahlungsbilanz der ehemaligen DDR*, p. 60; *Volze, Devisenverschuldung der DDR*, pp. 180 f. There also on the following. Calculation according to Statistisches Bundesamt, *Entstehung und Verwendung des Bruttoinlandsprodukts*, p. 89.

Brief Biographies

These brief biographies are confined to the principal heads in GDR economic history and to a few data on their origins and their main functions.

Erich Apel (1917–1965): engineer; in the war a member of Wernher von Braun's team developing the V2 at Peenemünde, after the end of the war compulsorily engaged by the Soviets; following his return from the Soviet Union in 1952 rapid rise: 1955–1958 Minister for Heavy Engineering; from 1954 candidate member and Party member from 1957; from February 1958 chief of the newly established Economic Commission at the Politbüro; from 1961 candidate member of the Party's Politbüro; 1961–1962 Secretary for the Economy in the Party's Central Committee; 1963–1965 chief of the State Planning Commission and deputy chairman of the Council of Ministers; committed suicide in 1965.

Erich Honecker (1912–1994): before 1933 Communist Youth functionary; during the Nazi regime in the illegal Resistance; arrested in 1935 and until 1945 imprisoned in the Brandenburg penitentiary; 1946 co-founder and first Chairman of the FDJ until 1955; 1950 to 1958 candidate, from 1958 member of the SED Politbüro, responsible for security and cadre matters; 1971 First Secretary, later Secretary General of the Central Committee of the SED and from 1976 Chairman of the GDR State Council; October 1989 resigned all posts; after 1990 sporadic detention while awaiting trial; charged; following the lifting of the arrest warrant in 1993, emigrated to Chile.

Bruno Leuschner (1910–1965): graduate industrial clerk, studied in various evening classes; became a Communist in 1931; imprisoned for illegal activity in several prisons and concentration camps until 1945; from 1945 head of the Department for Economic Policy in the Central Committee of the Communist Party of Germany; from 1946 head of the Department for Economics and Finances in the Socialist Unity Party Executive; 1947 head of the German Economic Commission's Department for Economic Matters; 1948 deputy chairman of the German Economic Commission and head of its Main Administration for Economic Planning; 1950–1952 First Deputy Chairman; 1952–1961 Chairman of the State Planning Commission; from 1953 candidate member and since 1958 member of the Politbüro; from 1962 Permanent Plenipotentiary of the GDR in the COMECON Executive.

Günter Mittag (1926–1994): railwayman; 1945 member of the Communist Party of Germany, various trade union and Party functions; 1953–1961 head of the Central Committee's Department for Railways, Transport and Communications; 1958–1961 Secretary of the Economic Commission at the Politbüro of the Socialist Unity Party; 1961–1962 Secretary of the National Economic Council; 1962–1973 and again 1976–1989 Secretary for the Economy of the Central Committee of the Socialist Unity Party; 1973–1976 First Deputy Chairman of the Council of Ministers; 1976–1989 Head of the Economic Commission at the Politbüro; October 1989 relieved of his functions; 1989–90 under detention; charges dismissed in 1993 on grounds of incapacity to stand trial.

Alfred Neumann (1909–2001): carpenter; 1929 member of the Communist Party of Germany; after 1933 illegal resistance, emigrated to the Soviet Union; 1938–1939 member of the International Brigade in the Spanish Civil War; 1939 arrested in France; 1941 handed over to the Gestapo; penitentiary; after 1947 various functions in the Socialist Unity Party; 1953–1957 First Secretary of the Socialist Unity Party's regional executive committee of Berlin; 1954 candidate member and 1954–1989 member of the Politbüro; 1957–1961 Secretary of the Central Committee; 1961–1965 Chairman of the National Economic Council; 1965–1968 Minister for Materials Economy; 1969–1989 First Deputy of the Chairman of the Council of Ministers; November 1989 resigned from his posts.

Heinrich Rau (1899–1961): prior to 1933 for many years Communist Party functionary; after 1933 illegal activity; 1937–1938 member of the International Brigade in the Spanish Civil War; 1942 handed over by France to the Gestapo; Gestapo and concentration camp prisoner; 1945 Second Chairman of Brandenburg Provincial Administration, responsible for economic issues; 1946–1948 Minister of Economic Planning of Land Brandenburg; 1948–49 Chairman of German Economic Commission; 1949 candidate member and from 1950 member of the Politbüro; 1950–1952 Chairman of the State Planning Commission; 1953–1955 Minister for Engineering; 1955–1961 Minister for Foreign Trade and Intra-German Trade.

Willi Rumpf (1903–1982): qualified insurance employee, working as accountant and treasurer; Communist Party member from 1925; resistance during Nazi period, arrested; 1948–1949 head of the Main Administration Finances in the German Economic Commission; 1949–1955 State Secretary in the Ministry of Finance; 1955–1966 Minister of Finance; retired for health reasons.

Alexander Schalck-Golodkowski (1932–): trained precision mechanic; after 1952 various positions in foreign trade; 1952–1962 head of a Main Administration in the Ministry of Foreign Trade; studied at the College for Foreign Trade; 1955 joined Socialist Unity Party; 1962–1966 First Secretary of the Party Headquarter in the same ministry; since 1966 chief of the division Kommerzielle Koordinierung ('Commercial Coordination', KoKo); from 1967 officer on special mission of the Ministry of State Security; 1967–1975 Deputy Secretary for Foreign Trade; from 1975 State Secretary in the same ministry; December 1989 escape to the Federal Republic; became, along with KoKo, object of an investigation committee of the Bundestag until 1994.

Gerhard Schürer (1921–): machine fitter; 1939–1945 Wehrmacht; after 1945 various activities; joined Socialist Unity Party in 1948; 1947–1951 industrial management school; 1951–1952 administrator and departmental chief in the State Planning Commission; 1953–1955 employee of Party Central Committee; 1955–1958 studied at the Party Academy of the Soviet Communist Party in Moscow; 1958–1962 deputy head, later head of the Department for Planning, Finance and Technological Development in the Central Committee; 1962–1965 deputy chairman of the State Planning Commission; 1965–1989 its chairman; from 1973 candidate member of the Politbüro, resigned November 1989.

Fritz Selbmann (1899–1975): miner; high-ranking functionary and Reichstag deputy of the Communist Party of Germany prior to 1933, then detained in prisons and concentration camps until 1945; since the autumn of 1945 Vice President of the Land Administration for Economy and Work for Saxony; 1946–1948 Minister for Economy and Economic Planning in Saxony; 1948–1949 Deputy Chairman of the German Economic Commission and Head of its Main Administration Industry; 1949–1950 Minister for Industry; 1950–1951 for Heavy Industry; 1951–1953 for Iron Smelting and Ore Mining; 1953–1955 for Heavy Industry; 1955–1958 Deputy Chairman of the Council of Ministers and Chairman of its Commission for Industry and Transport; in 1958 accused of 'managerdom' and 'creating factions'; 1958–1961 Deputy Chairman of the State Planning

Commission, and 1961–1964 of the National Economic Council; from 1964 author.

Walter Ulbricht (1893–1973): carpenter; 1919 member of the Communist Party of Germany, leading communist party official during Weimar period; 1929–1946 member of Communist Party Politbüro; 1933 emigration to Paris and then Prague, from 1938 in Moscow; 1946–1950 de facto Deputy Chairman of the Socialist Unity Party; 1949–1973 member of the Party's Politbüro; 1949–1955 Deputy; 1955–1960 First Deputy of the Chairman of the Council of Ministers; 1950–1953 General Secretary and 1953–1971 First Secretary of the Party Central Committee; from 1960 Chairman of the State Council.

Gerhard Ziller (1912–1957): electrical fitter and technical draftsman; 1930 member of the Communist Party of Germany, editor of a Communist paper; after 1933 repeatedly arrested for illegal activity; 1945–1948 Head of a department in the Ministry for Economy and Labour of Saxony; 1948–1949 Deputy and 1949–1950 Minister for Industry and Transport in Saxony; 1950–1953 Minister for Engineering and 1953–1954 for Heavy Engineering; since 1953 Secretary for the Economy in the Party's Central Committee; 1957 suicide after economic-policy arguments with and criticism of Ulbricht.

Bibliography

I. Primary Sources

A. Archives

Bundesarchiv Berlin (BA Berlin).

Stiftung Archiv der Parteien und Massenorganisationen der DDR im Bundesarchiv (SAPMO-BA).

B. Published Sources

Badstübner, R. and W. Loth (eds). 1994. *Wilhelm Pieck– Aufzeichnungen zur Deutschlandpolitik 1945–1953*. Berlin: Akademie-Verlag.
Behrens, F. 1957. 'Zum Problem der Ausnutzung ökonomischer Gesetze in der Übergangsperiode', *Wirtschaftswissenschaft* 5(3rd special issue): 105–40.
'Die Entwicklung der Lebenshaltungskosten im sowjetischen Besatzungsgebiet', in *DIW-Wochenbericht* 20, 1953, pp.107–9.
'Die gescheiterte Preisreform 1979 in der DDR. Protokoll einer Diskussion', in Rainer Weinert (ed.), *'Preise sind gefährlicher als Ideen'. Das Scheitern der Preisreform 1979 in der DDR. Protokoll einer Tagung.* (POLHIST Arbeitshefte der Forschungsstelle Diktatur und Demokratie am Fachbereich Politische Wissenschaften der Freien Universität Berlin. No. 10) Berlin 1999.
Direktive für den 2. Fünfjahrplan zur Entwicklung der Volkswirtschaft der DDR 1956 bis 1960. Beschluß der 3. Parteikonferenz der SED. 1956. Berlin (East): Dietz.
Dokumente zur Außenpolitik der Regierung der DDR, Vol. IX. 1962. Berlin (East): Staatsverlag.
Erler, P., H. Laude and M. Wilke (eds). 1994. *'Nach Hitler kommen wir'. Dokumente zur Programmatik der Moskauer KPD-Führung 1944–1945 für Nachkriegsdeutschland*. Berlin: Akademie-Verlag.
Fischer A. (ed.). 1985. *Teheran, Jalta, Potsdam. Die sowjetischen Protokolle von den Kriegskonferenzen der 'Großen Drei'*, 3rd Edition. Cologne: Verlag Wissenschaft und Politik.

Foitzik, J. 1995. 'Berichte des Hohen Kommissars der UdSSR in Deutschland aus den Jahren 1953/54. Dokumente aus dem Archiv für Außenpolitik der Russischen Föderation', in Deutscher Bundestag (ed.), *Materialien der Enquete-Kommission 'Aufarbeitung von Geschichte und Folgen der SED-Diktatur in Deutschland'*. Baden-Baden: Nomos, Vol. II/2, pp. 1350–542.

'Gesetz über den 2. Fünfjahrplan zur Entwicklung der Volkswirtschaft … vom 9.1.1958', *Gesetzblatt der DDR*, 1958, I, pp. 41ff.

Gleitze, B. 1956. *Ostdeutsche Wirtschaft. Industrielle Standorte und volkswirtschaftliche Kapazitäten des ungeteilten Deutschlands*. Berlin (West): Duncker und Humblot.

———. 1962. *Sowjetzonenwirtschaft in der Krise*. Cologne: Bund-Verlag.

Halbritter, W. 'Vermerk über ein Gespräch beim Generalsekretär des ZK der SED, Gen. Erich Honecker, am 29.10.1979 (anwesend Mittag, Jarowinsky, Halbritter)' in Rainer Weinert (ed.), *'Preise sind gefährlicher als Ideen'. Das Scheitern der Preisreform 1979 in der DDR. Protokoll einer Tagung*. (POLHIST Arbeitshefte der Forschungsstelle Diktatur und Demokratie am Fachbereich Politische Wissenschaften der Freien Universität Berlin. No. 10) Berlin 1999.

Hertle, H.-H. and G.R. Stephan (eds). 1997. *Das Ende der SED. Die letzten Tage des Zentralkomitees*. Berlin: Links.

Hoffmann, D., K.-H. Schmidt and P. Skyba (eds). 1993. *Die DDR vor dem Mauerbau. Dokumente zur Geschichte des anderen deutschen Staates 1949–1961*. Munich: Piper, pp. 152–58.

Judt, M. (ed.). 1997. *DDR-Geschichte in Dokumenten. Beschlüsse, Berichte, interne Materialien und Alltagszeugnisse*. Berlin: Links.

Köhler, H. 1965. *Economic Integration in the Soviet Bloc, with an East German Case Study*. New York: Praeger.

Kramer, M. 1957. *Die Landwirtschaft in der Sowjetischen Besatzungszone. Die Entwicklung in den Jahren 1945–1955. Textteil (Bonner Berichte aus Mittel- und Ostdeutschland)*. Bonn: Deutscher Bundesverlag.

Krause, W. 1958. *Die Entstehung des Volkseigentums in der Industrie der DDR*. Berlin (East): Verlag Die Wirtschaft.

Manz, G. 1990. 'Subventionspolitik als Teil der Sozialpolitik', *Wirtschaftswissenschaft* 38: 494–503.

'Preise und Lebenshaltungskosten im sowjetischen Besatzungsgebiet', in *DIW-Wochenbericht* 20, 1953, pp. 25 ff.

Protokoll der Verhandlungen des 2. Parteitages der SED. 20. bis 24. September 1947. 1947. Berlin: Dietz.

Protokoll der Verhandlungen des V. Parteitages der Sozialistischen Einheitspartei Deutschlands, 10. bis 16. Juli 1958. 1959. Berlin (East): Dietz.

Protokoll der Verhandlungen des VI. Parteitages der SED, 15. bis 21. Januar 1963, Vol. 1. 1963. Berlin (East): Dietz.

Protokoll der Verhandlungen des VIII. Parteitages der SED, 15. bis 19. Juni 1971, Vol. I and II. 1971. Berlin (East): Dietz.

Richtlinie für das neue ökonomische System der Planung und Leitung der Volkswirtschaft. 1963. Berlin (East): Dietz.

Scherstjanoi, E. and R. Semmelmann. 2004. 'Die Gespräche Stalins mit der SED-Führung im Dezember 1948 und im April 1952 (Teil 2)', *Zeitschrift für Geschichtswissenschaft* 52: 238–69.

Schürer, G., G. Beil, A. Schalck, E. Höffner, and A. Donda. 1992. 'Vorlage für das Politbüro des Zentralkomitees der SED. Analyse der ökonomischen Lage der DDR mit Schlußfolgerungen vom 30.10.1989', *Deutschland-Archiv* 25: 1112–20.

Selbmann, F. 1948. *Demokratische Wirtschaft*. Dresden: Dresdener Verlagsgesellschaft.

Suckut, S. 1986. *Blockpolitik in der SBZ/DDR 1945–1949. Die Sitzungsprotokolle des Zentralen Einheitsfront-Ausschusses. Quellenedition*. Cologne: Verlag Wissenschaft und Politik.

Tümmler, E. 1969. 'Die Agrarpolitik in Mitteldeutschland', in idem et al. (eds), *Die Agrarpolitik in Mitteldeutschland und ihre Auswirkungen auf Produktion und Verbrauch landwirtschaftlicher Erzeugnisse*, Berlin (West): Duncker und Humblot, pp. 1–167.

Ulbricht, W. 1962. *Zur Geschichte der deutschen Arbeiterbewegung. Aus Reden und Aufsätzen*, Vol. IV. Berlin (East): Dietz.

Ulbricht, W. 1963. *Das neue ökonomische System der Planung und Leitung der Volkswirtschaft in der Praxis*. Berlin (East): Dietz.

'Verordnung über die Bildung halbstaatlicher Betriebe vom 26.3.1959', *Gesetzblatt der DDR*, 1959, I, pp. 253 ff.

Weinert, R. (ed.). 1999. *'Preise sind gefährlicher als Ideen'. Das Scheitern der Preisreform 1979 in der DDR. Protokoll einer Tagung*. (POLHIST Arbeitshefte der Forschungsstelle Diktatur und Demokratie am Fachbereich Politische Wissenschaften der Freien Universität Berlin. Nr. 10). Berlin: Forschungsstelle Diktatur und Demokratie.

'Zu Grundproblemen der politischen Ökonomie des Sozialismus in der Übergangsperiode', *Wirtschaftswissenschaft* 5 (3rd special issue), 1957: 60–94.

C. Statistics

Bundesministerium für Arbeit und Sozialordnung (ed.). 1998. *Statistisches Taschenbuch 1998: Arbeits- und Sozialstatistik*. Bonn.

Deutsche Bundesbank (ed.). 1976. *Deutsches Geld- und Bankwesen in Zahlen 1876–1975*. Frankfurt.

Länderrat des amerikanischen Besatzungsgebietes (ed.). 1949. *Statistisches Handbuch von Deutschland 1928–1944*. Munich.

Melzer, M. 1980. *Anlagevermögen, Produktion und Beschäftigung der Industrie im Gebiet der DDR von 1936 bis 1978 sowie Schätzung des künftigen Angebotspotentials*. Berlin (West): Duncker und Humblot.

Staatliche Zentralverwaltung für Statistik (ed.). 1957. *Statistisches Jahrbuch der DDR 1956*. Berlin (East).

———. (ed.). 1963. *Statistisches Jahrbuch der DDR 1962*. Berlin (East).

———. (ed.). 1969. *Statistisches Jahrbuch der DDR 1968*. Berlin (East).

———. (ed.). 1971. *Statistisches Jahrbuch der DDR 1970*. Berlin (East).

———. (ed.). 1973. *Statistisches Jahrbuch der DDR 1972*. Berlin (East).

————. (ed.). 1977. *Statistisches Jahrbuch der DDR 1976*. Berlin (East).

Statistisches Amt der DDR (ed.). 1990. *Statistisches Jahrbuch der DDR 1990*. Berlin (East).

Statistisches Bundesamt (ed.). 1970. *Statistisches Jahrbuch für die BRD 1970*. Wiesbaden.

————. 1993. *Ausgewählte Zahlen zur Agrarwirtschaft 1949 bis 1989 (Sonderreihe mit Beiträgen für das Gebiet der ehemaligen DDR, No. 8)*. Wiesbaden.

————. 2000. *Entstehung und Verwendung des Bruttoinlandsprodukts 1970 bis 1989 (Sonderreihe mit Beiträgen für das Gebiet der ehemaligen DDR, No. 33)*. Wiesbaden.

Steiner, A., M. Judt and T. Reichel. 2006. *Statistische Übersichten zur Sozialpolitik in Deutschland seit 1945. Band SBZ/DDR (Bundesministerium für Arbeit und Soziales, Forschungsbericht 352)*. Bonn.

Wirtschaftsstatistik der deutschen Besatzungszonen 1945–1948 in Verbindung mit der deutschen Produktionsstatistik der Vorkriegszeit (Dokumente und Berichte des Europa-Archivs, Vol. 3). 1948. Oberursel: Europa-Archiv.

II. Secondary Sources

Abelshauser, W. 1983. *Wirtschaftsgeschichte der Bundesrepublik Deutschland 1945–1980*. Frankfurt: Suhrkamp.

————. 2004. *Deutsche Wirtschaftsgeschichte seit 1945*. Munich: Beck.

Ahrens, R. 2000. *Gegenseitige Wirtschaftshilfe? Die DDR im RGW – Strukturen und handelspolitische Strategien 1963–1976*. Cologne: Böhlau.

Augustine, D.L. 2007. *Red Prometheus. Engineering and Dictatorship in East Germany, 1945–1990*. Cambridge: MIT Press.

Baar, L., R. Karlsch and W. Matschke. 1995. 'Kriegsschäden, Demontagen und Reparationen', in Deutscher Bundestag (ed.), *Materialien der Enquete-Kommission 'Aufarbeitung von Geschichte und Folgen der SED-Diktatur in Deutschland'*. Baden-Baden: Nomos, Vol. II/2, pp. 868–988.

Baar, L., U. Müller and F. Zschaler. 1995. 'Strukturveränderungen und Wachstumsschwankungen. Investitionen und Budget in der DDR 1949 bis 1989', *Jahrbuch für Wirtschaftsgeschichte* 1995, 2: 47–74.

Bachman, D. 1991. *Bureaucracy, Economy, and Leadership in China. The Institutional Origins of the Great Leap Forward*. New York: Cambridge University Press.

Bähr, J. 1997. 'Die Firmenabwanderung aus der SBZ/DDR und aus Ost-Berlin (1945–1953)', in W. Fischer, U. Müller and F. Zschaler (eds), *Wirtschaft im Umbruch. Strukturveränderungen und Wirtschaftspolitik im 19. und 20. Jahrhundert*. St. Katharinen: Scripta-Mercaturae-Verlag, pp. 229–49.

Barthel, H. 1979. *Die wirtschaftlichen Ausgangsbedingungen der DDR. Zur Wirtschaftsentwicklung auf dem Gebiet der DDR 1945–1949/50*. Berlin (East): Akademie-Verlag.

————. 1984. 'Die Einführung des doppelten Preissystems für Einzelhandelsverkaufspreise in der DDR durch die Schaffung der HO-Laden von 1948 bis 1950/51 als komplexe Maßnahme der Wirtschaftspolitik', *Jahrbuch für Geschichte*, Vol. 31. Berlin (East): Akademie-Verlag, pp. 273–97.

Bauer, R. 1999. *PKW-Bau in der DDR. Zur Innovationsschwäche von Zentralverwaltungswirtschaften*. Frankfurt: Lang.

Bauerkämper, A. 1995. 'Problemdruck und Ressourcenverbrauch. Wirtschaftliche Auswirkungen der Bodenreform in der SBZ/DDR 1945–1952' in C. Buchheim (ed.), *Wirtschaftliche Folgelasten des Krieges in der SBZ/DDR*. Baden-Baden: Nomos, pp. 295–322.

———. 2000. 'Auf dem Wege zum "Sozialismus auf dem Lande". Die Politik der SED 1948/49 und die Reaktionen im dörflich-agrarischen Milieu', in D. Hoffmann and H. Wentker (eds), *Das letzte Jahr der SBZ. Politische Weichenstellungen und Kontinuitäten im Prozeß der Gründung der DDR*. Munich: Oldenbourg, pp. 245–68.

———. 2002. *Ländliche Gesellschaft in der kommunistischen Diktatur. Zwangsmodernisierung und Tradition in Brandenburg von 1945 bis zu den frühen sechziger Jahren*. Cologne: Böhlau.

Bezzenberger, T. 1997. 'Wie das Volkseigentum geschaffen wurde. Die Unternehmensenteignungen in der Sowjetischen Besatzungszone 1945–1948', *Zeitschrift für neuere Rechtsgeschichte* 19: 210–48.

Boldorf, M. 1998. *Sozialfürsorge in der SBZ/DDR 1945–1953. Ursachen, Ausmaß und Bewältigung der Nachkriegsarmut*. Stuttgart: Steiner.

Boyer, C. 2008. 'Politische Rahmenbedingungen 1981–1989', in C. Boyer, et al. (eds), *Geschichte der Sozialpolitik in Deutschland seit 1945*, Vol. 10: *Deutsche Demokratische Republik 1971–1989. Bewegung in der Sozialpolitik, Erstarrung und Niedergang*. Baden-Baden: Nomos, pp. 35–66.

———. and P. Skyba. 1999. 'Sozial- und Konsumpolitik als Stabilisierungsstrategie. Zur Genese der "Einheit von Wirtschafts- und Sozialpolitik" in der DDR', *Deutschland Archiv* 32(4): 577–90.

Broosch, K. 1998. *Die Währungsreform 1948 in der sowjetischen Besatzungszone Deutschlands. Eine Untersuchung zur Rolle des Geldes beim Übergang zur sozialistischen Planwirtschaft in der SBZ/DDR*. Herdecke: GCA-Verlag.

Bryson, P.J. and M. Melzer. 1991. *The End of the East German Economy. From Honecker to Reunification*. Basingstoke: Macmillan.

Buchheim, C. 1990a. *Die Wiedereingliederung Westdeutschlands in die Weltwirtschaft 1945–1958*. Munich: Oldenbourg.

———. 1990b. 'Wirtschaftliche Hintergründe des Arbeiteraufstandes vom 17 Juni 1953 in der DDR', *Vierteljahreshefte für Zeitgeschichte* 38: 415–33.

———. 1995a. 'Die Wirtschaftsordnung als Barriere des gesamtwirtschaftlichen Wachstums in der DDR', *Vierteljahrschrift für Sozial- und Wirtschaftsgeschichte* 82: 194–210.

———. 1995b. 'Kriegsschäden, Demontagen und Reparationen. Deutschland nach dem Zweiten Weltkrieg' in Deutscher Bundestag (ed.), *Materialien der Enquete-Kommission 'Aufarbeitung von Geschichte und Folgen der SED-Diktatur in Deutschland'*. Baden-Baden: Nomos, Vol. II/2, pp. 1030–69.

————. 1995c. 'Wirtschaftliche Folgen der Integration der DDR in den RGW', in idem (ed.), *Wirtschaftliche Folgelasten des Krieges in der SBZ/DDR*. Baden-Baden: Nomos, pp. 341–61.

————. 1998. 'Die Errichtung der Bank deutscher Länder und die Währungsreform in Westdeutschland', in Deutsche Bundesbank (ed.), *Fünfzig Jahre Deutsche Mark. Notenbank und Währung in Deutschland seit 1948*. Munich: Beck, pp. 91–138.

Buck, H.F. 1999. 'Wohnungsversorgung, Stadtgestaltung und Stadtverfall', in E. Kuhrt (ed.), *Die Endzeit der DDR-Wirtschaft – Analysen zur Wirtschafts-, Sozial- und Umweltpolitik*. Opladen: Leske and Budrich, pp. 67–102.

Ciesla, B. 1995. '"Intellektuelle Reparationen" der SBZ an die alliierten Siegermächte? Begriffsgeschichte, Diskussionsaspekte und ein Fallbeispiel – Die deutsche Flugzeugindustrie 1945–1946' in C. Buchheim (ed.), *Wirtschaftliche Folgelasten des Krieges in der SBZ/DDR*. Baden-Baden: Nomos, pp. 79–109.

————. and H. Trischler. 1999. 'Die andere "Verkehrsnot". Verkehrspolitik und Leistungsentwicklung des ostdeutschen Verkehrssystems', in L. Baar and D. Petzina (eds), *Deutsch–Deutsche Wirtschaft 1945 bis 1990. Strukturveränderungen, Innovationen und regionaler Wandel. Ein Vergleich*. St. Katharinen: Scripta-Mercaturae-Verlag, pp. 153–92.

Deutsche Bundesbank. 1999. *Die Zahlungsbilanz der ehemaligen DDR 1975 bis 1989*. Frankfurt.

Diedrich, T. 1994. 'Aufrüstungsvorbereitung und -finanzierung in der SBZ/DDR in den Jahren 1948 bis 1953 und deren Rückwirkungen auf die Wirtschaft', in B. Thoß (ed.), *Volksarmee schaffen – ohne Geschrei*. Munich: Oldenbourg, pp. 273–336.

————. and R. Wenzke. *Die getarnte Armee. Geschichte der Kasernierten Volkspolizei der DDR 1952–1956*. Berlin: Links.

Ebbinghaus, F. 2003. *Ausnutzung und Verdrängung. Steuerungsprobleme der SED-Mittelstandspolitik 1955–1972*. Berlin: Duncker und Humblot.

Ermer, M. 2000. *Von der Reichsmark zur Deutschen Mark der Deutschen Notenbank. Zum Binnenwährungsumtausch in der Sowjetischen Besatzungszone Deutschlands (Juni/Juli 1948)*. Stuttgart: Steiner.

Fäßler, P.E. 2006. *Durch den 'Eisernen Vorhang'. Die deutsch–deutschen Wirtschaftsbeziehungen 1949–1969*. Cologne: Böhlau.

Fisch, J. 1992. *Reparationen nach dem Zweiten Weltkrieg*. Munich: Beck.

Foitzik, J. 1999. *Sowjetische Militäradministration in Deutschland (SMAD) 1945–1949. Struktur und Funktion*. Berlin: Akademie-Verlag.

Frerich, J. and M. Frey. 1993. *Handbuch der Geschichte der Sozialpolitik in Deutschland*, Vol. 2: *Sozialpolitik in der Deutschen Demokratischen Republik*. Munich: Oldenbourg.

Gries, R. 1991. *Die Rationen-Gesellschaft. Versorgungskampf und Vergleichsmentalität: Leipzig, München und Köln nach dem Kriege*. Münster: Verlag Westfälisches Dampfboot.

Gruner-Domic, S. 1996. 'Zur Geschichte der Arbeitskräfteemigration in die DDR. Die bilateralen Verträge zur Beschäftigung ausländischer Arbeiter (1961–1989)', *IWK* 32: 204–30.

Haendcke-Hoppe-Arndt, M. 1997. 'Die Hauptabteilung XVIII: Volkswirtschaft', in S. Suckut et al. (eds), *Anatomie der Staatssicherheit. Geschichte, Struktur und Methoden (MfS-Handbuch* Vol. III/10). Berlin.

Halder, W. 1999. 'Prüfstein ... für die politische Lauterbarkeit der Führenden? Der Volksentscheid zur "Enteignung der Kriegs- und Naziverbrecher" in Sachsen im Juni 1946', *Geschichte und Gesellschaft* 25: 589–612.

———. 2001. *'Modell für Deutschland'. Wirtschaftspolitik in Sachsen 1945–1948*. Paderborn: Schöningh.

Hertle, H.-H. 1995. 'Die Diskussion der ökonomischen Krisen in der Führungsspitze der SED', in T. Pirker, M.R. Lepsius, R. Weinert and H.-H. Hertle, *Der Plan als Befehl und Fiktion. Wirtschaftsführung in der DDR. Gespräche und Analysen*. Opladen: Westdeutscher Verlag, pp. 309–45.

Hertle, H.-H. et al. (eds) 2002. *Mauerbau und Mauerfall. Ursachen – Verlauf – Auswirkungen*. Berlin: Links Verlag.

Hoffmann, D. 2002. *Aufbau und Krise der Planwirtschaft. Die Arbeitskräftelenkung in der SBZ/DDR 1945 bis 1963*. Munich: Oldenbourg.

Hoffmann, H. 1999. *Die Betriebe mit staatlicher Beteiligung im planwirtschaftlichen System der DDR 1956–1972*. Stuttgart: Steiner.

Hübner, P. 1995. *Konsens, Konflikt und Kompromiß. Soziale Arbeiterinteressen und Sozialpolitik in der SBZ/DDR 1945–1970*. Berlin: Akademie-Verlag.

———. 1998. 'Industrielle Manager in der SBZ/DDR. Sozial- und mentalitätsgeschichtliche Aspekte', *Geschichte und Gesellschaft* 24: 55–80.

———. 1999. 'Durch Planung zur Improvisation, Zur Geschichte des Leitungspersonals in der staatlichen Industrie der DDR', *Archiv für Sozialgeschichte* 39: 197–233.

———. and J. Danyel. 2002. 'Soziale Argumente im politischen Machtkampf: Prag, Warschau, Berlin 1968–1971', *Zeitschrift für Geschichtswissenschaft* 50: 804–32.

Industriezweige in der DDR 1945 bis 1985 (Jahrbuch für Wirtschaftsgeschichte, Sonderband 1988). 1989. Berlin (East): Akademie-Verlag.

Jeffries, I. and M. Melzer. 1987. 'The New Economic System of Planning and Management 1963–70 and Recentralisation in the 1970s', in idem (eds), *The East German Economy*. London: Croom Helm, pp. 35 ff.

Kaiser, M. 1990. *1972 – Knockout für den Mittelstand. Zum Wirken von SED, CDU, LDPD und NDPD für die Verstaatlichung der Klein- und Mittelbetriebe*. Berlin: Dietz.

Kaminsky, A. 2001. *Wohlstand, Schönheit, Glück. Kleine Konsumgeschichte der DDR*. Munich: Beck.

Karlsch, R. 1993. *Allein bezahlt? Die Reparationsleistungen der SBZ/DDR 1945–1953*. Berlin: Links.

———. 1996. 'Die Auswirkungen der Reparationsentnahmen auf die Wettbewerbsfähigkeit der Wirtschaft in der SBZ/DDR', in J. Schneider and W. Harbrecht (eds), *Wirtschaftsordnung und Wirtschaftspolitik in Deutschland (1933–1993)*. Stuttgart: Steiner, pp. 139–72.

————. 1999a. 'Die Reparationsleistungen der SBZ/DDR im Spiegel deutscher und russischer Quellen' in K. Eckart and J. Roesler (eds), *Die Wirtschaft im geteilten und vereinten Deutschland*. Berlin: Duncker und Humblot, pp. 9–30.

————. 1999b. 'Wirtschaftliche Belastungen durch bewaffnete Organe', in Deutscher Bundestag, *Materialien der Enquete-Kommission*, Vol. III: *Überwindung der Folgen der SED-Diktatur im Prozeß der deutschen Einheit*. Baden-Baden: Nomos, 2, pp. 1500–84.

————. and J. Bähr. 1994. 'Die Sowjetischen Aktiengesellschaften (SAG) in der SBZ/DDR. Bildung, Struktur und Probleme ihrer inneren Entwicklung' in K. Lauschke and T. Welskopp (eds), *Mikropolitik im Unternehmen. Arbeitsbeziehungen und Machtstrukturen in industriellen Großbetrieben des 20. Jahrhunderts*. Essen: Klartext-Verlag-Verlag, pp. 214–55.

Kluge, U. 1999. 'Die verhinderte Rebellion. Bauern, Genossenschaften und SED im Umfeld der Juni-Krise 1953 in der DDR', in W. V. Kieseritzky and K.-P. Sick (eds), *Demokratie in Deutschland. Chancen und Gefährdungen im 19. und 20. Jahrhundert*. Munich: Beck, pp. 317–35.

Kornai, J. 1986. 'The Hungarian Reform Process: Visions, Hopes, and Reality', *Journal of Economic Literature*, XXIV: 1728f.

Kühr, R. 1996. *Die Reparationspolitik der UdSSR und die Sowjetisierung des Verkehrswesens der SBZ. Eine Untersuchung der Entwicklung der Deutschen Reichsbahn 1945–1949*. Bochum: Brockmeyer.

Kusch, G., R. Montag, G. Specht. and K. Wetzker. 1991. *Schlußbilanz – DDR. Fazit einer verfehlten Wirtschafts- und Sozialpolitik*. Berlin: Duncker und Humblot.

Landsman, M. 2005. *Dictatorship and Demand: The Politics of Consumerism in East Germany*. Cambridge: Havard University Press.

Laufer, J. 1995. 'Die Reparationsplanungen im sowjetischen Außenministerium während des Zweiten Weltkrieges', in C. Buchheim (ed.), *Wirtschaftliche Folgelasten des Krieges in der SBZ/DDR*. Baden-Baden: Nomos, pp. 21–43.

————. 1998. 'Die UdSSR und die deutsche Währungsfrage 1944–1948', *Vierteljahreshefte für Zeitgeschichte* 46: 455–85.

————. 1999. 'Von den Demontagen zur Währungsreform – Besatzungspolitik und Sowjetisierung Ostdeutschlands 1945–1948' in M. Lemke (ed.), *Sowjetisierung und Eigenständigkeit in der SBZ/DDR (1945–1953)*. Cologne: Böhlau, pp. 163–86.

————. 2002. 'Politik und Bilanz der sowjetischen Demontagen in der SBZ/DDR 1945–1950' in R. Karlsch and idem (eds), *Sowjetische Demontagen in Deutschland 1944–1949. Hintergründe, Ziele und Wirkungen*. Berlin: Duncker und Humblot, pp. 31–77.

Lösch, D. and P. Plötz. 1994. 'HWWA-Gutachten. Die Bedeutung des Bereichs Kommerzielle Koordinierung für die Volkswirtschaft der DDR', in Deutscher Bundestag (ed.), *Der Bereich Kommerzielle Koordinierung und Alexander Schalck-Golodkowski. Bericht des 1. Untersuchungsausschusses des 12. Deutschen Bundestages. Anhangband 1994*. Bonn, pp. 3–158.

Loth, W. 1994. *Stalins ungeliebtes Kind. Warum Moskau die DDR nicht wollte*. Berlin: Rowohlt.

Mai, G. 1995. *Der Alliierte Kontrollrat in Deutschland 1945–1948. Alliierte Einheit – deutsche Teilung?* Munich: Oldenbourg.

Maier, C.S. 1997. *Dissolution. The Crisis of Communism and the End of East Germany.* Princeton: Princeton University Press.

Major, P. 2002. 'Innenpolitische Aspekte der zweiten Berlinkrise (1958–1961)', in H.-H. Hertle, K.H. Jarausch and C. Kleßmann (eds), *Mauerbau und Mauerfall. Ursachen – Verlauf – Auswirkungen.* Berlin: Links, pp. 97–110.

Matschke, W. 1988. *Die industrielle Entwicklung in der Sowjetischen Besatzungszone Deutschlands (SBZ) von 1945 bis 1948.* Berlin (West): Spitz.

Melzer, M. 1987. 'The Perfecting of the Planning and Steering Mechanism', in I. Jeffries and idem (eds), *The East German Economy.* London: Croom Helm, pp. 99–118.

Merkel, I. 1999. *Utopie und Bedürfnis. Die Geschichte der Konsumkultur in der DDR.* Cologne: Böhlau.

Mühlfriedel, W. and K. Wießner. 1989. *Die Geschichte der Industrie der DDR bis 1965.* Berlin (East): Akademie-Verlag.

Müller, A. 2006. *Institutionelle Brüche und personelle Brücken. Werkleiter in Volkseigenen Betrieben der DDR in der Ära Ulbricht.* Cologne: Böhlau.

Ostermann, C. 2001. *Uprising in East Germany 1953. The Cold War, the German Question and the First Major Upheaval behind the Iron Curtain.* Budapest: Central European University Press.

Port, A. 2007. *Conflict and Stability in the German Democratic Republic.* New York: Cambridge University Press.

Poutrus, P.G. 2002. *Die Erfindung des Goldbroilers. Über den Zusammenhang zwischen Herrschaftssicherung und Konsumentwicklung in der DDR.* Cologne: Böhlau.

Reichel, T. 1999. 'Konfliktprävention. Die Episode der "Arbeiterkomitees" 1956/58', in P. Hübner and K. Tenfelde (eds), *Arbeiter in der SBZ-DDR.* Essen: Klartext-Verlag, pp. 439–52.

Ritschl, A. 1995. 'Aufstieg und Niedergang der Wirtschaft der DDR: Ein Zahlenbild 1945–1989', *Jahrbuch für Wirtschaftsgeschichte* 1995, 2: 11–46.

Roesler, J. 1978. *Die Herausbildung der sozialistischen Planwirtschaft in der DDR. Aufgaben, Methoden und Ergebnisse der Wirtschaftsplanung in der zentralgeleiteten volkseigenen Industrie während der Übergangsperiode vom Kapitalismus zum Sozialismus.* Berlin (East): Akademie-Verlag.

———. 1984. 'Vom Akkordlohn zum Leistungslohn', *Zeitschrift für Geschichtswissenschaft* 32: 778–95.

———. 1990. *Zwischen Plan und Markt. Die Wirtschaftsreform 1963–1970 in der DDR.* Berlin: Haufe.

———. 1993. 'Privater Konsum in Ostdeutschland 1950–1960', in A. Schildt and A. Sywottek (eds), *Modernisierung im Wiederaufbau. Die westdeutsche Gesellschaft der 50er Jahre.* Bonn: Dietz, pp. 290–303.

———. 1997. 'Zu groß für die kleine DDR? Der Auf- und Ausbau neuer Industriezweige in der Planwirtschaft am Beispiel Flugzeugbau und Mikroelektronik', in W. Fischer, U. Müller and F. Zschaler (eds), *Wirtschaft im Umbruch. Strukturveränderungen und Wirtschaftspolitik im 19. und 20. Jahrhundert.* St. Katharinen: Scripta-Mercaturae-Verlag, 307–34.

————. V. Siedt and M. Elle. 1986. *Wirtschaftswachstum in der Industrie der DDR 1945–1970*. Berlin (East): Akademie-Verlag.

Rüden, B.V. 1991. *Die Rolle der D-Mark in der DDR. Von der Nebenwährung zur Währungsunion*. Baden-Baden: Nomos.

Sattler, F. 2002. *Wirtschaftsordnung im Übergang. Politik, Organisation und Funktion der KPD/SED im Land Brandenburg bei der Etablierung der zentralen Planwirtschaft in der SBZ/DDR 1945–52*. Münster: Lit.

Scherstjanoi, E. 2000. 'Die deutschlandpolitischen Absichten der UdSSR 1948. Erkenntnisstand und forschungsleitende Problematisierungen' in D. Hoffmann and H. Wentker (eds), *Das letzte Jahr der SBZ. Politische Weichenstellungen und Kontinuitäten im Prozeß der Gründung der DDR*. Munich: Oldenbourg, pp. 39–54.

Schevardo, J. 2006. *Vom Wert des Notwendigen. Preispolitik und Lebensstandard in der DDR der fünfziger Jahre*. Stuttgart: Steiner.

Schmidt, M.G. 2001. 'Grundlagen der Sozialpolitik in der Deutschen Demokratischen Republik', in Bundesministerium für Arbeit und Sozialordnung und Bundesarchiv, *Geschichte der Sozialpolitik in Deutschland seit 1945*, Vol. 1: *Grundlagen der Sozialpolitik*. Baden-Baden: Nomos, pp. 685–798.

Schneider, G. 1999. 'Lebensstandard und Versorgungslage', in E. Kuhrt (ed.), *Die Endzeit der DDR-Wirtschaft – Analysen zur Wirtschafts-, Sozial- und Umweltpolitik*. Opladen: Leske and Budrich, pp. 111–30.

Schöne, J. 2005. *Frühling auf dem Lande? Die Kollektivierung der DDR-Landwirtschaft*. Berlin: Links.

Schröter, H.G. 1996. 'Ölkrisen und Reaktionen in der chemischen Industrie beider deutschen Staaten. Ein Beitrag zur Erklärung wirtschaftlicher Leistungsdifferenzen', in J. Bähr and D. Petzina (eds), *Innovationsverhalten und Entscheidungsstrukturen. Vergleichende Studien zur wirtschaftlichen Entwicklung im geteilten Deutschland*. Berlin: Duncker und Humblot, pp. 109–38.

Schulz, D. 1984. 'Probleme der sozialen und politischen Entwicklung der Bauern und Landarbeiter in der DDR von 1949 bis 1955', Dissertation. Berlin: Humboldt-Universität zu Berlin.

————. 1990. 'Ruhe im Dorf? Die Agrarpolitik von 1952/53 und ihre Folgen', in J. âzerny (ed.), *Brüche, Krisen, Wendepunkte. Neubefragung von DDR-Geschichte*. Leipzig: Urania-Verlag, pp. 103–9.

————. 1994. *'Kapitalistische Länder überflügeln'. Die DDR-Bauern in der SED-Politik des ökonomischen Wettbewerbs mit der Bundesrepublik von 1956 bis 1961*. Berlin: Gesellschaftswissenschaftliches Forum.

Schwarzer, O. 1999. *Sozialistische Zentralplanwirtschaft in der SBZ/DDR. Ergebnisse eines ordnungspolitischen Experiments (1945–1989)*. Stuttgart: Steiner.

Sleifer, J. 2006. *Planning Ahead and Falling Behind. The East German Economy in Comparison with West Germany 1936–2002*. Berlin: Akademie-Verlag.

Staritz, D. 1981. 'Die "Arbeiterkomitees" der Jahre 1956/58. Fallstudie zur Partizipations-Problematik in der DDR', in *Der X. Parteitag der SED. 35 Jahre SED-Politik – Versuch einer Bilanz*. Cologne: Ed. Deutschland-Archiv, pp. 63–74.

———. 1995. *Die Gründung der DDR. Von der sowjetischen Besatzungsherrschaft zum sozialistischen Staat*, 3rd Edition. Munich: Deutscher Taschenbuch-Verlag.

———. 1996. *Geschichte der DDR*, New Enlarged Edition. Frankfurt: Suhrkamp.

Steiner, A. 1993. 'Sowjetische Berater in den zentralen wirtschaftsleitenden Instanzen der DDR in der zweiten Hälfte der fünfziger Jahre', *Jahrbuch für Historische Kommunismusforschung* 1: 100–17.

———. 1995a. 'Politische Vorstellungen und ökonomische Probleme im Vorfeld der Errichtung der Berliner Mauer. Briefe Walter Ulbrichts an Nikita Chruschtschow', in H. Mehringer (ed.), *Von der SBZ zur DDR: Studien zum Herrschaftssystem in der Sowjetischen Besatzungszone und in der Deutschen Demokratischen Republik*. Munich: Oldenbourg, pp. 233–68.

———. 1995b. 'Wirtschaftliche Lenkungsverfahren in der Industrie der DDR Mitte der fünfziger Jahre. Resultate und Alternativen', in C. Buchheim (ed.), *Wirtschaftliche Folgelasten des Krieges in der SBZ/DDR*. Baden-Baden: Nomos, pp. 271–93.

———. 1999. *Die DDR-Wirtschaftsreform der sechziger Jahre. Konflikt zwischen Effizienz und Machtkalkül*. Berlin: Akademie-Verlag.

———. 2002. 'Eine wirtschaftliche Bilanz der Berliner Mauer', in H.-H. Hertle, K.H. Jarausch and C. Kleßmann (eds), *Mauerbau und Mauerfall. Ursachen – Verlauf – Auswirkungen*. Berlin: Links, pp. 189–202.

———. 2006. 'Preispolitik und ihre Folgen unter den Bedingungen von Diktatur und Demokratie in Deutschland im Vergleich', in idem (ed.), *Preispolitik und Lebensstandard. Nationalsozialismus, DDR und Bundesrepublik im Vergleich*. Cologne: Böhlau, pp. 171–203.

———. 2008. 'Preisgestaltung', in C. Boyer, et al. (eds), *Geschichte der Sozialpolitik in Deutschland seit 1945*, Vol. 10: *Deutsche Demokratische Republik 1971–1989. Bewegung in der Sozialpolitik, Erstarrung und Niedergang*. Baden-Baden: Nomos, pp. 304–23.

Stitziel, J. 2005. *Fashioning Socialism: Clothing, Politics and Consumer Culture in East Germany*. Oxford: Berg.

Stokes, R.G. 2000. *Constructing Socialism. Technology and Change in East Germany, 1945–1990*. Baltimore: Johns Hopkins University Press.

Stolper, W.F. 1960. *The Structure of the East German Economy*. Cambridge: Harvard University Press.

Tatzkow, M. 1990. 'Privatindustrie ohne Perspektive. "Der Versuch zur Liquidierung der mittleren privaten Warenproduzenten"', in J. Čzerny (ed.), *Brüche, Krisen, Wendepunkte. Neubefragung von DDR-Geschichte*. Leipzig: Urania-Verlag, pp. 97–103.

Thieme, H.J. 1998. 'Notenbank und Währung in der DDR', in Deutsche Bundesbank (ed.), *Fünfzig Jahre Deutsche Mark. Notenbank und Währung in Deutschland seit 1948*. Munich: Beck, pp. 609–53.

Volze, A. 1996, 'Ein großer Bluff? Die Westverschuldung der DDR', *Deutschland-Archiv* 29: 701–13.

———. 1999. 'Zur Devisenverschuldung der DDR – Entstehung, Bewältigung und Folgen', in E. Kuhrt (ed.), *Die Endzeit der DDR-Wirtschaft – Analysen zur*

Wirtschafts-, Sozial- und Umweltpolitik. Opladen: Leske and Budrich, pp. 151–83.

Weber, A. 1999 'Ursachen und Folgen abnehmender Effizienz in der DDR-Landwirtschaft', in E. Kuhrt (ed.), *Die Endzeit der DDR-Wirtschaft – Analysen zur Wirtschafts-, Sozial- und Umweltpolitik.* Opladen: Leske and Budrich, pp. 225–69.

Werkentin, F. 1995. *Politische Strafjustiz in der Ära Ulbricht.* Berlin: Links.

Wettig, G. 2008. *Stalin and the Cold War in Europe. The Emergence and Development of East–West Conflict, 1939–1953.* Lanham: Rowman & Littlefield Publishers.

Wolkow, W.K. 2000. 'Die deutsche Frage aus Stalins Sicht (1947–1952)', *Zeitschrift für Geschichtswissenschaft* 48: 20–49.

Wolle, S. 1991. 'Das MfS und die Arbeiterproteste im Herbst 1956 in der DDR', *Aus Politik und Zeitgeschichte* B5/91: 42–51.

———. 1998. *Die heile Welt der Diktatur.* Bonn: Bundeszentrale für politische Bildung.

Wünderich, V. 2003. 'Die "Kaffeekrise" von 1977. Genußmittel und Verbraucherprotest in der DDR', *Historische Anthropologie* 11: 240–61.

Zank, W. 1987. *Wirtschaft und Arbeit in Ostdeutschland 1945–1949. Probleme des Wiederaufbaus in der Sowjetischen Besatzungszone Deutschlands.* Munich: Oldenbourg.

Zatlin, J.R. 2007. *The Currency of Socialism. Money and Political Culture in East Germany.* Cambridge: Cambridge University Press.

Zschaler, F. 1992. 'Von der Emissions- und Girobank zur Deutschen Notenbank. Zu den Umständen der Gründung einer Staatsbank für Ostdeutschland', *Bankhistorisches Archiv* 18: 59–68.

———. 1997. 'Die vergessene Währungsreform. Vorgeschichte, Durchführung und Ergebnisse der Geldumstellung in der SBZ 1948', *Vierteljahreshefte für Zeitgeschichte* 45: 191–224.

Appendix

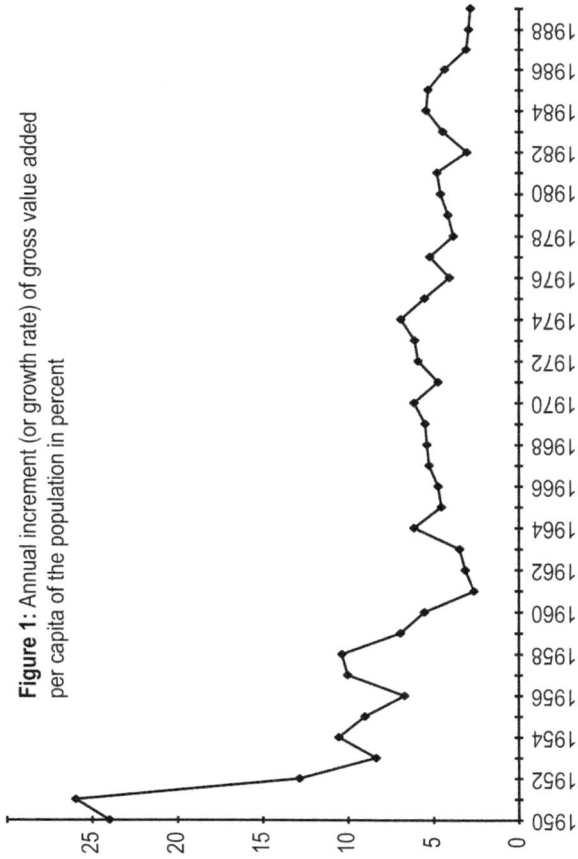

Figure 1: Annual increment (or growth rate) of gross value added per capita of the population in percent

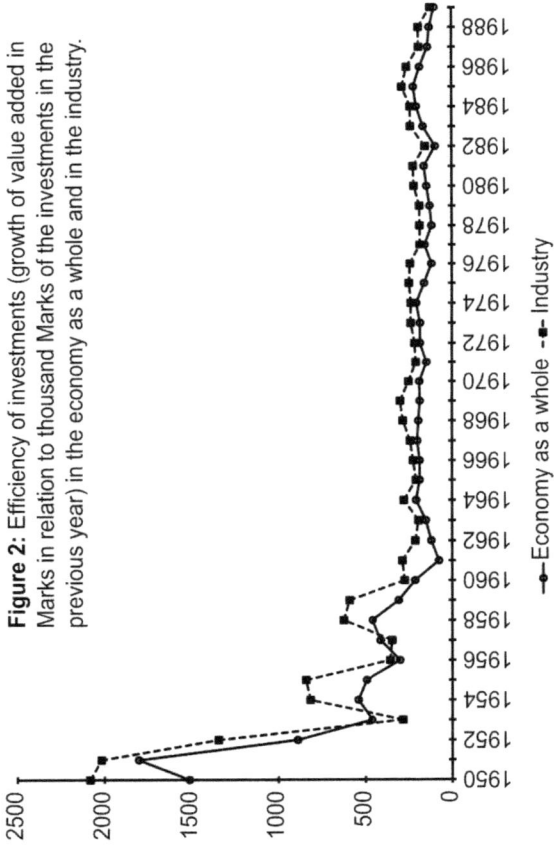

Figure 2: Efficiency of investments (growth of value added in Marks in relation to thousand Marks of the investments in the previous year) in the economy as a whole and in the industry.

Index

Schürer, Gerhard, 117, 162–64, 190, 198
Schwedt, 73, 127
science and technology, 71, 83, 116,
   118–19, 121, 152, 180
scientific–technological revolution, 119
Secretariat (of the Central Committee)
   see Socialist Unity Party of Germany
   (SED)
Secretary/-ies, 4, 81–83, 197–200
Secretary for Economic Affairs *see*
   Socialist Unity Party of Germany
   (SED)
Selbmann, Fritz, 29–30, 32, 45, 83, 90,
   199
shipbuilding, 50
shoes *see* footwear
shortage(s), 7–8, 27, 31, 34, 52–53,
   57–59, 69–70, 75, 77, 86, 89, 93, 98,
   120, 124, 128, 133, 142, 146–47,
   154–55, 158–59, 162–63, 171, 179–80,
   187–89
   of goods, 6, 42, 60, 109, 133, 143
   of raw materials, 7, 21, 70
Silesia, 13, 16, 33
Social Democratic Party (SPD), 17–18,
   25, 27
socialism, 3, 6, 25–26, 31, 56, 58, 60, 69,
   81–82, 90, 105–6, 109–10, 112, 119–20,
   123, 143, 160, 178, 191
   see also planned economy
Socialist Unity Party of Germany
   (SED), 1, 3, 4, 8, 17, 25, 30, 39, 41, 47,
   52–53, 58–61, 69, 72, 77, 81–83, 85,
   90–91, 93, 95, 97–98, 105, 108–9,
   111–13, 117, 122, 125–27, 130, 134,
   136, 141–42, 144, 147, 152, 156, 159,
   161–63, 178, 181, 183, 188–90, 197–200
   apparatus, 4, 110, 153
   Central Committee of the (ZK), 4, 25,
      81–83, 113–14, 117, 122, 132, 160,
      197–200
   conference, 56–57, 69, 71, 80
   congress, 1, 90, 143–45, 188
   Department for Planning and
      Finance, 132, 199
   leaders *see* Socialist Unity Party of
      Germany, Politbüro

leadership *see* Socialist Unity Party of
   Germany, Politbüro
meeting, 29, 82, 116–17, 157
organisations, 4
plenary session, 113, 160
Politbüro, 4, 8, 18, 29, 40–41, 48,
   56–63, 72, 74–75, 78, 80–83, 87,
   89–94, 98–99, 105–6, 108–10,
   112–13, 115–19, 122, 134–36,
   144–45, 147, 149–53, 155, 157, 160,
   162–64, 171, 173, 176–82, 184–85,
   187–88, 190–92, 197–200
   secretary/-iat, 4, 106, 197–200
   secretary for Economic Affairs, 83
soft budget constraint, 5, 79, 111
Soviet-type economy *see* planned
   economy
Soviet Communist Party, 83, 142, 177,
   199
Soviet joint-stock companies (SAG), 18,
   20–22, 29–30, 44, 62
Soviet Military Administration in
   Germany (SMAD), 16
Soviet Occupation Zone (SBZ), 12–18,
   20–25, 27, 29, 31–35, 39, 41–43, 48–51,
   56
Soviet Planning Commission, 71
Soviet Union/ USSR, 1–3, 7, 15–18,
   20–24, 26, 28, 31, 39–42, 49, 50, 55, 56,
   59–62, 69–72, 73, 78, 80, 82, 87, 88,
   91–92, 96–99, 105–9, 115, 116–119,
   122, 125, 127, 134–35, 141–42, 144,
   153, 161–64, 171–72, 175, 177, 180,
   181, 189, 192–93
Sputnik
   (magazine), 191
   (satellite), 90
Stalin, Josef, 2, 25, 29, 39, 56, 58, 60–61,
   69, 71, 80, 82, 85
standardisation, 74
standard of living, 3, 8, 34, 54–55,
   59–61, 69, 72, 83, 87, 89–90, 92, 94, 97,
   109, 122, 126, 129–31, 143–45, 157–58,
   171, 177–78, 186, 188, 191
State Bank *see* central bank
state budget, 5, 59, 63, 87–88, 94, 120,
   152, 158, 179, 181, 185